RENAISSANCE
HOMBRE

Reflections on a Well-Rounded Life

By

SCOTT W. PETERSEN

authorHOUSE

AuthorHouse™
1663 Liberty Drive
Bloomington, IN 47403
www.authorhouse.com
Phone: 833-262-8899

Cover illustration: Dante Alighieri and Virgil, details from a fresco by Luca Signorelli

Published by AuthorHouse 09/18/2020

ISBN: 978-1-7283-7235-8 (sc)
ISBN: 978-1-7283-7234-1 (hc)
ISBN: 978-1-7283-7267-9 (e)

Library of Congress Control Number: 2020916785

Print information available on the last page.

This book is printed on acid-free paper.

Scripture taken from the King James Version of the Bible.

CONTENTS

ACKNOWLEDGMENTS

There are so many people to thank for bringing this book to life. My wife, Donna, for reviewing each post and giving the nod. My daughter, Lauren, for being an inspiration and my granddaughters, Eve and Elin, who are amazing bright lights of joy. My extended family, my friends and anyone who laughs at my jokes. And a special thank-you to Pat Vaccaro for her editorial touch in bringing the posts to the page.

INTRODUCTION

My wife, Donna, tells me I have an *abbondanza* of interests and ideas. Endless topics capture my attention. So when I started my blog, I called it "Renaissance Hombre," in honor of those eclectic polymaths of bygone days.

My first post went up on July 23, 2011. Soon I was posting twice a week—Wednesdays and Saturdays. Over the next nine years, I shared an aggregation of information and observations. And now I'm sharing a compilation of my favorite posts.

Favorite meals. Music and movies. Recommended reading. Quotations. Vacations. Jokes. Magic tricks. Trivia. Stories from my life and reflections on the human condition. Sit back—or lie back—and read one or two. And come back again tomorrow for more.

~ Scott W. Petersen

The original date of each blog post is noted. Some posts have been updated or revised for this compilation.

1

GROWING UP

First Recollection

My granddaughters are *ever* so special. Since they were babies, I've sung to them, read to them, fed them, held them, talked to them and occasionally changed a diaper. And I sometimes wonder—will they remember *anything* of these times as they grow older? When does recall begin to kick in?

I have occasionally posed this question among friends when conversation stalls. "What is your very first memory when you were a child? What is the very first spark of cognizance that you remember?" The answers are very personal. And the question does prompt some interesting—and varied—responses.

My first three years were spent in a one-bedroom attic at 6036 W. Byron St. in Chicago. I remember the place. Clearly. And I remember—vividly—sitting by the lone street-side window looking out. And waving at a little boy (Georgey) across the street. This was in the days before *play groups*, so I never saw him up close (or anyone else for that matter). We never played together. We would just wave. Across the street.

I wonder if *he* remembers *me*.

August 16, 2012

Sweet Dreams

From the time I was 8 years old, my parents both worked. I'd walk home from school, let myself in the house, call my mother and let her know I was alive. I was what was called a *latchkey kid*. And then—being instructed not to watch television ("except for Cubs games")—I went down to the basement to play with toy soldiers, work on my stamp collection (my grandmother had bought me a small album and a bunch of foreign stamps) or read a book about rocks and fossils. And if the Cubs weren't on (which was most of the time), I would put old records on the record player.

I listened mainly to big-band music—Jimmy Dorsey, Tommy Dorsey, Benny Goodman, Dizzy Gillespie, Count Basie and so many others (that's all we had). I would sit and sing, memorizing the songs I heard as I played. Today I sing some of those songs to my granddaughters—from a memory of 60-plus years ago. Three of the favorites are "If That Phone Ever Rings and It's You," "The Whiffenpoof Song" and "The Hut Sut Song."

You want to hear what I listened to when I was 8 years old? Give it a whirl:

"If That Phone…"

https://www.youtube.com/watch?v=FFNqTrf6pdw

"The Whiffenpoof Song"

https://www.youtube.com/watch?v=RJVUTHLFdQ0

"Hut Sut Ralston"

https://www.youtube.com/watch?v=7kKU1S0lWxo

And then came "Oh Shenandoah," which won the fraternity sing 11 years later at Augustana College. *That* song I sang to my daughter, Lauren, *every night* from that first night home from the hospital. And it was played for the daddy-daughter dance—at her wedding. Sweet memories. Sweet dreams…

March 17, 2019

CLearbrook 3–75 _ _

My pal Darryl lived across the creek from my home. Darryl and I would walk across a narrow footbridge to play catch or just hang out. Darryl's telephone number was CLearbrook 3-75_ _. Sometimes I would call him. We'd chat. And hang up.

One bright day—I must have been about 10 years old—I called Darryl's number. *Ring. Ring. Ring.* And a woman answered, "Hello."

I said, "Hello, is Darryl there?" Sounds pretty innocuous, eh? Well, it was the wrong number.

This woman began screaming into the phone, "You #$&*$X.... You have the wrong $%@&@X number!" I sat there listening. Mouth open. *Mesmerized.* I realized I'd dialed a 6 instead of a 7.

I got on my bike and rode over to Darryl's. Darryl answered the door, and I pushed inside, grabbed Darryl, picked up the phone and said, "Listen to this." And I dialed the wrong number again. *Ring. Ring. Ring.* And a woman answered, "Hello." I said cheerfully, "Hello, is Darryl there?" And she began screaming again. This was *really* something special. We shared the "wrong number" with our pals. It seemed entertaining (at the time), and we all learned new four-letter words in the process.

Mind you—these were the days before *caller ID.*

June 16, 2016

The Ushers

Growing up, I attended St. Mark Lutheran Church in the Chicago suburb of Mount Prospect. It was a big church, offering three services on Sunday morning: 8, 9:30 and 11. The 8 a.m. service was relatively new. And as you might imagine, it was sometimes a challenge to staff the early service with ushers.

The head of the ushering program, Mr. Wendt, often had to attend all three services, filling in as needed. Finally, perhaps in some desperation, he approached the head of the church's youth program and asked if there were some high school boys who could "help out" with the early service. The answer? "Sure." So Chuck, Wayne, Randy, Dave and I were tapped to usher the 8 a.m. service—*every Sunday.*

On the first Sunday, the five of us showed up early. Suits. Ties. We each donned a white carnation and got an ushering lesson from Mr. Wendt. He guided us through the service, offering a running commentary. ("Smile....

Greet people by name if you can.... When collecting the offering, walk backward—never turn your back on the altar.")

After a few weeks of this, the five of us had the protocol down pat. And a few weeks later, Mr. Wendt said, "Keep up the good work, boys."

He never showed up again.

July 9, 2017

Don't Get Off the Train 'til Denver

When I was 10 years old, my parents put me on a train with two of my friends—Kurt and Steve. We were headed for Denver. A camp in Estes Park, Colorado. Skyline Ranch. The three of us were alone. No adult supervision. My father admonished, "Son, don't get off the train 'til Denver." He handed me a $10 bill for food. And that was it.

Once at camp—after the homesick tears ended—I settled in pretty well. Riding horses, hiking, swimming and shooting every day. The big day came when we all participated in a junior rodeo in Estes Park. And I won. I still have the trophy. The events were pretty tame. Barrel races. Flat-out races.

And then there was the potato race. Each kid mounted his horse and got a spoon and potato. The potato went in the spoon. And you trotted toward the finish line. If the potato fell, you had to dismount, pick it up, put it on the spoon and get back in the saddle. I won the event. No one told me I couldn't put my thumb on the potato to hold it in place.

Then there was the balloon pop. Every kid had a balloon tied to his saddle. And each got a sharpened 9-inch nail. When the starting gun went off, everyone flurried into the mix, trying to pop the other kid's balloon. Once popped, you had to move out. Well, I figured I was toast if I got in the mix, so I slung one leg over the saddle horn. And waited. When there were two boys left—going round and round, stabbing and yelling—I said "giddup" and suddenly appeared. And I popped their balloons. I won that event too. I won't tell you how I won the barrel race....

I'm told these instincts probably have helped me as a lawyer.

May 25, 2014

900 Pounds of Bull

After winning a junior rodeo, I was given the task (with Marvin, also age 10) of rounding up the horses each morning. We had to rise at 5:30 a.m., walk out past the corral fence off a dirt road and walk into a high plains pasture of several hundred acres. There were cows, horses and a bull. "Flap your poncho at the bull if he charges you," was the advice given to us. So two 10-year-old boys headed off alone. On foot—into the high grass. Looking for horses in the gray twilight of dawn.

The cows paid us little mind. The bull mercifully stayed away (*it's those punks*). When the horses would see us, they would cock their ears back (*danger!*) then forward (*huh?*) then normal (*oh, it's them*) and begin galloping past us toward the corral. They *knew* we would feed them. So we hiked the mile or so back to the corral with a weather eye on the bull—who kept a weather eye on us.

All the horses—Arab, Bubbles, Chief, Dakota, Eagle, Hi Boy, Indian and the others—would be standing at parade rest in the corral. Marvin and I would put 2 cups of oats in each feed bag and slip it over their ears. Then we'd lead them (*come on, Bubbles*) to the fence, tether and saddle them. No adults were ever around.

Kids today have a tough time developing independence. You don't need to do it on a ranch. At dawn. With a 900-pound bull giving you the evil eye. But I believe there must be challenges for kids to face or they will have trouble as adults. Today we move in the direction of no grades (*they can damage egos*), no playing tag (*too rough*), no dodge ball (*too violent*), no pointing your finger like a gun (*eeek!*). We hear about *safe spaces*. Teachers cannot raise their voice at a child, and of course no—however well-earned—corporal punishment (see "A Sixth Grade Lesson").

It's one thing to protect. It's another to insulate. As I see it, *insulating* kids from challenge has negative consequences. For *everyone*.

September 30, 2018

Patrol Boys

During sixth and seventh grade, I was a patrol boy. After careful instruction, I was given a white Sam Brown belt (a 3-inch white belt with an angled strap from one hip to the opposite shoulder). And I was given power. I was the *capo di tutti capi* (or one of them) for Lincoln School in Mount Prospect. (My wife, Donna, was a patrol *girl* back in Rye, New York.)

I stood at the street corner. When kids wanted to cross the street, I would thrust my arms out to the sides. (*Don't go!*) When traffic slowed, I would step into the street and shove my arm into the air. (*Stop!*) And cars would slow and stop. (*It's a patrol boy.*) Kids would cross. I would step back and motion the drivers with a wave. (*As you were.*) *Yeah.* Sixth grade.

Today you see crossing guards who are older than dirt. Some look old enough to be my *grandparents.* Now that's *old.* Not as nimble as a patrol boy. They wear iridescent vests and reflective hats, and they carry a monster STOP sign. A few look as if they're geared up for a SWAT team. I remember seeing one old guy wearing a helmet.

I always wondered why the patrol boy era came to an end. Probably lawyers. And helicopter parents who worry about giving their (or someone else's) child authority. Autonomy. Power. Risk. I frankly think it would be great if we could resume the patrol boy (and girl) era. Think about the sense of responsibility. Confidence. Growing up. *Yeah.*

I know, it's a different time. But it's still the old tug of war between protecting and insulating children. We want to give children *wings*— and *roots.*

November 20, 2014

Sandlot Baseball

As a kid, I played sandlot baseball. We would get 15 to 20 guys on any given Saturday morning in the park by Sunset School. Two of the older boys (age 12 or 13) would pick the teams. "Meyer." "Shutt." "Kaspari." "Wilkes." "Knox." "Barsi." "Hudson." And so on. "Petersen" was usually one of the last picked. But no hard feelings. And the game would begin.

Boys ran the game. There were no adult coaches or overseers. When a kid slid into second base and the tag was close, 10-year-old boys would decide *safe* or *out*. Sometimes there would be an argument. A shove. Then it was back to baseball. It worked like a charm. Regulations were not needed. We made the rules as we went along—and they were fair.

Government, however, is different. Counties. Cities. Districts. Municipalities. Townships. School districts. Each with its own rules. The government does not trust its citizens to play sandlot baseball. The government doesn't trust people to make decisions for *themselves*. Sound cynical? I have a bridge in Brooklyn I'd like to sell you....

December 20, 2018

Fireworks

So what do you think about fireworks? Firecrackers? Cherry bombs? Should they be legal? I was in Wisconsin this last weekend, and the fireworks stores seemed to outnumber cows. And the weekend festivities were punctuated by the occasional staccato of firecrackers or *boom* of something larger.

From 9 years old on, I *loved* firecrackers and fireworks. *Loved* that smell of cordite. We used to break open firecrackers, shake the fulminate of mercury powder into cigar tubes with homemade fins, balance them on an incline and then light a fuse, sending the "rocket" skyward (often with an enormous explosion). We would pack match heads into the tubes, pouring in the powder for more incendiary displays. And bombs. It was *wonderful.*☺ Every guy had a supply of firecrackers, cherry bombs, M-80s and such.

I am *keenly* aware of all of the arguments of the armchair howlers. ("What about accidents?" "They can blow your finger off!") But I still feel that fireworks (at *least* firecrackers) have a place in a young boy's life.

October 10, 2012

Intelligence Testing

In sixth grade, apart from being the local expert on creating and detonating bombs, launching rockets and making Molotov cocktails (see "Fireworks"), I cut lawns to make a few bucks. And kept my eyes glued to the ground for stray pennies (more on that later). *And* I sold Kool-Aid on the local golf course for a dime (sprinting into the weeds when the ranger came zooming toward me in his golf cart).

Another occupation of mine involved creating nine different "intelligence tests" for classmates. I would type (from scratch—one finger at a time) 10 questions on a sheet of paper and give it to a classmate in exchange for a quarter. If my classmates could answer the questions, I'd give them their quarter plus *another* quarter. ("You win....") If they didn't, I kept their quarter. No one ever won.

The questions included things like, how many gorillas were in the U.S. in 1919? (One) What King of France tinkered with locks? (Louis XVI) How many American Indians served in World War I? (17,313) What was the parcel-post rate on packages going to Manchuria in 1924? (12 cents a pound) And so on. I earned a *lot* of quarters. The reason for my success was that I had a *book*. It was *Answers to Questions* by Frederic J. Haskin (Grosset & Dunlap, 1926). The book had all of these questions—and so many more.

Do you know how many of the mules sent to France in World War I were killed? If you can answer *that* one, I'll give you a quarter. No fair Googling.

September 10, 2015

Put Your Head on My Shoulder

The first time I ever danced with a girl was in my sixth grade classroom. Our teacher, Mrs. S., put on some music and drafted my classmate Marilyn to dance with me. Poor girl. To say I had two left feet would be a compliment. They felt like two left flippers. I was scared to death. And I remember stepping on this poor girl's feet in my pathetic effort to "dance." I'm sure the experience soured poor Marilyn on the male of the species.

By seventh grade, I had danced maybe three or four times. So I was an old hand. Seventh and eighth graders were invited to "Rec," as it was called, on Friday nights. At the park district. It was a dance....

Few of the guys I knew ever danced. They just stood on the sidelines. Joshing. Joking. Snorting. And acting like immature boys. That is, until *Sharon* walked over to me during one "slow" dance and asked me out on the floor. My friends were stunned. They stared. I was nearly apoplectic inside. But that was only a taste of what was to come....

We went out on the floor and began dancing. And Sharon promptly pressed her head against my head. I remember immediately beginning to perspire. Heavily. Notwithstanding, her head remained glued to mine. Sweat dripping down the both of us. The music ended, and she walked back to the line of girls. And I sheepishly went back to the line of boys, feeling like I'd just emerged from a swimming pool. And got glares. And snickers. And when the slow music began again, I saw her moving in my direction. Uh-oh. And we danced. Her head pressed against mine.

I don't think we exchanged a single word. Ever. But after a few times, dancing with Sharon wasn't so bad....

September 19, 2015

A Sixth Grade Lesson

One afternoon between classes, I saw my classmate Tim in the hall. In a show of sixth grade bravado, I grabbed him and pushed him bodily into the girls' bathroom. And I held the door closed—*chortling*—while screams of girls and cries from Tim resounded down the hall.

What happened next occurred in a kind of slow motion, though I'm sure it took place in a flash. I felt a hand on my shoulder, which spun me around. Suddenly, a bright light exploded on the side of my face. My teacher, Mrs. S., had *slapped* me. *Hard.* "Don't you ever do that again."

Tim escaped. I wobbled back to the classroom. When I got home, my mother was there—arms akimbo. She *knew*.... Instead of hugging me and spitting about the mean teacher, my mother simply commented that she hoped I'd learned my lesson. I had.

I learned a lesson. It was epiphanic. I learned there are lines that are not to be crossed.

I tend to think our educational system needs options for teaching lessons—without the consequence. After all, who wins? *I sure did....*

Gum Behind the Ear

When I was a kid, I would chew gum on the way to school. Upon entering class, I would stick the gum behind my right ear. Just behind the lobe. At recess I'd pull out the gum and start chewing. I was reasonably efficient in this task, and I could probably nurse a penny piece of Double Bubble chewing gum for the entire day. Ear. Mouth. Ear. Mouth. And so on. I do recall that by the end of the day, the gum was always a little grittier—and saltier—than in the morning. But hey—it was good chewing gum.

Fast forward to last year. I'm sitting on the train. Reading. And a couple gets on the train and plops down in front of me. Probably in their late 50s. My gaze sharpens. At first it looks like the guy has a large and ugly mole on the back of his ear. Just behind the lobe. But then it comes to me ... *Oh my socks and shoes—this guy has a piece of gum behind his ear!* Now mind you, I haven't put a piece of gum behind my ear since last October (yes, I'm kidding), and I haven't *thought* about the subject for about 50 years. But wow! It all came roaring back.

I couldn't resist. I took a picture with my phone. And when the guy heard the distinctive *click*, he turned slightly, took the gum and put it in his mouth.

Scout's honor.

2

SCOUTING DAYS

For Want of a Nail

If there was a pivotal moment in my life, it was becoming an Eagle Scout. I owe a lot to that boyhood achievement: Going to college. Going to law school. Getting a job. Meeting my wife. Having a daughter and grandchildren. And knowing how to deal with different "situations."

The fact that I was an Eagle Scout was *sine qua non*—the indispensable thing—for my acceptance to Augustana College (more on that later). At Augustana, I chatted with a couple of pals who talked about *law school*. *Sooo*, I went to law school. At Augustana, I met Diane—who, a year after my graduation, introduced me to Donna. ("Scott, I have a girlfriend from New York I think you should meet.") And because of Donna, we have Lauren and her family. When I interviewed to be a state's attorney, the first 15 minutes of conversation was about *Boy Scouts*. (I'd put "Eagle Scout" on my resume.) And I was offered the job.

Being an Eagle Scout taught me a lot. An Eagle trajectory got me a job at age 14 (for three summers) on staff at Camp Napowan, a Boy Scout camp in Wild Rose, Wisconsin. The experience provided a *major* education and provided friends I have to this day.

All in all, I have to say that being an Eagle Scout was the "nail" (Benjamin Franklin, *Poor Richard's Almanac*, 1758) that made all the difference in the world for yours truly. And you know what? That achievement has made—and will continue to make—*all the difference in the world* for a universe of young men.

December 3, 2015

Collecting Meteorites

When I was a Boy Scout, I subscribed to *Boys' Life* magazine. I read it cover to cover. Sometimes twice. Great tips on *everything*. If a dog attacks someone, pick up the dog's hind legs (it will stop) or wrap your belt around him. Drowning people rarely splash—watch their heads. Polaris, the North Star, never moves in the sky. It is true north and determines your precise north latitude. Great articles. Good stuff. Even a page of humor.

One article that I remember to this day is how to collect meteorites. Yes, *meteorites*. Every day, the Earth is bombarded with cosmic debris—including an avalanche of tiny meteorites. Not the big splashy ones that *whooosh* through the air, leaving trails of brilliant light, and make the news when they smack into a house. I'm talking about *dust*. Meteorite dust—and particles.

So how do you collect this cosmic detritus? *Boys' Life* said to get a large tin pan, put a piece of cloth in the bottom and set it outside—perhaps in the garden. And leave it there for a week. Then go out with a magnet and run it through the particles that have collected. Those that stick—especially the pencil dot–sized nuggets—are likely small meteorites. (There may also be remnants of fly ash from coal-burning stoves or fireplaces.)

Good articles and videos about this subject are available today online. The best (probably quickest) way suggested for collecting meteorites is to put a bucket under a gutter downspout—and then hose down the roof. The roof is a good collector of such material. The water from the downspout pours into the bucket. The heavy stuff (as when you pan for gold) settles to the bottom. Pour out the water and (unless your roof is metallic) use your magnet to pick up these visitors from outer space.

July 25, 2019

1913 V Nickel

The Liberty Head 5-cent piece (also called the V nickel because of a Roman numeral 5 on the reverse) was made from 1883 to 1912. It was America's second nickel. In 1913, the United States Mint produced Liberty Head nickels, but they were never intended for circulation. Colonel E.H.R. Green (the son of the famous Gilded Age financier Hetty Green) owned five strikes of the 1913 nickel. These five rarities have since been dispersed to collectors.

Around 1960, I was a Boy Scout working on a coin collecting merit badge. The merit badge counselor was a gentle man named Mr. Noll. He had an *amazing* collection of coins housed in a walk-in closet off his living room. Apart from quizzing me on and helping me with the merit badge requirements, Mr. Noll generously gave me some assorted coins for my collection.

I remember him telling me that his father was an employee of the U.S. Mint that produced the 1913 V nickel. And that his father took a few—apparently beyond those belonging to Mr. Green. Mr. Noll never told me where the remaining 1913 nickels were or what had been done with them.

In 2018 a 1913 V nickel sold for $4.5 million. It was described as one of five ever made. I wonder if they know about Mr. Noll….

I wish I'd asked a few more questions.

August 3, 2011

The Slop Bucket

As I've mentioned, I worked at Camp Napowan in Wisconsin. Before being accepted for the staff, a young man would serve as a trainee for a month. Trainees would rotate through the various camp areas. Doing the grunt work. *And* spending a fair amount of time in the kitchen, peeling potatoes, doing dishes and cleaning up.

After meals in the mess hall, scouts and trainees would bus the tables. We would throw *paper* garbage into one garbage can. And we would put *food* waste into another. The food barrel was called the slop bucket. We were always careful about putting food scraps (no bones, no paper) in the slop bucket because each day we would give that bucket to a local farmer, who would use it to feed his pigs. Uneaten food was *used*.

I have written frequently on environmental issues. And I have touted my registered trademark—JUST TURN IT OFF'—a motto that applies to cars, lights, water and energy.

When I read about how the Earth is being *inundated* with waste, oceans are overflowing with garbage, rivers and lakes are turning toxic, yet many folks *still* remain heedless of our environment—I get a wee bit steamed. But then I simmer down—and start *thinking* about what we can do.

It's one thing to *just turn off* your water, lights, car, energy. But there is also merit in *reusing* bags, bottles, containers. And not polluting. Not to mention *recycling*. And *composting*. Taking food waste and carefully mixing it with soil. In the garden. Or backyard. You don't need a slop bucket.

We *all* really need to get on board with this idea of helping our limping planet along. *Pronto*. We live here. But we also have generations of souls who yet have no voice—who will *have* to live here too. And they will have no choice but to take what we give them.

April 25, 2019

Riding With Joe M.

When I worked at Camp Napowan, the chap who owned some of the property was Joe M. Joe had an ancient olive drab pickup truck that (Scout's honor) had no doors. Floor stick shift. And of course there were no seat belts and no handle above the door to grab.

His favorite line—while cruising, weaving and wobbling on the back roads of Wild Rose—was, "If there's no one coming around that bend, we'll see the sun rise tomorrow." I swear if we were driving with Joe, we'd grab *under the glove compartment* and hang on for dear life.

Today, there'd be a lot of *tsk-tsking*. There would be newspaper articles. There'd be an *inquiry*. Joe would be criticized. Maybe given a ticket. Unsafe vehicle. Endangerment. Et cetera. The usual assortment of plaintiffs' lawyers would sue anyone and everyone.

Now, I would definitely not want—or allow—my child or grandchild to be one of Joe's passengers. But looking back on it—I'm privately glad that *I rode with Joe M.*

June 4, 2013

A Lifebuoy Lesson

When I was 12 years old (1959), I spent part of the summer at Camp Napowan—a great Boy Scout camp in Wild Rose, Wisconsin. One hot sunny afternoon, I was loping back to my campsite when I saw a fellow camper named "Wiley." I looked at him and called him a "_____."

It was a highly offensive and nasty slur. What prompted my outburst, I don't recall but from the moment the words left my lips, things began moving verrry quickly. And with great and lasting impression.

The senior patrol leader, age 14, heard my comment and yelled an order to other Scouts. They grabbed me and dragged me shouting and struggling to the wash stand. The senior patrol leader took a well-used cake of Lifebuoy's finest and pushed it into my mouth. Then—without a word—I was released. I ran back to my tent on the verge of tears, spitting soap shards. When I emerged, the matter was forgotten.

But you know what? From that time on, I never used an epithet like that. I learned. Some might say "the hard way." But I disagree. I wish other young people could learn like this—from their peers. I look at this lesson (and others I've had) as being key to my development. I'm glad I learned.

Oh and that senior patrol leader? He and I went on to become Eagle Scouts. We worked together on staff at Camp Napowan for the next three years. He became one of my two closest friends (along with my great pal "Colonel Ox"—another Eagle Scout). Today, he's the finest veterinarian in the State of Kentucky. And to this day, I've rarely heard my friend utter anything stronger than a (usually appropriate) "doggonit."

February 2, 2012

Eagle Scout Politicians

I am an Eagle Scout. I grew up with—and was inculcated with—the Boy Scout Oath: "On my honor, I will do my best to do my duty to God and my country and to obey the Scout Law; to help other people at all times; to keep myself physically strong, mentally awake, and morally straight."

The Boy Scout Law added further obligations: "A Scout is trustworthy, loyal, helpful, friendly, courteous, kind, obedient, cheerful, thrifty, brave, clean, and reverent." All of the Eagle Scouts I know continue to try and live their lives according to these solemn vows, though Donna doesn't always feel I'm obedient when she asks me to take the garbage out or clean the garage. (I'm not really cheerful about that stuff either.)

When I see gridlock in Washington, I am sad we don't have more Eagle Scout–types running the country. I would wager that Democratic and Republican Eagle Scouts would get along a far sight better and work a lot more diligently.

They would sing campfire songs while drinking beer at the Old Ebbitt Grill (D.C.'s oldest saloon). They would hike to the office with backpacks, doing good deeds along the way. And most importantly, they would take seriously—very seriously—their duty to this great country, their obligation to be thrifty and the promise to "help other people at all times."

October 6, 2013

Girl Scouts

I said before that being an Eagle Scout was likely the *sine qua non* that got me where I am today. It got me into college. Where I met Donna and from there had our daughter, Lauren, and two granddaughters. College led me to a great job. *Yada yada.*

And I believe that *no one* should be allowed to become a politician unless they were an Eagle Scout, or a Girl Scout Gold Award recipient—*or share the values thereof.*

So how do I feel about having girls becoming Eagle Scouts? I think it's *great.* It is a *wonderful* idea. While I prefer that this achievement be accomplished under the auspices of the *Girl* Scouts of America, if it's done through the *Boy* Scouts, so be it. The important thing is to develop a universe of young women who achieve the Eagle Scout rank by meeting all of the challenging requirements and living up to the values. It would be a *major* plus for them. And for America.

I would want *them* to run for office. And *win*.

February 1, 2018

3

FURTHER ADVENTURES

College

At 16, well into my senior year of high school, I went to see my guidance counselor. Mr. Hillman. Mr. Hillman told me (the words are etched in my brain), "I think I can get you a job as an assistant plumber." I sat. And wanted to cry. An honorable profession. But I didn't want to be an assistant plumber. I left his office. Sad about my impending future. But some of my friends talked about *college*. *College* sounded pretty good.

My father never finished high school, and my mother never went to college. So we never talked much about college at home. I would finish high school and then go to work. Even so, I mentioned *college* to my father. "College?" he said. "The only guy I know who went to college is Mr. Swanson." He looked at me. "You wanna talk to him?" I nodded.

So we went to see Mr. Swanson. He said, "I went to Augustana College. Maybe I could get you an interview." My dad said, "You want that?" and I nodded … not entirely sure what *that* meant. My parents and I drove out to Rock Island, Illinois—home of Augustana College—and I had an interview with Mr. Henning, the director of admissions. It was April or May, around the time of high school graduation. Mr. Henning said the class was full. And my grades were not great.

But he liked that I was an Eagle Scout. He had a couple of discretionary spots. So he offered to admit me on academic probation. If I didn't have a C average first semester, I was *out*. So I signed on. A few months later, I was in *college*. My first semester, of six courses, I had five C's and one B (in swimming). I was in. The second-youngest freshman in my class (I'd skipped second grade).

I owe Augustana College for taking a flier on a just-turned-17-year-old kid with mediocre grades. I was given a chance.

This fall, I will have my 50ᵗʰ reunion. It will be good to be back. See old friends. My fraternity brothers. And visit … my *college*.

May 17, 2018

A Big Lesson

September. Freshman year. My second or third week of college. On academic probation. Dr. Erickson was teaching a course in political science. I had been slouched in my chair, probably doodling and not paying much attention to the class. Suddenly, I heard my name. "Mr. Petersen." It was Dr. Erickson asking me to answer a question. With considerable ease, I looked up and offered, "I'm not prepared," and I went back to whatever it was I was doing.

Dr. Erickson padded over and stood by my seat. "Stand up," he said. I looked up. "Stand up," he repeated. So I stood up. He continued.

"Mr. Petersen, you're not prepared? Well, let me tell you—if you're not prepared to answer a simple question, you will probably not be prepared to answer the tough ones. You're not prepared today, so I would bet, Mr. Petersen, that you will not be prepared tomorrow either. Perhaps you don't care. And if that's the case, I feel sorry for you."

The sweat began trickling down my neck. And he went on.

"Mr. Petersen, you have two choices in life. To try to be prepared for what needs to be done. Or not."

Dr. Erickson finished his comments, and from that day forward, I was never again unprepared for his class. I was generally quick to raise my hand, and I was usually ready with an answer. Others in the class had learned a lesson that day too (at my expense). I ended up getting a C in the class, and I took four more courses from Dr. Erickson (A's and B's). Poly sci became my major, and he was my faculty advisor. No—I didn't whine because he badgered me. I was *truly* grateful for the lesson. More kids should have such lessons.

October 17, 2013

Typing

I had some good courses in college. But the most useful was a yearlong course on *advanced first aid*, which ended with me getting a civil defense medical responder card (remember, this was 1966). I thought, "I'm an Eagle Scout. This'll be a snap." It was *not*. But the knowledge gleaned from this course has come in *very* handy over the years.

Of all the subjects I endured in high school, far and away the best course I ever took was *typing*. It was called "touch typing," a method developed by Frank Edward McGurrin (a Salt Lake City court stenographer) in 1888. Thank you, Mr. McGurrin! I use this skill *every* day. In abundance.

I am able to type the way one was meant to type. Accurately. Fast. Fingers flying. *Whooosh!* None of this two-finger business. I often type my own letters, lengthy reports and loquacious emails at a speed of perhaps 60 words a minute with minimal error. Rarely looking at the keyboard. *Typing.* What a value-added learning tool for a young person today. Do schools teach typing the way I learned? I dunno, but it belongs on the menu.

By the way—do you know the longest word in the English language that you can write using the letters on the top row of a keyboard?

Typewriter. Yep.

August 9, 2018

Brothers

Behold, how good and how pleasant it is for brothers to dwell together in unity. It is like the precious ointment upon the head … and as the dew that descended upon the mountains of Zion. (Psalm 133)

I have a hundred brothers. They are scattered to the four winds. They are my *fraternity* brothers from Augustana College. Members of the Gamma Alpha Beta—GAB—fraternity.

I wasn't destined for college. My future was to work after high school. Frankly, it's a fluke that I even applied (after graduation) and got into *college*. And came to know my brothers.

Last weekend, we had a reunion of brothers from the GAB fraternity. Donna and other wives attended. It started Friday night and went to Sunday afternoon. What a slice. I am truly grateful for the opportunity of meeting, knowing and loving the men who are my *brothers*. There are amazing memories and stories (many of which are gladly remembered—and a few that won't be repeated). I remember one dark night when my *entire* pledge class was corralled by police and taken off to jail. One astute pledge escaped by pulling himself up onto a fire escape. Me.☺

The GABs won the Homecoming Sing with the ballad "Oh Shenandoah" (more on that later). One brother—my roommate for three years, "Colonel Ox"—has been a glue that helped hold together the hundred or so GABs on our mailing list. It's interesting how when you meet old friends, you kinda pick up where you left off. It's as if time stood still and you're back being 19 years old again.

In my brain, I'm still 19. Now if only my body would cooperate…

_____

July 5, 2015

Hitchhiking

Does *anyone* hitchhike anymore? I can't remember the last time I saw someone standing on the side of the road. Arm extended. Thumb pointed up. Back at Augustana College in Rock Island, Illinois, when I wanted to go home, my options were to take the train (to the tune of 20 bucks) or hitchhike. I nearly always chose the latter option.

My *modus operandi* was to Magic Marker a sign: *Augie student to Chicago*. And on the back: *Augie student to Mount Prospect*. I'd stand on the street outside my dorm. And hold up the sign. And stick out my thumb. And always got a ride. *And* I lived to tell the tale.

The first rides would usually cart me to Interstate 80 and drop me off. There, I'd stand at the entrance ramp, looking forlorn and holding my sign. And I was always picked up.

Once (Scout's honor), a big tractor-trailer stopped. I hustled up and climbed in. The driver said, "I'm sick, and need to sleep. If you wanna drive, I'm going to Route 47." *Sooo...* I traded places with the driver. He shifted a few of the floor gears, and off I went, piloting this big rig. The driver conked out instantly, leaning against the door. At Route 47, I slowed to a stop. The driver took over, and I hopped out, walked to the down ramp and held up my sign.

Hitchhiking was so popular back in the day that Marvin Gaye wrote a song with the title "Hitch Hike." The song was recorded in 1962 and released in Gaye's *That Stubborn Kinda Fellow* album. In 1965 the Rolling Stones released their own version. Both are available online. They take me back....

September 4, 2016

The Turtle in the Tire Track

In 1969 I was in Tucumcari, New Mexico. I've always been interested in American Indian artifacts, so I took a drive to *look around*. Outside of town, I took the long road of the Chappell Spade Ranch along the Canadian River. I pulled up to the ranch house, where a man was standing. I asked if there was a place one might find such artifacts and was told "Mr. Griggs" might help, but he was out walking. "Out there," the man pointed. I was driving my 1964 Ford Falcon Sprint—ragtop. Top down. So I headed off into the desert, driving on a two-tire-track "road."

I bounced along and found Mr. Griggs about 2 miles out, walking with a young girl who was on horseback. I asked about artifacts, and he shrugged. "You just have to look." Big help *he* was. He asked if I'd drive him back to the ranch. "Sure," I said, and he hopped in.

We came to the top of a rise. Below, the two tire-track ruts were full of water from rain the night before. He said, "You better gun it, or we'll get stuck." So I did. *Whoosh!* Down the hill. And then I suddenly jammed on the brakes—skidding and splashing to a stop with water up to my hubcaps. He said, "What the ..." I got out of the car, and about 20 feet in front of us, a big turtle was cooling himself. In the water. In the tire track. If I'd continued, I would have crushed him.

I held up the turtle to show Mr. Griggs. I set the turtle on the side of the road and got back in the car. He stared at me. I looked at him somewhat defensively and said, "I didn't want to kill the turtle."

He nodded and thought a moment. "You did the right thing. You want Indian artifacts? Go that way," he pointed. I slushed out of the water, and we lurched across the desert in another two-tire-track "road." We stopped and climbed to the top of a butte, and he showed me an American Indian burial ground. He told me the story of the Anasazis who had lived there. I found some neat things—some of which I took.

Today I have in my office a well-used *mano* (corn-grinding stone), one of three I found that day, along with a *metate* (the stone on which corn was ground). Every time I walk in my office—and glance at the *mano*—I think of the turtle in the tire track ... and that very special day.

February 13, 2012

Just for a Half Hour

In July 1970, my college roommate and great friend Ox and I were driving out West in my 1964 Ford Falcon Sprint ragtop. We were destined for Spokane, Washington, to drop Ox off at Fairchild Air Force Base for survival training before he headed off to Vietnam. On the way, we were cruising an interstate, approaching Las Vegas from the east. It was probably 1:30 in the morning. Pitch dark. But when we were still 75 miles away, we could see the arched glow of Vegas in the distance.

We drove through Vegas and continued north to Nellis AFB. Ox checked us into the base VOQ—Visiting Officers Quarters. Ox, an Air Force second lieutenant; I, a retired Boy Scout. By then It was about 2 a.m. Once we got to the room and dropped our bags, Ox's first words were, "Let's go into town."

My response: "Are you kidding? I'm tired."

Ox said, "Oh c'mon let's go in for just a half hour." I thought, half hour. I looked at my watch. We'd still be back by 3:30 or so. And so I capitulated. A half hour.

When we arrived in downtown Las Vegas, we were mesmerized by the famous corner with four casinos. And we sauntered into the Golden Nugget. A 25-cent slot machine called my name. *"Scotty ... come to me...."*

I fished in my pocket and found one quarter. I put it in, pulled the handle, and bells began ringing. And lights, flashing. I had won a $47.50 jackpot. I was rich. I looked at Ox and said, "Ox, we're gonna leave here millionaires."

Later on—around 10 a.m.—we drove back to Nellis. Considerably poorer than we had arrived. We slept for a few hours and headed to Reno to try our luck again. Regrettably, I won no further jackpots. At least at a casino...

August 17, 2019

Blind Date

When I was in law school, a great friend from Augustana College—Diane—was living nearby while going to grad school. One day, Diane said to me, "Scott, I have a girlfriend from New York I think you should meet." I probably said something like, "Duhhh ... OK." And drooled.

A few weeks later, at the appointed hour, I knocked on the door of my blind date. This cute girl opened the door and smiled, and I fumbled for words (*"Duhhh ... humna humna ...* Nice pad ya got here...." Those *were* among my first words). She probably wondered what sort of bozo Diane had fixed her up with. ("Yes ... *uhmmm* ... thank you.") I remember sweating a lot and making a lot of *duhhh* sounds, but for some inexplicable reason she must have found these qualities endearing. So we went out. Double-dated. To the racetrack of all places. And then dinner.

A few months later, the most *cosmic* of coincidences occurred, which probably sealed the deal. A couple of years later, we were married, and we're still at it. *Duhhh...*

September 9, 2018

Coincidence

You meet someone you know in a faraway place. *Wow!* What a coincidence. You meet someone that has *your* name. *Wow!* What a coincidence. We've all had that moment of coincidence when we slap our forehead and go, *That's pretty cool.*

I've had my share of coincidences but none more profound than happened when I was dating this girl I'd met on a blind date. Donna. I was in law school, and she was in grad school. Donna had a subscription to the Lyric Opera. One seat in the upper balcony. I asked her where she sat. "Maybe I'll come join you one of these evenings," I offered. She handed me an old ticket stub, and I stuck it in my pocket. A few weeks later, a night class was canceled, and I had the evening off. I thought, *Tonight's Donna's opera night. I'll go to the opera.*

So I walked over to the Lyric's box office and was directed to the seventh floor, where there was a ticket office. I pulled out the dog-eared ticket stub and handed it to the woman behind the counter. "I'd like to get the seat next to this one for tonight."

The woman looked at me like I was an idiot. "Sir, tonight is *Rigoletto*. We've been sold out for six months. And we have a *looong* waiting list."

At that moment, the stars and planets fell into alignment. All of the sages of the ages seemed to nod in somber agreement. At that very moment, as I was about to turn away, a woman walked from behind a partition and said, "Here's a cancellation." And handed the woman in the ticket office a piece of paper. The woman looked at it. And then at my ticket stub. "Oh my…" was about all she could say. The cancellation happened to be precisely, exactly, the seat next to Donna's.

The woman looked at me. "I know we have a waiting list, but I'm not sure I could give this to anyone else … under the circumstances." And she sold me the ticket for *Rigoletto*.

I arrived late. The lights were out. And I sat down, waited a brief moment and grabbed Donna's leg. She jumped and let out a whoop like Gilda, the soprano. And the rest—as they say—is history. What a *coincidence…*

August 2, 2013

The Antique Crutch

Soon after Donna and I were married, we took a drive out to western Illinois. We stopped at an antique shop outside a small town. After wandering around—and finding nothing—we strolled outside and headed to the car. Suddenly, we heard shouts and yells from the store. The door banged open, and a man—running—burst out, covering his head. He was being chased and pummeled by another man with an antique crutch(!!). *Whack! Whack!*

Having no clue what to do—if anything—I pointed and yelled, "YOU'RE UNDER ARREST!" The two stopped—one in midswing—and turned toward me. Like a deer in the headlights. I yelled and pointed, "YOU—OVER THERE. AND YOU—OVER THERE." The two parted and began babbling animatedly—and angrily—about what the other had done. ("He was …" "No you were …")

A woman stepped out on the porch of a house. I pointed at *her* and yelled, *"YOU*—CALL THE POLICE." She immediately popped back into the house. The two men continued to explain whatever the issue was. But I sensed they were starting to wonder—*who is this guy?*

After a few minutes, off in the distance, I saw a police car—emergency lights flashing—speeding down the road. Under my breath I hissed to Donna, "Get in the car." She did. And I calmly walked to the car got in and drove away—just as the police car pulled into the driveway.

I really had *zero* curiosity about staying to see how it all turned out.

November 7, 2011

True Confessions

Shortly after I passed the Illinois bar exam, Donna and I flew to Portland, Oregon, to visit my aunt and uncle and their family. One weekend, we rented a car and drove south into the hinterlands of Oregon.

Upon leaving a small town, I saw birds on the road ahead. I announced to Donna in my best John Wayne voice, "Watch this," and I stomped on the accelerator. The car sped up 80, 90, 100…. Donna was shouting at me to slow down, but—hey, I was 25 and macho. As I approached the birds, they looked up and casually flew off. I *rocketed* over the carrion they'd been chewing on (*guess I showed them*).

About that time, I looked in the rearview mirror and was surprised to see a car behind us. A police car. *#&X@*!* I pulled over and stopped. And got a ticket. For doing 108 in a 65 mph zone. *#&X@*!*

The bad thing was that I was to appear in court at the same time I was to appear before the Character and Fitness Committee of the Illinois Bar (*sorry, fellows, I have a court date*). Donna was silent. *Stewing.* At the next town, I stopped. The judge's name was on the ticket. So I ... called the police station from a pay phone.

Me: Hello? Officer, I'm trying to reach Judge _____. Can you call him and ask him to please call me?
Officer: It's Sunday.
Me: I know, but it's important (I gave him the pay phone number).
Officer: I'll see (*click*).

I waited for 30 minutes. The sun was setting. Quiet. Birds chirping their evening hymns. Then the pay phone rang.

Me: This is Scott Petersen (I figured that was better than "hullo").
Judge: This is Judge _____. You wanted me to call (*sounds of splashing and children in the background*).
Me: Your Honor, I'm from Chicago. I just graduated from law school and passed the bar. I was just pulled over by two officers for speeding—108 in a 65 zone. I am guilty. But I am supposed to appear in court, and I am also supposed to appear before the Character and Fitness Committee of the bar at that time. I was wondering ...
Judge: Just a minute (*long silence*). All right, Mr. Petersen. Raise your right hand. Repeat after me. "I promise that I will never speed again."
Me: I will never speed again.
Judge: I want you to promise. I want you to swear to me...
Me: I swear (*raising my hand in the phone booth*) ... I swear ... I will never speed again.
Judge: Send me your ticket. Mark it "personal." Remember, Mr. Petersen—you promised me (*click*).

It was a "not guilty" over the phone. No fine.

The judge could have said, "Tough, kid. You show up or else." But he didn't. The lesson therefore became all the more powerful. *Seriously.* And since then, I have never taken a car much beyond the speed limit (except maybe when I'm in a hurry to play golf). When tempted, I am always tugged back to a fall day in 1972 ... when I made a promise....

August 16, 2011

Do You Play Golf?

Years ago, when I was a state's attorney, I played golf with seven other guys. *Every* Saturday morning for several years. From April to October, we played at Cog Hill in Lemont, Illinois. Number 4. Dubsdread. Reserved tee times at 6:30 a.m. or so, depending on sunrise. We were the second and third foursomes off the tee—often after Larry Lujack and a group from his radio staff.

From my house, this meant traversing 45 miles to Lemont. Every Saturday morn. To arrive by 5:45 a.m. Thus, each Saturday, I was up at 4 a.m. Showered, dressed and on the road by 4:30.

When I left my house, I would not waste time. If you get my drift. I gunned the car when I left the driveway, and by the time I hit Lake Street, I was doing maybe 50. In a 30 zone. Never a soul on the highway. Except one morning when in the black of night, way back, I saw flashing lights moving *swiftly* in my direction. *#&X@*!*

I slowed. Stopped. Got out of the car and stood there. Holding up my license. A police cruiser ground to a stop, and an officer got out. I was wearing shorts and a golf shirt, so I didn't look like much of a threat.

"Do you know how fast you were going?" he asked as he approached.

I handed him my license. "Yes sir, I do. I was going too fast." And then I offered, "Are you a golfer?"

He looked at me. "Yeah. Why?"

I responded, "I live back there." I turned and pointed. "Every Saturday morning, I play golf at Cog Hill in Lemont. We tee off in about an hour. And I confess that I sometimes go faster than I should when I leave the house."

The officer looked at me. Chewing on my comment. "Well, most Saturdays, I'm sitting right back"—he turned and pointed—"there. Keeping an eye on things. Do me a favor. Go the speed limit from now on." And he handed me back my license.

"Hit 'em straight," he said. And walked back to his cruiser.

March 19, 2017

Did You Shave?

I golf a couple times a week. If I get up early, I hop in the shower, dry off and dress in the space of 7 or 8 minutes. I normally don't shave unless I have to "go somewhere." Last weekend, I went off to play golf. Donna was up. She gave me a quizzical *look.*

"Did you shave?" she asked. "Nah. I'm just playing golf." "Don't you think you should shave?" she asked. "Nah. Nobody notices," I replied. She gave me another *look,* and I made a hasty exit.

Now I have to say that I have never—*never*—said to my golfing buddies, "*Pssst!* Did you see Norm? He didn't shave this morning." I have never observed that one of my brethren had not taken Barbasol and Schick to face. Frankly, I probably wouldn't notice if a guy hadn't shaved unless he started to look like Billy Gibbons of ZZ Top. ("Hey Mark, did you shave this morning?" "Scott, I haven't shaved in six months." "Golly, I never noticed.")

I'm not sure what the big deal is about shaving. But whenever we go *anywhere,* I inevitably get the question "Did you shave?" *Most* of the time, I come up with the right answer.

In my house, I make all of the *big* important decisions. Donna makes all of the *piddly* ones. However, *Donna* is the one who decides what decisions are *big* and which are *piddly.* Shaving, it seems, is one that borders on piddly.

May 20, 2018

Who May I Say Is Calling?

When you place a telephone call and the receptionist says, "Who may I say is calling," you give your name. Right?

One day years ago, I got this question when I called a close friend. My eyes narrowed, and I responded, "This is his parole officer." A few weeks later, I identified myself as "his tap dance teacher." A few weeks ago, I said, "I'm from the Garden Shop, and I wanna know, do I dump this load of manure on his driveway or in the front yard?"

I called my Boy Scout pal Dr. Bill in Lexington, Kentucky. ("Who's calling please?") I said I was putting the new roof on his house. Well, patients took a back seat for the moment. He quickly answered and said, "WHAT??" Apparently, he'd just asked for a *quote* on a new roof and was debating the subject.

We all get the *who's calling please* business and—maybe it's just me— one day I decided to be different. "My name is Marv McClurg from the *Reader's Digest*. I'm calling about his million-dollar prize." And I hear in the background, "Sir, this man's calling about your million-dollar prize."

At this point, when I call and say, "This is Nelson Snodgrass from the White House," receptionists will giggle and tell the recipient—always with a smile—"Scott's on the phone."

March 8, 2015

Finding Pennies

As a kid, I lived in the one-room attic of a Chicago bungalow on Byron Street. I remember with clarity that my family didn't have much money. I decided to do something about it. At the age of 4, I sold water in front of my house for a penny. The water came from a garden hose and was dispensed in one of four small colorful, hard-plastic cups.

My father seriously advised that I should pick up any stray pennies (or nickels or dimes) I might happen across. My big score was finding a crisply folded dollar bill lodged under a counter at Sears Roebuck at Six Corners in Chicago. I gave it to my mother, and she called me her "hero."

To this day, I still pick up pennies and dimes and wallets and watches and cell phones and rings and other jewelry and even (once) a hundred-dollar bill, all found lying in public places. I always repatriate the personal (identifiable) items. But the few that have no claimants (like the wedding rings), I keep. Some items are *verrry* nice....

My habit is to put "found" money in my left pocket (my change is in my right) and toss it into a bowl when I get home. And each year, I donate the proceeds (plus some extra) to a charity. Both my granddaughters now keenly watch for pennies on the street. Eve found a pair of eyeglasses and a nickel under a table in a restaurant. Elin has picked up nails found on the street (another penchant of mine). I've told Donna that when I retire, I will simply walk the streets. And come home with bags full of coins, bills and diamond rings....

May 26, 2019

Picking Up Nails

When I walk from my house to the train station in the morning, I walk in the *street*. Every day. I *like* the street. There's little traffic, and while conscientious folks hoof on the sidewalk with a 48-inch path, *I* have my own white carpet boulevard—20 feet wide. I walk against traffic. Near the curb. And as I walk, I keep my eyes peeled. I've found coins, bills, wallets, watches, cell phones, jewelry, a diamond ring (yep). And *nails*.

Watching for nails in the street was inspired by my parents. And I still pick up *nails*. Whenever. Wherever. On my walk to the train station. Or downtown. Or on vacation. I stoop over and pick 'em up. The file cabinet in my office at home sports a few of the more exceptional specimens (including a 9-inch monster).

Why do I still pick up nails? Maybe it's my upbringing (we can't escape some things). Maybe it's the Boy Scout in me. I don't want you, your child or my daughter to drive over one of those sharpies and have a (potentially big) problem. Over the years, I've picked up *hundreds* of nails. And pitched them in the garbage. *And* displayed a few on my file cabinet.

32

We are told that small things we do can make a big difference. I know that everyone who reads these words does small things. Big things. And *more*. Picking up nails doesn't sound like a big thing. But who knows?

January 8, 2017

Run Over

My parents taught me early to keep my eyes open. And to watch for coins on the street or sidewalk. I've picked up pennies, nickels, dimes, dollar bills—as well as cell phones, wallets, watches and fine jewelry (some *mighty* fine). My eyes are glued to the ground. All monetary finds go into a bowl for a year-end charitable donation. It's really a game. A personal challenge. To see what I can find.

During the week, I catch the train and go downtown to my office. Each day as I walk across the train tracks, I slow. *Looking.* I have never put a coin on the railroad tracks (to do so would probably invite several years in the penitentiary). But I'm on the scout for those errant "run-over" coins that have been placed on the tracks—and lost—by *others*.

Over the years, I have acquired a nice collection. *Nineteen* flattened coins to be precise. A few quarters. Dimes. Nickels. Pennies. Each one I'm sure has a story. Just as each lost coin has a story. The good thing is that if I ever run low on cash, I can always take these run-over coins to the bank and trade them in for unscathed versions. One dollar and 36 cents by my count.

December 11, 2014

The Wedding Ring

In January 2013, I was at O'Hare airport with my family. Terminal 3, American Airlines. Standing in front of a self-service check-in thingy. Going through the ritual. And I looked down. There was a circular object on the floor. At first it looked like a small bare key ring. My gaze sharpened. I bent down and picked it up. It was a *wedding ring*. A man's wedding ring.

I looked around then squinted at the inside. There was an inscription—a date in 2002 and the name *Rosa*.

I raised my voice inquiringly to those nearby—"Rosa?" The only looks I got were the curious—not the *that's me or someone I know* look. I padded over to one of the AA stations (No. 39 as I recall), and I told the woman behind the counter I'd found a wedding ring inscribed *Rosa*. I asked if she could make an announcement. And she did. Inside the entire terminal. "Anyone losing an item that relates to Rosa, please report to Station 39."

Now, I had to catch a plane, so I gave the woman my card and a few details on the ring and went on my way. Ring in my left pocket. As we walked, I heard the announcement a second—then third—time.

Since reporting the find, I heard nothing. I called the TSA and AA lost-and-found stations. Gave them the details. American Airlines posted the find on Facebook—and it generated more than 600,000 hits. Yet— no response.

I kept the ring on my desk at home. Waiting. In the bowl where I keep "found" money—and things. I *wanted* to get a call. I could envision Rosa standing there, arms akimbo, asking her hubby, "Where did you leave your wedding ring?" and the poor soul going, "*Duhhh* … I dunno."

Update: The ring remained on my desk for several years. It has now— regrettably—been deaccessioned and the funds donated to a charity. Sorry, Rosa.

February 17, 2019

Flying Commercial

On May 6, 1982, Donna was on United Airlines flight 911 (ironic flight number) from New York to Chicago's O'Hare International Airport after her grandfather's funeral. In those days, anyone could wander out to the arrival gate, to welcome friends and loved ones. So I parked in the lot and hoofed out to the gate. The flight was due to arrive at 10:09 p.m. but was running late. It finally arrived at 10:40 p.m.

Waiting in the gate area, I noticed a few *suits* standing around. Whispering into little walkie-talkies. I figured they were there to make sure I didn't get rambunctious when I saw Donna. The plane docked. The gangway door opened, and people began streaming out. And then there was Donna....

She came up to me and said, "You won't believe who's on the flight." I said, "Donald Trump?" (Just kidding.) And she said, "No—Gerald Ford." And indeed, as we started walking toward the baggage claim, I looked back, and out from the gangway popped the 38th president of the United States. Surrounded by a fast-walking security diamond of Secret Service. *Well...*

I have quite an interest in autographs and manuscripts. So I asked Donna for her ticket. And I slowed down—positioning myself to be in the center of the security diamond as it advanced. Suddenly, I was caught up on the edge of the diamond. I was one agent away from number 38. "Mr. President," I asked, "may I have your autograph?"

He had papers under his arm, and he responded, "Kinda tough with my arms full"—and I handed him my ticket and a pen. He slowed, put the ticket on his papers, and scribbled his name. I exited the diamond. *Zing!*

I remember the story of Harry and Bess Truman. When they left the White House, they took a *train* back to Independence, Missouri. And the two lived on Harry's $112.56-a-month Army pension. *Without* Secret Service protection. I am keenly aware that we're in a different world. But it would sure be nice if our current leaders—*and* their spouses—could be safe. *And* economical. Taking the train like Harry. Or flying commercial like Jerry.

December 28, 2017

Stay Out of Highwood

Shortly after the movie *Ghostbusters* was released (that was 1984), Donna, Lauren (then age 8) and I were on a flight from LaGuardia to Chicago. We were sitting in my least favorite spot—the bulkhead (no leg room). So we took off, and we were flying along when Donna announced that she was going to the bathroom. Since we were sitting at the opposite end of the coach-section bathrooms, the flight attendant said Donna could go up to first class.

When she returned, she sat down and said, "You will not believe who is sitting right in front of us. Bill Murray!" Now, Lauren was keenly aware of *Ghostbusters,* and she immediately had to go to the bathroom. And she whisked through the curtains. I could see her standing in the aisle—staring at the person directly in front of us (presumably Mr. Murray). She giggled—went to the bathroom—and returned.

"He made a funny face at me!" she exclaimed. Soon thereafter, she had to go to the bathroom again. And *again.* And *again...*

After we landed and pulled into the gate, I asked Lauren if she wanted his autograph. Embarrassed, she said no. We walked through the terminal toward baggage claim—with Bill Murray (now wearing a large floppy hat) a few feet ahead. As we got to baggage claim, I told Lauren this was the last chance. "Do you want his autograph?" And she said, "Yes. But you go first."

So I approached Mr. Murray—Lauren behind me, peeking out. "Hello, Mr. Murray. We are from Wilmette [where he grew up], and we are fans of your new movie. May we bother you for an autograph?" Bill Murray looked at Lauren behind me—grabbed her and picked her up and gave her a gentle shake. "Whatsa matter? Can't you talk?" And Lauren melted.

He signed a large card: *To Lauren—Stay out of Highwood* (the place in our area known for taverns). So far, she has. I think....

September 29, 2016

TWA Emergency

Years ago, I would flit off to Spain and Portugal every few months. One Wednesday, I was returning on a TWA flight from Lisbon to Chicago. The flight was scheduled to leave at 1:10 p.m. I arrived at the airport in good order (probably 90 minutes ahead of departure) and got in the check-in line. There were no clerks checking in passengers. So we stood. 12:15 pm. 12:30. 12:45. No clerk. No nothing. People were grumbling. Looking at watches and the marquee with flight information.

Finally, at about 1 p.m., a man emerged from the back—behind the counter—and advised that the flight was oversold and was taking no passengers (which was odd since some folks had stood there for two hours).

36

"Come back on Friday, and we'll make sure we get you on a flight." And the clerk beat a hasty retreat.

The Portuguese travelers picked up their suitcases and shuffled off for the exits. Not so the 14 Americans who remained. *Fuming.* We huddled. Brief introductions. Two of us went off in search of answers and help. I left my luggage with a bunch of complete strangers. After a call to TWA from the American Embassy (*please take care of these folks*), we were offered lunch. TWA personnel took our names—promising to call family to let them know of the glitch in service. The plan was to fly us to Frankfurt that afternoon and put us up in the airport hotel. Next morning, we would head off to our respective destinations.

Lunch was passable, and the BOAC flight to Frankfurt, uneventful. I checked into a nondescript hotel room in Frankfurt. Showered. And headed down for a late dinner. Then back up to the room. And sleep. Next morning, I was on a flight through London to New York. I arrived home—*finally.* Lauren seemed especially glad to see me.

Later I learned that the TWA folks in Lisbon had called my home. Donna was playing tennis, and Lauren (age 10) was home alone. Lauren answered the phone. "This is a TWA emergency! I must speak with Mrs. Petersen. *TWA emergency.*" Lauren said her mom was not home and—*click*—the line went dead.

Lauren called the tennis center. Hysterical. Donna rushed home and after an hour of calling—and waiting—learned that I was not deep-sixed into the Atlantic but simply delayed. Lauren was relieved. When Donna arrived home, Lauren had been sobbing. Holding my picture. *TWA emergency.*

September 28, 2014

'Oh Shenandoah'

From the day we brought our newborn daughter home from the hospital—and for years—I sang to her. Every night before she went to bed. I would play my guitar and sing "Froggy Went a Courtin'," "This Little Light of Mine," "Trouble in Mind" and a host of others.

But I would also lapse into some old songs that we used to sing in the Gamma Alpha Beta fraternity at Augustana College. And I would often close the evening, as Lauren was closing her eyes, with the GAB "Sweetheart Song"—"Oh Shenandoah," a song the GABs sang at a homecoming event one year (and won).

When Lauren was married just over two years ago, I thought long and hard about what song should be played for the daddy-daughter dance at the reception. Then it hit me. And I smiled. Lauren had some general notion about the universe of songs from which I would select. "Dad, you're not going to have them play 'Froggy Went a Courtin',' are you?" *No....* Instead, I picked that melancholy favorite I'd sung to close each evening—"Oh Shenandoah."

The music started, and we both had tears in our eyes as we danced to this song that will forever be in our hearts.

August 14, 2011

4

FAMILY MATTERS

Setting a Bad Example

My daughter, Lauren, was about 3 years old. I remember the moment. It was a sunny day. We were standing on a bridge, looking down on a bubbling stream. Several rocks jutted out from the rushing water—just below the bridge.

Now, understand that when a guy is standing on a bridge, looking down, there is a genetic hardwiring that impulses him to do something. *Spit.* So, without thinking, I did, and hit a rock down below.

Lauren thought this was *really* neat. She giggled, and she puckered her lips and began drooling royally. Smiles.☺ Laughs.😄 More drool.😊

"Nooo, sweetheart. This way." *Pffft.* And I hit the rock again. More drool. Laughs. Smiles. More drool. Maybe this wasn't such a good idea. I guess it really is a guy thing....☺

January 27, 2013

Fasty and Slowy

When Lauren was very small, Donna and I would often need to keep her occupied while sitting in the car, a restaurant or store. One evening we were sitting in a Greek restaurant in Evanston, just north of Chicago. Lauren was getting a little bored, so I took my right hand and—using my fingers as "feet"—began walking my hand toward her. She squealed with delight.

And of course the hand walked up her arm, over her head and down the other side. Big smiles.😊 Big laughs.😆

After awhile I got the other hand into play. Where the right hand was light and quick, the left hand was slow, lumbering and ponderous. And *heavy.* My index fingers would be raised to serve as "heads" of the two critters. And so, "Fasty" and "Slowy" were born. Fasty was nimble, dancing lightly over the table and all over Lauren (even bouncing on top of Slowy), while Slowy plodded along. Slowly. Heavily. And when Slowy stepped onto our daughter's hand, he was ... well, heavy. Lauren thought it was *hysterical!* And so Fasty and Slowy were regular visitors from then on.

Fasty and Slowy have been in hibernation for quite a few years. But I have a feeling that pretty soon they'll be making a reappearance....

November 27, 2011

T.T.T.

When Lauren was little, my great friend David devised a challenging "test" for her and his son Dave. It was called the Tickle Tolerance Test.

The object was for the little one to lie on the ground face up. While far above, a father's wiggling finger would begin its descent. Right toward Lauren's or Dave's tummy. Now, the finger never touched Lauren or Dave. It would just descend. Slowly. Wigglingly. The wiggling finger rarely got within a foot or two before the giggling and squeals of laughter began. Anyone who could stifle their laughter until the wiggling finger got within an inch or two of the tummy would get a treat. But no one survived—or passed—the Tickle Tolerance Test.

I have begun the Tickle Tolerance Test with my granddaughters, Eve and Elin. And—as expected—the laughter begins when my wiggling finger is far over my head. Beginning its descent.

Heck, I'm not sure *I* could pass the Tickle Tolerance Test.

December 18, 2014

Is There Anything in My Teeth?

How often do you go in the bathroom, look in the mirror and give yourself a quick open-mouthed grimace? Just to make sure there's nothing stuck in your teeth? I sometimes do. Occasionally, I will find, lodged in my pearly whites, something the size of a small fishing lure.

When Donna and I go out for dinner with our daughter and her family, I will sometimes use my tongue to position a large hunk of lettuce to cover my front upper teeth. Then I'll open my mouth with a Cheshire cat grin and say to the crowd, "Do I have anything in my teeth?" My granddaughters think this is *hysterical.* They laugh and giggle. Even my daughter (who is accustomed to such tomfoolery) will laugh.

Donna, however, will narrow her eyes, tighten her gaze and say, "That's not funny." I disagree. It has *got* to be funny if the people at the next table are laughing too....

February 2, 2017

Nice Mustache

Donna and I will take off in the summer and go up to Wisconsin. Or somewhere. Long weekends. Getaways. These are the times when I tend to be lazy about shaving.

I have no strong inclination to shave. Given my druthers, I'd probably look like Billy Gibbons. Or Dusty Hill. I shave to look neat. Presentable. But most importantly, I shave to please a certain member of my family. If you get my drift. Over the last few weeks, I have let the caterpillar on my upper lip grow. And expand. Maybe it's the manly levels of testosterone that pulse through my body, but my 'stache is looking quite cool. At least *I* think it is when I look at myself in the mirror. I give the edge a little twirl. Smirk. *Nice 'stache, Studly.*

From people who haven't seen me for a few weeks, I get a quizzical look. As if to say, "What the ..." Time skips a beat or two. They recover and blurt out the words, "Nice mustache!" *Nice mustache.* At first I would do a fist pump and think,*!* But I have come to realize that "nice mustache" is really the only civil observation a friend might offer when confronted

41

by someone with mangy-looking facial hair. And I have come to the conclusion that "nice mustache" probably translates to "Petersen, you look like a #%&*X! idiot."

That has been the conclusion of *everyone* in my family, who now—led by my granddaughters—routinely chants, "Shave it, Popi, shave it!" My hearing isn't so good lately. So all I hear is "Save it, Popi, save it!"

August 21, 2016

Gus Edwards

I went to the veterinarian to pick up my daughter's dog, who had been boarded for a few days. I walked in and said, "I'm here to pick up Gus." The young woman looked at me. "Last name?"

It was then I realized dogs have last names that must be trotted out on special occasions. If you asked me whether I had a dog, I'd say, yes. If you asked me her name, I'd say, "Daisy." And that would be it. If I responded that my dog's name is "Daisy Petersen," you'd probably look at me, roll your eyes and start edging away....

At the veterinarian though, it's customary for dogs, cats, gerbils and the occasional fish to have last names. "I'm here to pick up my hamster—Butterscotch Petersen." And the receptionist nods and checks the records. And sends a note to the back room to bring out "Butterscotch Petersen." No rolled eyes. No edging away. Just a $184 hotel bill for Butterscotch Petersen.

January 26, 2017

Daisy

My wife and I have a 10-pound gray miniature poodle named Daisy. To say Daisy is smart would be an understatement. Daisy is smarter than some lawyers and most politicians I know. And probably brighter than me on some occasions. When you talk to her, she looks you right square in the eye as if she's trying to figure out ... *Just what language is he speaking?*

Daisy is a certified therapy dog—certified with the Canine Therapy Corps in Chicago (www.caninetherapycorps.org). Canine Therapy

Corps has nearly 75 dogs working in 15 area hospitals. It is a wonderful program that provides animal-assisted therapy, often in collaboration with physicians and attending staff.

Daisy went to school for nearly two years to get certified. She and Donna work on Wednesday afternoons at the Rehabilitation Institute of Chicago. Since Daisy responds to voice and motion commands (both of which Donna says I have trouble with), Daisy works with stroke and spinal cord–injury patients who may need help with speech and movement.

To watch Daisy "on the job" is a treat. She dances, twirls, sits, stays, barks, marches and does Level 1 calculus, all while working with the patients. When she's working with children, sometimes a little boy or girl will just want to hold her. And that's just fine too.

When Daisy gets home, she takes off her blue vest and kicks back, knocking down a few liver treats and taking a walk. Then—exhausted from the day—Daisy heads upstairs to bed, to dream of table scraps and fire hydrants....

On July 19, 2018, Daisy left us. She was a wonderful dog—who will be greatly missed. It's very hard to say goodbye.

August 24, 2011

Roots and Wings

Good parenting is critical for the development of children. *Nature* and *nurture* play a significant role. It is best to *guide* children to achieve their greatest and highest potential, rather than to *steer* them into a parental choice of interests, profession and schools.

I once attended an insightful presentation by psychotherapist Alice Virgil. She spoke on the things parents and grandparents can do to participate in this development. Tops on her list were:

Relationships. It's important to have them. Develop empathy with others in the sense that we are all in this together.
Creativity. Help children stretch their thinking: Learn how to make a meal, how to play with a cardboard box, how to be occupied *without* an iPhone or television.

Awareness. Develop social awareness such that a child learns to "read" situations and social cues.

Initiative and courage. Learn to do the right thing at the right time. Learn how to work hard and put in effort to achieve.

Morality. Develop a moral code. Learn what is right—*and* what is wrong.

Spirituality. Develop a sense of purpose. Learn that we all have a reason to be in this world. Say grace at meals.

So what can parents and grandparents do to build strong and resilient kids?

Express gratitude. Discuss the best of the day—and the worst. Teach joy and appreciation.

Practice mindfulness. Give attention to the present moment with kindness, curiosity and compassion. This helps children respond *reflectively* rather than *reflexively*.

Be an emotion coach. Help children understand their emotions.

Free up play. Forget the gimmicks, complex toys and oversight. Allow *unstructured, unsupervised* free play.

Support the right way. Praise a child? Absolutely. But never praise results or outcome. Always praise *effort*.

Build from the basics. Develop a strong marriage and family home.

In a Sunday sermon, our pastor added further inspiration for parents, using a famous quote of Henry Ward Beecher: "The greatest bequest we can give our children is roots and wings." The book *Hot Chocolate for the Soul* expands on this admonition—and provides context: "Good parents give their children roots and wings. Roots to know where their home is, and wings to fly and put into practice what they have learned."

It's a tough job being a parent (a wee bit easier being a grandparent ☺). Little words of wisdom like those can't help but help.

April 23, 2012, and
January 24, 2019

Hennessy 3-Star

My father's parents were both gone before I was born. My mother's father died when I was 3 years old. While I have some old photos, I have only one memory of him—sitting on the floor with me as I played with toy cars. Fortunately, I got to know my mom's mother, Ruth, a sweet lady who would save stamps and coins for my collections.

My dad had an aunt and uncle—Anna and Axel Larsen—who had no children. From an early age, they were my "Grandma" and "Grandpa" Larsen. They were happy with these monikers. Grandpa Larsen passed away when I was in college, and Grandma Larsen went into the Danish "old people's home."

One day, while in college, I went to visit her. We talked, and as I was leaving she asked if, the next time I came to visit, I would bring her a little Hennessy 3-Star cognac. I said sure and left. I got in the car and thought … and then drove to a liquor store, where I bought a half pint of Hennessy 3-Star. And drove back to the home.

Now, I couldn't tell which made her happier—my return visit or the half pint of 3-Star. Either way, I resolved to pay a visit whenever I could. And I did. And each time brought a pint bottle of Hennessy 3-Star.

When Grandma Larsen passed, I'm sure she licked her lips. And smiled.

July 18, 2020

Uncle Walter

I wonder if every family has an "Uncle Walter." *My* Uncle Walter was my father's father's brother. He was born in Denmark and moved to the United States just in time to be conscripted into the United States Army—and shipped off to France—in World War I.

When Uncle Walter finally got home, he behaved strangely. He only wore white clothes, and he refused to sleep in a bed. He always slept on the floor. He was committed to a veterans hospital in Milwaukee. My father (Willy) said Uncle Walter was *shellshocked*—PTSD—from the war. And that was that for Uncle Walter. My father's family never talked about him, and only once that I recall did anyone go to visit.

I'd heard about Uncle Walter, but I'd never met him. So when I was in my late 20s—rebel that I was—I decided to go *find* him. I called the Veterans Administration and learned that he was in a halfway house for veterans on South 27th Street in Milwaukee. And I drove up to see him.

As I approached the address, there was an old man in white clothing walking slowly on the sidewalk. I stopped the car. Got out. "Are you Walter Petersen?" He looked at me. I said, "I am Willy's son." And Uncle Walter began crying....

A few months later, I brought my father up to see Uncle Walter. And just about every week from my first visit, I sent him a care package of Copenhagen snuff (he loved it), some candy and a couple of dollar bills. When he died at the veterans home in King, Wisconsin, he left me "everything": his large-print Bible, his veterans benefit (about $1,700), the cross on his coffin and a brand-new stuffed bunny for my daughter. The Bible remains on my shelf. The cross is on the wall in my den. The bunny is still in Lauren's old room. And the money purchased a tree that sits in our yard.

I'm glad I reached out to *my* Uncle Walter. Though I'd bet there are more than a few Uncle Walters out there....

December 14, 2017

5

LEGAL BRIEFS

On Being a Lawyer

I
Do
Not
Find
Every
Detail
Notably
Exciting.
Courtroom
Litigation
Nonetheless
Demonstrates
Unadulterated
Satisfaction
Adventurous
Strategies
Arguments
Sidebars
Lengthy
Briefs
Windy
Talk
And
Me
2

September 14, 2014

So This Guy

So this guy is up delivering a speech to a large group of people. He begins to rant, "All lawyers are jerks!" (Or you may select your own epithet.)

From the back of the room, a guy raises his hand and yells, "I really take offense at your words."

The guy giving the speech asks, "Are you a lawyer?"

"Absolutely not," the guy says defensively. "I'm a jerk!"

Lawyers *do* get a bad rap from the public. In a 2013 Pew research poll, lawyers ranked at the bottom of ten professions. Only 18% of responders felt that lawyers contributed "a lot" to society's well-being. And that's down from 23% in 2009. In a December 2013 Gallup poll on "Honesty/Ethics in Professions," lawyers were at the bottom of the list—just above members of congress, lobbyists and car salesmen.

While there are a lot of good lawyers, I tend to think that much of the criticism of lawyers is deserved. We don't police the profession as we might and … wait … *shhh* … Sorry, gotta run! I hear a siren.

September 14, 2014

My Biggest Case

When I was a young(er) lawyer, my father got a speeding ticket. "I wasn't speeding," he protested. "I wanna fight this thing. You wanna be my lawyer?" he asked me. I'd never handled a speeding ticket, but I said, "Sure, Dad."

On the appointed day of the court hearing for my father's speeding ticket, we showed up and sat toward the back of the courtroom. The room was crowded, and people milled around. The judge entered. Everyone rose. And the judge got down to business. "Anyone who wants to plead guilty, I'm willing to give you supervision—which means you pay a fine, but if you get no ticket in the next six months, the conviction is wiped out."

The judge directed those interested toward a window where they would pay a fine but get their "supervision." My father—who had been deaf since World War II—didn't hear, but I knew he wasn't interested ("I wanna fight this thing").

After a while, my father's case was called. I took my father's arm, stood—and we walked to the front. And stepped before the judge. "Good morning, your honor," I said. "My name is Scott Petersen, and I'm here representing the defendant Peter Petersen."

The judge got a glint in his eye and looked at me. Smiling. "Is he your father?"

"Yes, your honor," I replied seriously. The judge chuckled. Looked at the ticket and said, "Case dismissed." I thanked the judge for this amazing gift—and started to lead my father away. He pulled back. "Wait, I wanna say …"

"*DAD*," I hissed—and put a finger to my lips.

I've had a few cases in my career, but none gave me the satisfaction of that one. Once outside the courtroom, I explained that the case had been dismissed. He smiled. "You're pretty good," he said. *Yep.*

May 13, 2018

Streets and Sanitation

For five-plus years, I was an assistant state's attorney—Felony Trial Division in Chicago. My daughter was born in the middle of a brutal two-week murder jury trial (for which I go back every three years to testify in parole hearings to argue *against* release of the killer).

My wife, Donna, went into labor at about 2 a.m. on a Thursday morning. I called my friend and partner in the case and said, "Charlie, Donna's having the baby. You're gonna have to handle things today." His response: "Congrats, but be here tomorrow." The next day, I showed up at the office with my arms full of files and three boxes of cigars.

So picture this—I was in my office passing out cigars, smiling, yabbering, guys wandering in and out, when suddenly a large chap appeared at my door. He was wearing bib overalls, high rubber boots, a thick shirt and a hat. He leaned against the door frame. "Is there a Scott Petersen here?" he asked. We all turned.

I raised my hand. "Yeah. That's me."

"You missin' anything?" he asked. I felt pockets. Jacket. My checkbook! It's gone. "My checkbook," I said.

He held it up waggling it between two fingers. "I found it on the street."

I quickly dipped into my wallet for a twenty. "Here," I said, taking the checkbook. "Thank you. I apprec—"

"No. That's OK," he held up his hand. "I'm with Streets and Sanitation. I want you guys to know—we have a lot of good people in Streets and Sanitation."

I then said, "My wife just had a baby. Can I offer you some cigars?" He looked at the open box. "That I will take." He grabbed a large handful of stogies and disappeared.

It's funny how things happen—and there are moments of intense clarity. Obviously, I'll never forget the birth of my daughter (I was there☺), but I'll also never forget the integrity of that stranger. Streets and Sanitation...

October 28, 2012

Threat Level

The first time someone threatens to kill you, it gets your attention. The second and third times it does, but not as much.

In my other life, I dealt with bad people. Bad crime. Pretty intense stuff. A few of the bad guys I dealt with took the enthusiasm I showed for my job personally. When that happened, they were apt to lash out.

Threats were rare. But they happened. The first time for me was Robert A., North Shore punk who had a string of armed robberies. He had cases all over. So I followed him. From courthouse to courthouse. Courtroom to courtroom. Informing the judges of *all* the other cases. *And* what a bad guy he was. So Robert A. remained in custody—ultimately going down for the count.

After perhaps half a dozen of these expeditions, as he was being led away—he screamed at me. Lunging. Held back by court bailiffs. He described in detail what he planned to do to me—and my family—when he got out.

Our usual protocol was to report such threats to the chief of the Criminal Division. He would ask us to fill out a 3-by-5 card detailing the case, the parties and the threat. That way, if one morning I was found floating in the Sag Canal, investigators could thumb through the file cards and have a heads-up on where to start. ("Lemme see.... Petersen.... Here he is. Petersen was threatened by ...")

January 19, 2017

"I'm Goin' to Trial

When I was in Chicago's Felony Trial Division at 26th and California, every day was *let's make a deal*. Each courtroom had about 400 *felony* cases on call—with perhaps 20 coming up each day for status or trial. There was *no* way we could handle trials on all these cases, so we played *let's make a deal*.

A killing that took place in a bar fight might be reduced from murder to voluntary manslaughter *if* the guy pleaded guilty. But go to trial for murder? You're looking at 14 years on the bottom (and in a few cases after 1976, the death penalty). *Let's make a deal.* Most everyone did.

Isaac R. was charged with armed robbery. He walked into a rental car agency at Lake and Wabash in the Loop, swinging a sawed-off shotgun along his right leg. A car hiker, sitting in a chair leaned up against the wall, saw Isaac walking toward the glass-walled office. And he called the police. Isaac entered, raised the gun, and the seven women behind the counter all raised their hands.

Police arrived on the scene almost immediately and could see the goings-on through the glass walls. Guns were drawn. Aimed. A Channel 7 news crew was driving by, saw the activity, stopped and began *filming*. When Isaac walked out, he was immediately arrested—*on air*—and taken into custody.

When his case came up, we assumed Isaac would plead guilty (can we *please* make a deal?) but he wanted a *jury* trial. *And* he wanted to represent himself—*pro se*. A lawyer was assigned to sit with him and help. My partner Al and I put on six of the seven women as witnesses. Two were *nuns* from a local order, and two were teachers with second jobs. Al and I wanted to put the Channel 7 video on, but the judge asked—smiling—"*Why?*" So we didn't.

The jury was out for an hour and 20 minutes. The reason it took so long was—the jury had *lunch*. And Isaac (who had three other felony indictments pending) went away for a long, *long* time. I *hope* he's still there.

April 8, 2018

Groundhog Day

Last Wednesday was "Groundhog Day." I was asked to testify—again—in a 1976 murder case. What's left of the family was there. Very emotional.

Ernie S. stabbed Susan H. to death in the 5000 block of South Ellis. She was stabbed in a kitchen. Ernie S. ran out. Susan sat down at the kitchen table. Bleeding out. Her screams brought two friends who were upstairs. Beat cops arrived and scooped her up and raced her in the squadrol to the hospital. No time for an ambulance. But Susan was DOA.

Ernie S. got 100 to 300 years after a 2½-week jury trial. The U.S. moratorium on the death penalty (for which he would have been eligible) did not end until June 1977. Interestingly, Ernie had done the same thing the week before to Jasmin G., a nursing student (Jasmin lived). Some years later, he escaped from a prison van, ran into Joliet West High School and yanked a 14-year-old girl out of a classroom. He did stuff to her in a stairwell. He was recaptured. But now Ernie wants out.

Because the sentence was "indeterminate," every two or three years we go back and testify that Ernie S. should never see the light of day again. Some folks will say, "Ohhh, just let him go. He's a victim." Just wait. Until it's their child. Grandchild.

On March 24, 2016, the parole board voted 12-0 to deny parole. They agreed on a three-year "set." Ernie would not be up for parole again until 2019.

In 2019 Ernie was released.

March 26, 2016

52

Lawyers

A police officer was being cross-examined by a defense attorney during a felony trial. The lawyer was trying to undermine the police officer's credibility.

Q: Officer, did you see my client fleeing the scene?

A: No sir. But I subsequently observed a person matching the description of the offender, running several blocks away.

Q: Officer, who provided this description?

A: The officer who responded to the scene.

Q: So a fellow officer provided the description of this so-called offender? Do you trust your fellow officers?

A: Yes, sir. With my life.

Q: With your life? Let me ask you this then, officer. Do you have a room where you change your clothes in preparation for your daily duties?

A: Yes sir, we do.

Q: And do you have a locker in the room?

A: Yes, sir, I do.

Q: And do you have a lock on your locker?

A: Yes, sir.

Q: Now, why is it, officer, if you trust your fellow officers with your life, you find it necessary to lock your locker in a room you share with these same officers?

A: You see, sir, we share the building with the court complex, and sometimes *lawyers* have been known to walk through that room.

July 6, 2017

Facilitating Payments

Let's say you're a trucker. And you have arrived at your destination in Canada to deliver a load of paper. The official at the paper plant says quite plainly, "You may not unload your truck … unless you give me $50." You hem and haw, and he tells you that unless you fork over the 50, you will have to drive back to Oklahoma City. You then agree and hand him a $50 bill. Is that a bribe?

You want to influence a public official to admit only your company's product into a particular city in Costa Rica. You offer the official $1,000 to keep your competitors out of the city. She accepts the grand. Is that a bribe?

Answer? The first situation is *probably* legal. It might be considered a "facilitating payment" under American federal law. The second is a bribe. Hands down. And you can go to jail. There is a clear difference between the two situations. While a facilitating payment (or "grease payment") might be considered a questionable business ethic, there is nothing legally wrong with it.

A "facilitating payment" is defined by the Foreign Corrupt Practices Act (1977) as a payment to a foreign official, political party or party official for "routine government action" (such as processing papers, issuing permits or other duties) that are *nondiscretionary* and that an official is already *bound* to perform. The payment is not intended to influence the outcome of an official's action—only the timing thereof. Facilitating payments are one of the few exceptions from anti-bribery prohibitions of the law.

I sometimes suggest to my wife that a payment on her part might be in order to facilitate my doing the dishes or organizing a closet. Unfortunately, it normally takes a bribe on my part to *avoid* such tasks.

As a lawyer, I have to say, this is *not* legal advice (*except* perhaps when dealing with your spouse).

January 17, 2013

I Am One of the Donkeys Here

A *long* time ago, I studied a bit of Mandarin Chinese. Then some years ago, I got back in the game with a three-month Berlitz "immersion" course. I continued for several years with my tutor—Weixin—who came to my office once a week. And we would work on Mandarin.

Chinese is not as easy as it looks. It can be … *challenging*. There are four different tonal sounds such that each word can be pronounced four different ways—with perhaps a dozen different meanings, depending on context. Thus one must be *very careful* when saying *anything*. The only word resembling an English equivalent is the word *mama*. And that will only get you so far.

After the Berlitz immersion and a few months of tutoring, I had occasion to host several Chinese judges and lawyers at my firm. I thought to myself, I will *wow* them with my resurrected knowledge of Chinese. I took them on a tour of our offices and brought them into our boardroom for a meeting. At one point in my presentation, I noticed some polite laughter, which I thought might be a result of my excellent elocution or my Shanghai accent. However, as they were leaving, their translator pulled me aside and commented that when I tried to say, "As one of the partners at Holland & Knight," I had actually said, "As one of the donkeys at Holland & Knight." ("You should say *lu shi*—not *lu zi*. Partner. Donkey." *Great...*)

I have a feeling that my *contretemps* was one of the highlights of their trip, such that the story will be retold with smiles and great enthusiasm. Probably for years (*sigh*)...

December 13, 2018

Did You Ever Pick Your Toes in Poughkeepsie?

In a classic scene in the 1971 movie *The French Connection*, Gene Hackman as Detective "Popeye" Doyle chases down a suspect. He throws him up against a wall and asks, "Did you ever pick your toes in Poughkeepsie?" The perp looks at him like, *WTF?* And Doyle repeats it. And the guy answers.

The question wasn't meant to be funny. The purpose was to disorient the subject and change the *situational dynamic*. Next time you have a disagreement with someone, ask a random, unrelated question (at the right moment of course). And see what happens.

When you read of the failures of our prison system and the collateral damage of incarceration, you wonder if changing the *situational dynamics* of rehabilitation might provide better results. Breaking the *patterns* of troubled youth might be just the ticket. For first and even second offenders, this could include *mandatory* programs for:

Socialization—singing, acting, dancing, debating, doing stand-up comedy, counseling others and so on.

Scholastics—reading, writing and arithmetic, and also languages, computer programming and skills like cooking.

Discipline—toeing the line, sticking with the program and cooperating.

Sports—learning the *atypical* such as golf, tennis, skiing, squash, handball (rather than basketball or football).

Responsibility—caring for plants and animals, working with therapy dogs, visiting senior centers, getting jobs, etc.

Nutrition—eating healthy and learning *why* to eat healthy.

You read of boot camps where young offenders are pushed by drill instructors. They do pushups, lift weights and toe the line—just as they would in prison. But just think about getting young men to learn ballet, play golf, prepare spaghetti *carbonara* or perform in a Shakespearean drama.

Modifying *situational dynamics* can enhance levels of success for a lot of things (marriage, politics, parenting, academics, business). Creative thinking—inside and *outside* the box—can pay dividends.

_____

October 31, 2018

6

GOOD TO LEARN

Try? Win. Don't Try? Lose.

My father was born in 1913. In the late 1920s, he was a caddy at North Shore Country Club in Glenview, Illinois. He would take the streetcar from the Portage Park neighborhood on Chicago's northwest side up to Waukegan and Glenview roads. From there, he and his chums would hoof east to the club.

He would do one or two "loops" and then go home on the streetcar, which ran down the middle of Waukegan Road. His best tip as a caddy was a $5 dollar bill from one wealthy (and apparently grateful) member. He said he felt *rich*.

What's interesting was my dad's clear recollection of what happened *after* work. He and several other neighborhood boys would exit from the west end of the club onto Glenview Road and walk around the corner. Streetcars ran every hour or two. Thus if a streetcar was approaching, there was lots of incentive to traverse the quarter mile or so as quickly as possible. My father said it was often the same conductor.

If he *saw* the boys—and saw them *running*—he would look at his watch and hold the other arm in the air. Holding up the streetcar. Standing on the pavement. Arm in the air. One eye on the watch. One eye on the boys. *However*, if one of the boys lagged, or slowed to walk, Mr. Conductor would look up. Twirl his arm in the air (*go!*) and hop on the streetcar. And off it went. And the boys would have to wait for an hour for the next streetcar home.

If they *tried*, and ran, or at least made an effort, the streetcar would be held up for a few minutes for the boys to arrive. And then go. My father said he learned a lesson here. About *trying*. That nameless conductor of nearly a century ago appreciated *effort*. He also knew something about *charity*. It was simple. Try? Win. Don't try? Lose.

April 12, 2015

The Road to Character

When I tutored for Chicago Lights, each week I would put a "character" quotation on a 3-by-5 card for my students. To me, the reading, writing and arithmetic are all important. But developing *character* is just as important. Perhaps more. For students, friends, family and politicians.

I just finished David Brooks' wonderful work *The Road to Character*. Brooks opens with a reference to the end of World War II—a victory of epic proportion. He observes that our parents and granadparents did not go around telling each other how great they were. The collective impulse was to warn themselves against pride. And self-glorification.

But Brooks observes that there has been a shift in ensuing generations. From a culture of humility to a culture of *I am the center of the universe*. Brooks calls it the "Big Me." Fame and fortune used to rank low as life's core ambitions. Today, those goals have skyrocketed to the top, while there's a push to censor the teaching of virtue, character and integrity in schools.

The word "sin" was always a moral tug that helped remind us life is a moral affair. But as Brooks comments, "When modern culture tries to replace sin with ideas like error or insensitivity, or tries to banish words like 'virtue,' 'character,' 'evil,' and 'vice' altogether, that doesn't make life any less moral; it just means we have obscured the inescapable moral core of life with shallow language."

Words to think about, whatever road we're on.

January 26, 2012

Frames of Mind

Most individuals have a level of competence with various skill sets. I have reasonable eye-hand coordination, which allows me to play a passable game of golf. And perform magic. I play the guitar, speak Spanish and express myself with some clarity. But don't ask me for directions. And do *not* ask me about algebra. I have the mathematical IQ of a chipmunk (I'm sure I'm insulting some very nice chipmunks).

In the original edition of his classic book *Frames of Mind*, Howard Gardner speaks of the *basic intelligences* that all people share: linguistic; musical; logical/mathematical; spatial; bodily/kinesthetic; interpersonal; and intrapersonal. While everyone has a modicum of each of these intelligences, some folks are more heavily endowed with one or more of these capabilities.

It thus becomes important for parents to recognize—and nurture— the natural intelligence of their children rather than skew development with subjective expectation. And demand. ("My boy will play football." "My daughter will be a lawyer." "My child will go to [XYZ] college.") It's one thing to *encourage* a natural athlete to study physics or a math whiz to take speech classes. But it is quite another to discourage and thereby defeat a young person's natural gifts. Or skills. In cases like that, it seems, everyone loses.

March 8, 2018

Teaching to the Test

"Teaching to the test" is an educational practice that focuses teachers on preparing students for standardized testing. The practice forces teachers to limit curriculum to a fixed set of knowledge or facts. There is an emphasis on excessive repetition of simple and isolated skills. A student's rote memorization then translates to a possible ability to *score* on a test—but an inability to understand *why* answers are what they are.

The big problem is that students suffer—greatly—by losing out on creative and abstract thinking, general knowledge and overall concepts (that's why they call it "drill and kill"). So why do teachers "teach to the test"? The answer is simple—because teachers are often themselves graded on this false metric of student success. These skewed results then reduce the validity of standardized tests and create an incorrect profile of a student's achievement. What could be *worse* for our children? For students?

June 8, 2014

Life After High School

Social studies. Reading comprehension. English literature. P.E. Chemistry. Trigonometry. These are all courses I took in high school. But the *best* course I took in high school was typing. I can type flawlessly at about 60 words a minute. The other courses? Physical science? Chemistry? What the heck is a *beaker*?

OK, *OK*. These are all good courses—and worth taking. But for my money, I think high school students should all be *required* to take a course in "Life After High School." It would be a one-year curriculum and involve seminars on balancing a checkbook, shopping, performing simple first aid, spending money wisely, building respectful relationships, acing job interviews, understanding nutrition, cooking simple meals, raising babies, investing and so on. Topics that help a young person acclimate and will actually be put to good use after high school.

Many kids will go to college. Many will not. But learning how to respect a spouse, showing your best to a prospective employer and dealing intelligently with a screaming baby will benefit *everyone.*

These are not topics that are in conflict with parents, so there should be no pushback. And it might create a broader universe of students and grads who are more able to socialize, interact and thrive.

September 7, 2014

Once Upon a Time

Once upon a time, there was a beautiful princess. She lived in a big castle and had a cat. The cat's name was Flashy. One day, the beautiful princess stepped outside the castle with her cat—and *then* ...

My wife, Donna, and I happily entertain our granddaughters with regularity. It's always special to share time with them. When we have a meal, we normally encourage some sort of interaction. It's more than "How was your day?" or "Do you like your spaghetti?" Donna or I will *whirrr* our arms around and point to one of our granddaughters and say, "You begin a story."

The 3- or 6-year-old will begin a story—often like the four lines above. Sometimes they'll start a story on their own. After "and then," the obligation shifts to the *next* person at the table to *continue* the story. We've had some *verrry* interesting adventures come out of this roundtable authorship. I often include the beautiful—yet powerful—princess going to the local golf course and shooting a subpar round from the back tees.

Another staple for dinnertime discussion is *rose and thorn*. Everyone is asked the *rose* of their day—the happiest or most exciting part of the day. Then we will ask if there was a *thorn* in their day—something that *wasn't* pleasant or happy. We learn a lot—from our granddaughters and from *each other*—from these simple yet insightful interactions of dialogue.

What was the *rose* of your day?

_____

September 13, 2018

Miles Ahead

Donna and I were driving in Wisconsin with one of our granddaughters, then 3½ years old.

"There' s a field of corn." "There's a field of wheat." "Those are cherry trees." "Look at the cows. They're called Holsteins." Some words we added in Spanish.

We went to a petting farm and fed the pigs and goats and cows. Learned about Texas longhorns, Brahma bulls, sunflowers, wells (complete with bucket). Counted bags of corn used to feed the goats and sheep. Looked at wild turkeys. Discussed the purpose of silos, and ... and on. And on.

I pondered the fact that our granddaughter at age 3½ is likely ahead of disadvantaged kids—who may not have the *hands-on* tutelage of parents, grandparents, caregivers and friends. I read an article that said children from middle- and upper-socioeconomic families will hear *millions* of words more than children born into welfare families. And this *abbondanza* of words forms a critical base for future learning, performance and advancement. Add to this that children from middle- and upper-income families receive hundreds of thousands more affirmations of *encouragement* and fewer of discouragement (the reverse of families on welfare).

Betty Hart and Todd Risley penned an incisive book on this troublesome situation—*The Early Catastrophe: The 30 Million Word Gap by Age 3*. The big question is, *What do we do about it?*

September 4, 2015

Palindromes

Can you say "Anna backward"? The usual response is "Anna." But the correct answer is "Anna backward."☺

Anna is a *palindrome*, a word that reads the same forward and backward, like Otto, Eve, Hannah and Elle. "Anna sees Anna" is a palindrome. "Did Hannah see bees? Hannah did." Sure, she did—backward and forward. One of the first palindromes I learned was "Madam, I'm Adam." Then there was "A man, a plan, a canal—Panama," referencing Teddy Roosevelt.

I began using palindromes at Chicago Lights Tutoring. "Read this backward," I would say to the student. And get blank stares. And then suddenly—the lights (and smiles) went on.

Cigar? Toss it in a can. It is so tragic.
Enid and Edna dine.
Hey Roy! Am I mayor? Yeh!
My gym.
Never odd or even.
Now I won.
Too bad I hid a boot.
Was it a car or a cat I saw?
Too hot to hoot!
Live not on evil.
Mr. Owl ate my metal worm.

So Ida, adios.

Tuna roll or nut?

Stella won no wallets.

The earliest recorded palindrome dates to A.D. 79 In Latin, it is *Sator Arepo tenet opera rotas* (the sower Arepo holds works wheels). The longest palindrome? It's 17,826 pretty random words. No, I won't repeat it here....

April 16, 2012

American Sign Language

I was sitting on the train a few weeks ago, waiting to pull out of the station. Three young girls (probably high school) came in and sat in the four-seater ahead of me. They began conversing animatedly. Laughing. Giggling. And I watched. Fascinated.

What caught my attention was—*they didn't make a sound*. One of the girls was deaf. And the three were mouthing words to each other *and* using sign language. Signing. They were fast. And fluent.

American Sign Language (ASL) originated in the early 19th century at the American School for the Deaf in Hartford, Connecticut. Today it is used by around a million people. I have two friends who are conversant in ASL: my partner Dave D. and my former priest the Rev. Bob M. (both Eagle Scouts, by the way).

Watching these three young women signing was something of a wake-up for me. Since then, when I have lunch at my desk (which is often), I will sometimes log on to an ASL site just to stretch my brain. (The site is http://lifeprint.com.) I can say, "I am a grandfather" and a few other things in ASL. It is pretty cool to crack open this door. I even looked into the cost of a class at a Loop college a few blocks away.

If you want to stretch *your* brain, this would be a great way to do it. I guess I have a special reason to look into ASL. You see, my father was clinically deaf from World War II. And he never learned ASL. And neither did I....

February 23, 2014

The Taste Test

As I said, Donna and I are frequent, happy hosts for our granddaughters (ages 3 and 6). *A sleepover at Nonni and Popi's* is usually a Saturday evening. It means Japanese food (which they love) or pizza. *And* a "movie night." Last Saturday, it was *The Lion King*. It's always a delight. Sunday morning it's up and off to church and Sunday school and then—*shhh!* do *not* tell our daughter—we go to McDonald's for lunch. Then on the drive home, we "get lost," allowing our granddaughters to guide the car ("left," "right," "straight") until we have no clue (*wink, wink*) where we are.

One of our activities for a Saturday afternoon or Sunday morning is the *taste test*. I prepare by purchasing various organic juices (cherry, blueberry, pomegranate, grape, apple or whatever). And we sit at the table with three or four little Solo cups, each with a splash of different juice. We then taste the offerings. And try to discern what it is we are drinking. And what our preferences are. And why.

Pomegranate juice always prompts a wrinkled nose. We've done the same with different fruits and (*yuck*) vegetables—with eyes closed. There is no tiring of the taste test. It is always fun, and our granddaughters never know just what Popi has on the menu.

February 25, 2018

7

WHAT'S COOKING

Honey

One of my primo recipes is Swedish pancakes. My secret: I don't use sugar in the mix. I use *honey*. To me, honey adds a subtle, gentle sweetness to the flavor. In baking (or even grilling onions), when I have the choice, I use honey. A healthy dessert that I make for myself is Greek yogurt and almond (or peanut) butter, topped with honey. How sweet it is!

We all know that bees make honey, but did you know that honey is the result of continuous regurgitation by the bees? It goes up and down until it reaches a desired consistency then—*splat!*—it goes into the honeycomb. Interestingly, most microorganisms don't grow in honey because of the low water content, so honey normally does not spoil—even after decades or even centuries of sitting around (that's true). Just like Twinkies.☺ Honey gleaned from different flowers and plants results in varied flavor and qualities. Honey is a healthier choice than sugar (except for infants), and it contains no cholesterol.

Our ancestors were collecting honey 10,000 years ago. The Old and New Testaments refer to honey (Judges 14:8 and Matthew 3:4), and the Quran devotes an entire Surah to honey (*Al-Nahl*: The Honey Bee). Sore throat? Honey in hot water. MRSA bacteria? Honey (New Zealand manuka) can make them more sensitive to antibiotics, according to the World Health Organization. Good stuff, honey.

November 19, 2011

Avocados for Breakfast

I try to eat a healthy breakfast. Oh I *know*—if there's leftover pizza or spaghetti carbonara in the fridge, I'll likely grab that and some coffee. But that stuff does *not* make for a sparky day. Usually, I have high-fiber (bran) cereal, blueberries or banana and coffee. Lotsa coffee… Maybe once or twice a week, I have an avocado (with a little salad dressing) and a banana. And the obligatory coffee. More and more, though, I'm drifting toward avocados for breakfast.

I know what you're thinking. *Avocados for Breakfast* sounds like the title of a steamy romance novel set in Northern California. "Hey Martha, would you like an avocado for breakfast?" "Oh Henry, you sweet talker…"

But avocados are a magnificent food. One of the healthiest you can eat. And avocados are among the least contaminated, so there is really no need to buy organic (see the "Dirty Dozen" foods you do *not* want to buy "conventional"). And avocados are simply delish. I make my own guacamole (smooshed avocado, finely chopped cilantro and lime juice) and have it for a meal.

Heck, guacamole for breakfast? It doesn't get any better.

August 20, 2013

Bacon

When I head to the golf course on weekends, I usually drive by two popular breakfast spots (Ridgeview Grill and Sarkis Cafe for those of you in the North Shore 'hood). I have all I can do to *not* stop. And have a second breakfast.

It is the smell of *bacon*. Cooking. That starts twisting the wires in my primitive brain. Gets me blinking. Drooling. Twitching. *Bacon*. Is there anything better than the smell of *bacon*? Yes—the *taste* of bacon. I *love* bacon. Well-done and usually piled alongside an omelet *or* a stack of French toast. *And* a stack of French toast is OK too.…

But alas my bacon consumption has been severely limited by a breakfast regimen of high-fiber cereal and fruit. And dinners featuring two-legged or no-legged protein and vegetables. But once a month or so, Donna and

I will go out for dinner. And go to Walker Bros. Pancake House. And it is *there* that I let my hair down (no wisecracks) and tear down the fences. "I'll have the bacon and cheese omelet, hash browns and six orders of bacon—well-done." I'm sure my heart is going, *The man is CRAZY again! Let's get pumping....* Then there's spaghetti carbonara ... BLT sandwiches (hold the lettuce and tomato) ... and those appetizers made with thick bacon and maple syrup. Be still my heart. But not too still...

June 5, 2016

Breakfast Tips

Lemme ask this. You go into a restaurant and order a cup of coffee for $1.50. What would you leave as a tip for your server? A tip of 15% is 22½ cents (round that up to a quarter). Yes? Maybe 30 cents if you leave 20%? Your server would probably give you the *big spender* look, shake his head and walk away. Me? I'd probably leave a buck. Or two. Especially if I'm nursing five refills of java while reading the newspaper.

I remember reading an article a few years ago that has guided me on tipping. Especially for breakfast. Breakfast service, the article said, deserves a higher percentage tip than dinner service. Why? Because bacon and eggs with toast, hash browns, coffee and orange juice may cost you nine bucks. And you walk out of the restaurant stuffed to the gills and smiling for the day. Dinner may cost you three sawbucks and a fin. Who gets more tip for the same work? *Yep....*

I don't want to seem frivolous, but on those occasions when I've gone out for breakfast, and the bill for Donna and me is $20, I may leave a $5 tip. Maybe $6. Why? Because the server works just as hard (probably more so) filling the coffee cups, water glasses and balancing multiple plates. Of course if service is bad, I'm quick to adjust downward too.

In restaurants where I am known (*uh oh—it's Petersen*), I will also be generous. After all, why not? Again, I am *not* being frivolous. I believe I'm being smart.

A generous tip makes for a happy server. And it seems to make me welcome when I come back.

May 2, 2013

The Greasy Spoon

When I was a kid, we rarely went out for dinner. But when we did, my folks would take me to different places, mainly burger joints. One night—I was maybe 7 years old—we went to a place on Milwaukee Avenue in Chicago. I don't remember much about the place or the food. But I remember—*keenly*—my father's reaction. "Man. This is really a greasy spoon." *Greasy spoon*. I looked around on the table. *No spoons*. I thought—*wow!* That is a *cool* term.

The next time we went out for dinner to one of the regular sit-down burger joints, the waitress came over and took our order. I looked up at her and asked—quite seriously—"Is this a greasy spoon?" I don't recall the waitress's reaction, but I remember my father laughing and trying to wriggle out of my inquiry.

The "greasy spoon" comment probably pales to the time when my father's boss—Mr. Lovell—came to the house for dinner. And I said, quite innocently, "Gosh, we oughta have company more often. This food is really *good!*"

January 5, 2017

Wisconsin Supper Clubs

Have you ever been to a Wisconsin supper club? If you haven't, you're missing a major life experience. Wisconsin supper clubs have a presence in most parts of (*yep*) Wisconsin. Little, sometimes out-of-the-way towns will have good restaurants that feature four-course meals: soup, salad, main course and dessert. And of course there are the obligatory beverages: beer, spirits and jug wine (though sometimes one is surprised by a genuine wine list).

When you enter a supper club, you usually pass the bar. The trick is—*do not pass the bar*. Ever. There's a protocol. In most places, you go to the bar, say hello to the bartender and indicate you would like a table. He (or she) will then give you the once-over. Make a mental note that you want a table. And ask if you want a drink. You must always say yes to the drink. Or you may still be sitting at the bar at closing time. At some point, a table will open, and you'll be escorted into the dining room. Immediately, a relish tray, menus, water, bread and butter will be plopped on your table.

Menus contain the usual assortment of two-, four- and no-legged protein. My suggestion is go for the fish. Usually perch or walleye. Interestingly, walleyed pike from Wisconsin may not be served in Wisconsin. Walleye all comes from Canada. Regulations...

Your entree includes mashed or baked potatoes and vegetables (sometimes canned). Soups are usually onion or some "cream of" soup. There's often a salad bar. Served salads can be disappointing. If that's the option, have the blue cheese dressing. I mean, *what the hey?* But the spigot is on—from the bar to your table—so you may have as much firewater as you want. Dessert is usually a chocolate sundae in a shiny tin cup.

I've been to my share of supper clubs, mostly in Door County and northern Wisconsin. The Guide's Inn in Boulder Junction and Birmingham's Bar & Cottages in Sturgeon Bay are favorites. These are two I would go back to again. And again. And order the fish....

October 6, 2016

Chinese-Style

The Berghoff Restaurant in Chicago's Loop is an old, German, family restaurant. The Berghoff has been in business since 1898. The classic "men's bar" survived until 1969. The Berghoff received the city's liquor license No. 1 in 1933 when Prohibition ended. And three classic scenes from *The Dark Knight* (Batman) were filmed there.

I once hosted three attorneys from Beijing for meetings in my office. At the conclusion of the meetings, I offered to take them to lunch. They accepted, and we walked across the street to the Berghoff.

We sat down at a table and perused the menu. I asked my guests what kind of food they liked. None had any limitations. And no particular preferences. They smiled. And suggested *I* order for them. Talk about *pressure*....

So I ordered three meals: a duck platter, stuffed sole and a sausage trio. And we placed the three plates in the center of the table and dined. Chinese style. I stifled my appetite a bit, deferring to my guests. Bottom line—everything was devoured. But it did have me wondering how many times in its 120-year history the Berghoff had seen Chinese-style dining with Chinese visitors.

Frankly, I *like* Chinese-style dining. Next time Donna and I have dinner with you, don't be surprised if I reach across the table and fork a slice of your filet. Make sure you order it medium-well....

June 17, 2018

Grilled Peanut Butter

Did you ever have a special dish of your own creation added to a restaurant menu? I did.

When I was at Augustana College, I was a night owl. I would study (or play cards) until the wee hours. And often, as the second hand approached midnight, I would hitchhike with a few other guys to the Round the Clock restaurant in downtown Rock Island. And I would order a *grilled peanut butter sandwich*. With a dill pickle on the side. *And* a tall glass of milk. The interesting thing was that grilled peanut butter was *not* on the menu.

One evening at Round the Clock, I had noticed a *Peanut Butter and Jelly Sandwich* on the menu. I didn't want a PB&J, but it occurred to me that a *grilled* peanut butter sandwich might be just the ticket. We slid into the booth, and I ordered a "grilled peanut butter sandwich." The waitress looked at me like I was a moon rock. I said, "Same as a grilled cheese but use peanut butter instead of cheese." I felt like Jack Nicholson in the *Five Easy Pieces* diner scene. The waitress walked away shaking her head. She used gestures to explain the order at the window to the kitchen. And she pointed at the goofy-looking kid in the booth.

After a few weeks of this, when I walked in the door, the waitress would give me that knowing look. "Grilled peanut butter?" she would ask. I'd nod and smile "yes, ma'am." A few months later, *Grilled Peanut Butter Sandwich* made its debut on Round the Clock's menu. And I became a legend. At least in my own mind.

December 1, 2016

Chicken Potpie

When I was in law school, I lived at State and Oak just off of Rush Street in Chicago. It was a dingy walk-up apartment across the street from the old Mister Kelly's nightclub and kitty-corner from Papa Milano restaurant. At night, massive cockroaches would invade the kitchen, and in the morning there would sometimes be a mouse in the trap.

Being occupied with school prompted me to shortchange meals. Cereal in the morning. A sandwich on the go for lunch. And then came dinner. My staple dinner consisted of two frozen chicken potpies, to which I would add a can of corn or peas. To save on dishes, I would rip the label off the can. Then I would open the can part way, fold back the top and set the can on the burner. When it started bubbling, I figured it was done. I'd drain the water and pour the corn over the potpies that by then were upside down on a plate. And devour the mix. Pretty much every night.

Fast forward a few years. I'd married, settled down, gotten a job and taken to having more creative dinners. I was about to hustle off to the courts at 26th and California when Donna asked, "What do you think you'd like for dinner?"

I thought. "I got an idea," I said, "How 'bout a couple of frozen chicken potpies covered with corn?" That night I got home, looked at my plate—and there it was. I realized then, *I never want this meal again.* And since then, years ago, that old standby has been off the menu.

May 6, 2020

Donna's Favorite Meal: Meatloaf, Beets and Potatoes

A few years ago, my wife, Donna, mentioned over dinner that her favorite meal as a little girl was meatloaf, fresh beets and mashed potatoes. Ever the quick-witted spouse, I made a mental note. A few weeks later on a Sunday, I stopped at the nearby Fresh Market—a go-to for us—and secured the "fixings" for the "favorite meal." Then I went home, donned my red "Mr. Excitement" apron and put on the eye of the tiger. Iron Chef Petersen…

The beets are straightforward: Clip the long stems, wash and boil for 25 to 50 minutes depending on size. Remove, peel and slice (yes, they will be *hot*!).

Then a small bag of yellow (or red) potatoes. Boil for 30 minutes and mash along with ¼ stick of butter, a splash of skim milk and about 5 ounces of chopped garlic cheddar cheese. Add salt, garlic powder and pepper. Mercy!

The meatloaf is tricky. I always chop a Vidalia onion and grill the pieces in olive oil. Roll them into 2 pounds of lean ground round. Add an egg or two, ¾ cup of Italian breadcrumbs, ½ cup of barbecue sauce, salt, pepper and garlic powder (Donna suggests adding onion soup mix), then shape and bake for an hour at 350 degrees. A rack is probably better than a meatloaf pan to drain juice.

While the meatloaf is arguably a work in progress, I score major points with this meal *every* time I make it (which is more and more often). Love those points....

October 28, 2011

Winning at Squash

I am an aspiring chef. Or *perspiring*. Anyway, I enjoy cooking and devising new creations. And I hit a home run on Saturday night. It wasn't just a perfect "10," it was a *you gotta write this down* 10....

We were granddaughter-sitting, so I volunteered to make dinner. I stopped off at the market and reconnoitered the aisles. I was inspired. I got four 5-ounce lobster tails (half-off special), a large butternut squash, a yellow onion, some portobello mushrooms and a bag of organic potatoes. And some fresh, pitted Kalamata olives.

The potatoes, I did in my usual way (see "Donna's Favorite Meal"). For the lobster tails, I cut the shells (all the way, to allow expansion) and *baked* them for about 11 minutes at 400 degrees. But it was the butternut squash that raised the roof. This is the secret.

Cut and dice the squash, chop the onion and cut up the portobello mushrooms in 2-inch pieces. Throw it all into a saute pan with olive oil (I like Colavita). Simmer over low heat with some pepper and three garlic cloves finely sliced. Add chopped Kalamata olives. Sauté for about 35 minutes. Then leave it covered while the rest is finishing. When all is done, add some *honey* to the squash and turn up the heat. And let things caramelize....

I had the usual melted butter with lemon quarters for the lobster. The mashed potatoes were perfection. We had a dandy malbec on hand, and a gelato to finish things up.

But the squash dish I had divined was the unknown. I was perspiring as Donna began to delve into the meal. She took a bite. Another. Another. And looked up.... "You gotta write this down." It was a "10." Next stop? *Top Chef.*

November 3, 2013

Let's Talk Tilapia

I made dinner last night. Baked tilapia, mashed potatoes and my own creation of sauteed baby bella mushrooms and carrots. Key lime sorbet with *fresh* mango for dessert.

Tilapia does not have the omega-3 star power of some other fish, but it is good, healthy and relatively free from the chemicals that plague larger fish. Here's how I did a pair of tilapia filets.

Marinate in olive oil (tilapia is a somewhat porous fish) and roll in finely grated Romano cheese and Italian breadcrumbs. Next saute the filets (in olive oil) for about two minutes a side, then bake them in a 400-degree oven for 10 minutes. *Perfecto!* (My wife, however, advises against sauteing. She'd stick with baking....)

The mashed potatoes were the small, white organic kind (see "Donna's Favorite Meal" for the recipe). To go with them: two bunches of carrots—washed, peeled and cut in small pieces—plus the chopped baby bella mushrooms (carefully washed). Put the mix in a frypan. Sautee with olive oil, some tarragon, salt and pepper. Add some honey to caramelize and enhance the flavor. Cover the pan and stir often to keep the mix from burning. Once the carrots are *al dente*, it is done.

A wee bit of pinot noir was the *perfect* accompaniment. It doesn't get any better. And the points rolled in.

June 14, 2012

Walleyed Pike

I go fishing once a year, though not *every* year. Up near Minnoqua, Wisconsin, with my friend Dan. We get a guide—often Jim, who is excellent—and head out onto the deep waters. Looking for walleye. It's often so early the loons are not even awake (*what are* they *doing here?*).

To catch walleyes, you need big worms and a small jig with a medium-sized hook. You string the worm onto the hook so most of the worm trails behind. Then you cast and reel in slowly, waiting for a little tug. There are times when I've fished and had not so much as a nibble. And then there are times when the fish are biting so fast and furious you have to bait your hook behind a tree.

At the end of the day, Jim will clean the fish and portion them into filets. As with tilapia, not much needs to be done. A quick roll in some olive oil, Italian seasoning and breadcrumbs and saute over medium heat until the fish is flaky. (I swear there isn't a better-tasting fish on the planet when it's fresh out of the lake.)

Add some homemade hash browns (I cut organic potatoes thin then saute in a squidge of olive oil, some butter, salt and pepper, and chopped Vidalia onion), steamed broccoli and wagon-wheel chocolate chip cookies for dessert. Oh yes, and some cabernet. You'll have a north woods meal fit for Paul Bunyan.

June 28, 2012

Flounder Filets

Last Saturday, Donna asked if I would make dinner. I was quick to say, "Sure." And I trotted off to the market to reconnoiter. The result was a 9.5.

I took flounder filets, rolled in gluten-free breadcrumbs, basted lightly in olive oil and then baked for 14 minutes at 375 degrees. Flounder is a buttery, tasty fish. Hard to go wrong. My vegetable medley was a takeoff on a prior theme. Take fresh shiitake mushrooms, washed, dried and sliced; a sweet onion, also sliced; and some organic carrots, chopped. Put them all into a covered skillet, smother in olive oil and nip with pepper and turmeric. After about 40 minutes (stirring frequently), drain and add a wee bit of honey to caramelize.

Finally, I whipped up my fresh guacamole (avocado, cilantro and lime juice), served with gluten-free hummus chips. And a few slices of fresh mango. We enjoyed a pinot noir and some San Pellegrino. Dessert was a pistachio gelato, to which I added small chunks of 72% dark chocolate.

It didn't hurt that I handcrafted a menu with my usual artwork, put on a little Gato Barbieri, lit a few candles. *And* did the dishes.

I *know* what you're thinking.… "Petersen, you &@^\$x#!%, you're making me look bad." Hey, just follow the recipe.

April 19, 2015

Seafood and *Perfecto* Potatoes

I scored a point or two by asking Donna if she wanted to go out for dinner on Friday (*ka-ching*). "No.… How about if we stay home and have something simple." Now I have come to realize that *simple* in Donna's parlance means plain chicken, rice and asparagus. Three of my favorite things. *Not.* So I offered to make dinner.

I went to the market looking for inspiration and bought ¾ of a pound of wild Atlantic sockeye salmon for Donna. Simple. But I got three crabcakes for myself (a regular crabcake; the "ultimate" crabcake; and a salmon cake). I wanted to try them all. Then (be still my heart) I got organic white potatoes, organic carrots and some shiitake mushrooms. (Shiitakes are healthier and have less toxicity than other mushroom varieties.)

When I got home, I went ahead to …

Drench the salmon in olive oil, season with turmeric and pepper, and bake for 20 minutes at 400 degrees. Saute the crabcakes in olive oil until brown.

Here's where it gets good.…

Dice the potatoes thinly and saute in butter. Top with ground pepper, turmeric, kosher salt and garlic powder. Wash the carrots and shiitakes, skin the carrots, dice everything and saute in olive oil. Took about 40 minutes on low(er) heat.

Candles. A little Gato Barbieri crooning in the background. "Well?" I asked. Donna looked up. "This is probably a nine-and-a-half." She paused. Savored a bite. "Actually, a 10" (*ka-ching*). And then—the pièce de résistance—I whipped out a pistachio gelato to close the meal. And did the dishes. *Ka-ching! Ka-ching!*

July 3, 2016

Pasta with P's

Well, I've done it again. Donna spent much of Saturday with our daughter helping out with the baby. Donna called midafternoon and said she was tired and that she'd be home around 6. "Would you like me to fix dinner?" I asked. "Would you?" she responded. I smiled. "Just you wait."

I went out and bought about ¾ pound of fresh **prosciutto** (sliced thick), a Vidalia onion (what else?), Le Sueur **peas** and some Laurel Hill fire-roasted red peppers. We had spaghetti in the house. Putting it all together is simple enough.

Chop the prosciutto and onion into small pieces. Saute them slowly (covered, stirring often) with some shaved garlic in a nice olive oil, so the prosciutto is brown and the onions are somewhat absorbed.

Heat the peas and toss in one of the red **peppers** (cut up) for color. Cook up the spaghetti (*al dente*) and when it's done, mix it all in a bowl with a jar of artichoke lemon **pesto** (heated with extra olive oil). Roast some breadcrumbs in olive oil to sprinkle on top of the dish, and serve grated parmesan on the side. *Voila!*

The table was set. The candles were lit. Sinatra was crooning in the background. Donna walked in. She smiled and sat down. A red wine was the *perfect* accompaniment. We had a caramel gelato for dessert.

In retrospect, the lemon artichoke pesto made the dish *too* lemony (though it was still very good). Next time, I may stay with olive oil and some extra garlic or peperoncino. But hey—I scored some points. *Major points after doing the dishes.*

January 16, 2017

Mexican Fiesta

I made dinner on Sunday. And I scored a perfect 10 … *and* got the gold medal.

It's clear I enjoy cooking—and experimenting. Last Sunday's dinner was up in the air. So I volunteered. And Donna quickly agreed. I went to the market and got the fixings for a Mexican fiesta—*la cena*. It's a simple recipe with a twist.

Marinate and bake two chicken breasts. Chop and saute a large yellow onion and some shiitake mushrooms in olive oil over low heat in a covered pan for about 45 minutes. Heat taco shells 5 minutes at 350 degrees (I like the Garden of Eatin' organic blue corn variety). Slice the chicken and place strips within each shell. Then add a slice of garlic cheddar cheese. On top, spoon some of the shiitake and onion combo (*after* draining the olive oil and browning slightly). Warm the shells in the oven for another 5 minutes.

I made my usual guacamole recipe (smooshed avocado, cilantro and lime juice—that's it). To go with, I prepared some fresh quinoa on which I spooned some organic black beans (I confess—from a *can*). I had some green tomatillo sauce on hand for the tacos.

We had a great cabernet and some San Pellegrino to wash things down. My daughter, Lauren, and her husband, Trent, joined us for the experience. The sauteed shiitake and onion combo was a 10-point triple lutz. The combination of quinoa and black beans—with fresh guac on the side—was a graceful double axel that landed perfectly. The wine was a magical double toe loop. The entire meal was a *flawless* triple salchow *nailed* by *the Renaissance Hombre.*

Donna and Lauren both looked up from their plates and said seriously, "This is your best yet." *Awww shucks….*

February 27, 2014

Rice and Beans

Rice and beans is a food staple in much of the world. And for me, rice and beans has *always* been a staple. But not just *any* rice and beans.

Last weekend, I started with a container of RiceSelect Royal Blend. This wonderful mix combines Texmati˚ white, brown, wild and Thai red rice. Just boil 1 cup of rice mix in 2¼ cups of low-sodium chicken broth for about 30 minutes. In a saucepan, wash—then heat—a 15.5-ounce can of organic black beans.

But this addendum brings *rice 'n' beans* to a whole new level of gastronomy. In a frypan, heat some olive oil. Toss in a diced onion, two minced garlic cloves, two finely chopped celery stalks and a large carrot (or two), also finely chopped. For seasoning, use 2 teaspoons of minced fresh oregano, 1 teaspoon of ground cumin and 2 teaspoons of chopped, fresh parsley. Optional: Tap in a light dusting of cayenne pepper to give an added kick.

The combo came together nicely. I mixed everything together and— *voila!* A rice and beans extravaganza. For the side, I drenched some wild Atlantic salmon in olive oil, shook on some turmeric and baked at 450 degrees for about 10 minutes. Bake time naturally depends on the thickness of the salmon.

When it came time for the obligatory gelato, Donna and I looked at each other, smiled and dug into more rice and beans for dessert.

December 10, 2015

40-Minute Dinner

I volunteered (as I frequently do on weekends) to make dinner. I drove to the market, walked in and stood. My eyes narrowed. I rubbed my chin. Drooled. And then the lights flickered and went on. I got the fixings and went home to boldly go where no man had gone before.

I took a cup of RiceSelect Royal Blend original (see above) and got it going in a pot of water. (You can use chicken stock—flavorful but *salty*.) With the clock ticking, I proceeded to ...

Chop some organic carrots. Wash and slice some shiitake mushrooms. Dice an acorn squash and chop a sweet onion. Saute the mix on low heat in a drench of olive oil. Shake on some pepper, turmeric and Sunny Spain Seasoning. Stir frequently. Spoon on some honey to caramelize.

The side was a wild Atlantic salmon covered in olive oil, turmeric, pepper and more Sunny Spain Seasoning. Dinner was *finito* in about 40 minutes. We sat, listening to Gato Barbieri, sipping merlot and dining on a dish that I have absolutely no idea what to call.

January 17, 2016

Orange You Wonderful

Sunday night I decided to make a memorable dinner for my whole family. I think I did.

I toddled off to the market and wandered around. Looking for inspiration. There were foods of many colors. Red. Green. Yellow. And orange. *Orange. Hmmm…* My eyes narrowed. What if I prepare a dinner where everything is *orange*—or a close facsimile. I was sure my granddaughters would love it.

So I seized on crab and salmon cakes and chicken strips for the main course. Orange-*ish*. With an orange remoulade sauce. For the accompaniment, I chose organic carrots, diced sweet potato and shaved butternut squash. *Orange.*

I sauteed the squash over low heat in olive oil for about 45 minutes (and then caramelized with some Maine maple syrup). I chopped up a cantaloupe and sliced a mango for side dishes. There were orange corn chips in a bowl on the table. Dessert was an (orange) sea salt caramel gelato. Though in deference to the chef, the wine was a cabernet. No orange juice…

There were leftovers. And I did the dishes. As a result, I scored points big time. *Ding-ding-ding-ding!* The best compliment was when I asked my granddaughters what they wanted for dinner tomorrow night. They yelled, "*Orange!*"

August 24, 2017

Carrots a la Punt

I made dinner on Saturday. It was two filets of flounder turbot, which really can't go wrong. Marinate in olive oil then coat with gluten-free breadcrumbs. I sprinkled this dish with ground pepper, garlic powder and turmeric. For the first time, I opted for *roasted* potatoes—the South Florida white variety—in an Ina Garten theme. To wit:

Wash the potatoes and cut them into 1-inch chunks. *Soak* them in olive oil and add salt, pepper and turmeric. Lay them out on a flat pan and bake at 400 degrees for about 45 minutes (or until tender and browned).

It was the vegetable dish that was the challenge. I golfed Saturday morning and all I could think about was hitting the ball straight and pureed carrots. *Don't say it.* When I got off the course, I bought a batch of organic carrots and proceeded to …

Peel the carrots. Peel and cut a fresh mango. Sliver two cloves of garlic. Melt ½ stick of butter. The plan was to put the mix in the blender. Blend the carrot and mango into a puree, pour it into a glass bowl, then set that bowl in a bowl of water. Put it in a 350-degree oven for perhaps 25 minutes. What could go wrong? *Well…*

Long story short, the black plastic thingy that turns the blender blade broke. The smell of heated plastic was the clue. So there I was with half the stuff in the glass jar smooshed and half not. So I switched on the fly to an unplanned Plan B. I poured out the glop, diced the carrots and put the whole thing in the microwave ("vegetable" setting) and let 'er rip.

What could have been a real culinary downer actually turned out to be a *whew* moment. Dinner was *wonderful.* A little cabernet to wash things down. And the gelato for dessert didn't hurt. What sealed the deal as usual—I did the dishes.

May 18, 2015

The Great Hash Brown Cook-Off

Donna and I spent a long weekend in Park City, Utah, with some good friends. One evening, we planned to make dinner and dine in. *Sooo* I volunteered to make my world-famous hash browns. No big thing.

Well, my friend Jack said, "I make hash browns too. Why don't we have a cook-off?" I thought, *Hmmm … a cook-off.* With that, the gloves were down, the aprons on and the skillets ready. We went to the market, where I bought some large (ideally organic) yellow potatoes (I used eight) and two large yellow onions. I was ready. Jack bought similar ingredients. We went back and fired up the stove.

This is how I do hash browns. Halve, then thinly slice the onions. Wash the potatoes and pit any "eyes" or rough spots (gotta be perfect). Then cut the potatoes into small chunks. Put the onions and potatoes with olive oil into a large frypan. Cover and cook on low heat. The object: to cook the potatoes slowly by *steaming* them with the onions. Stir frequently. This is a slow process, 45 minutes or more.

Gradually, the potatoes soften, and the onions begin to darken. Add garlic powder, pepper, salt and a little Italian seasoning. Then toss in a large spoon of butter. *Mmmm…* When the potatoes are ready, turn up the heat and take off the lid to do a little pan roasting for perhaps six or seven minutes. At this point, well-done chopped bacon is an option. The result is wonderful.

Jack's offering was a counterpoint to mine. He first *boiled* the potatoes and chopped them small, then tossed in finely chopped onions. He used butter only. His were more traditional flat hash browns with a delicious buttery taste. Mine were chunky and more of a roasted potato dish. The gathering happily devoured both. No winner was declared. It was a toss-up!☺

September 10, 2013

Weekend Lunch

Searching for a decent lunch on Saturdays, I usually feel like Diogenes searching for an honest man. *Good luck.* It's often been PB&J on pita or crackers. Occasionally, I'd dash to the Treasure Island grocery (RIP) to grab three squares of spanakopita (from which I'd whittle off the tasteless phyllo crust).

Lately, I've been teeing up a Saturday lunch that is a *keeper*. It is corn tortillas with smoked salmon, a squirt of honey mustard, Monterey Jack cheese, fresh avocado and Frontera Foods' Salpica brand Good to be Green cilantro green olive salsa with roasted tomatillos. Oh my...

Toast the tortillas for a few minutes. Remove, lay flat then layer some smoked salmon, a slice of Monterey Jack and fresh avocado. Nuke it all on "reheat" for a bit, remove and slather with salsa. I have died and gone to heaven. For a dinner portion, you might use larger tortillas and add some grilled onions and fresh guacamole (avocados, squeezed limes, well-chopped cilantro).

If you add a side of black beans and rice (brown rice is tastier) with a tad of salsa on top, and perhaps a glass or two of cab, you will have an *exquisite* Sunday (or any day) dinner. If you make it, invite me over.

March 4, 2018

Winner Sunday Dinner

I *enjoy* cooking and look forward to prowling the aisles of Fresh Market or Whole Foods, seeking inspiration for new dishes. This Sunday was no exception. Here's the skinny on a new squash dish.

Dice and skin a large acorn squash. Dice two bunches of organic carrots. Slice a dozen large shiitake mushrooms. Then chop up a yellow onion. Saute the mix in olive oil (high heat to begin, then low heat for about 40 minutes). Stir frequently. Seasoning is optional, depending on the crowd. I'm partial to light pepper, turmeric and garlic powder.

I also made a salad with mixed greens—heavy on the arugula. Add fresh mango, papaya and banana. Top with a light avocado dressing.

For the main course: grilled chicken breasts marinated for a few hours in mango sauce. (Pound the chicken lightly; a wine bottle usually works better than one of those kitchen hammers.) The meal was accompanied by a nice merlot. Dessert—as a concession to my granddaughters, who joined us—consisted of gluten-free double chocolate chip cookies.

Pow! This Sunday dinner was a winner.

June 8, 2017

Port Wine

Port (*vinho do Porto*) is a "fortified" wine that comes from the Douro Valley in the north of Portugal. The Douro Valley was established as a protected wine area (or appellation) in 1756, making it the oldest wine region in the world. The wine received its name from the *port* city of Oporto—hence, "port."

Port became popular in England in the early 1700s, when England and France were at war—thus depriving the Brits of French wine. Merchants tried importing wine from Portugal, but the long, rough ship journey—and extremes of temperature—would often cause the wine to spoil. Add a bit of brandy to "fortify" the wine before shipping, and *voila*—or, should I say, *aí está*—the wine arrived in good order and with a slightly higher alcoholic content (about 20%). Today, *aguardente* (it's like brandy) is added to this classic dessert wine (best served with cheese).

The ongoing British involvement in the port trade can be seen in the names of many of the shippers (Cockburn, Dow, Warre, Taylor, Croft and so on). There are different kinds of port (white, ruby, tawny, crust), but the king of ports is the *vintage* port. Do *not* expect to enjoy a *vintage* port if it is less than 15 years old and you are less than 21....

December 9, 2011

These Cookies Aren't Very Good

Each year, Donna and I host a Christmas Eve celebration for family. It's always a smorgasbord dinner, exchange of gifts and a special appearance by Santa Claus. It is a relaxing and happy time.

A few days after one of those special days, I was grazing in the pantry, looking for goodies. I happened upon a neat plastic bag, festooned with ribbons and bows. Inside were cookies made by one of my cousins. *Hmmm...* Well, it didn't take long for me to rip open the bag and shovel a cookie into my mouth. *Chomp, chomp, chomp... Hmmm...* The cookie was not very good. I had another. Hoping to glean some nuance of sweetness. Or chocolate. But it was no-go.

At that moment, Donna walked into the kitchen and saw me with the bag. I said, "These cookies are not very good." She looked at me like I was an idiot. Arms akimbo, she shook her head. And offered, "Scott ... those cookies are for Daisy." *Hmmm...* No wonder. I took another bite and then handed the rest to Daisy, who sat at my feet. Wagging her tail.

Maybe if I had put peanut butter on them...

October 12, 2019

How Can You Eat That Stuff?

De gustibus non est disputandum is a favorite phrase of mine (I know, *get a life*). It means, in matters of taste, there can be no disputes. We all have different tastes—in food, activities, temperature, friends, work, politics and other things. Your taste in food may be *way* out of my wheelhouse, but that doesn't make it wrong. Or right. It's just *your* taste.

I love spaghetti carbonara with lean bacon, pancetta and peas. I crave avocados and smoked salmon. You may hate the stuff (you poor soul). But hey, brother—*de gustibus non est disputandum*.

I know a lot of folks swear by soft-shell crabs. But what is tasty about chewing on what tastes like shards of broken plastic? I never order and rarely consume corned beef and cabbage. On occasions when it has been served to me, I will nibble a piece of cabbage and bury the rest under a roll. And pat my stomach. "Delicious!" Ribs? I mean, what's the point?

I'm not afraid to try new things. I've eaten worms, brains, innards and goat tongue—often in business settings. But when given the choice, I'll tee up something I *like*. Or tolerate.

What are *your* most *un*favorite foods? *There's* a topic for dinner conversation....

August 3, 2017

Cold Desserts

As you may have noticed, all the desserts on these menus are cold. There's a reason for that. *De gustibus non est disputandum.*

Sure, I like blueberry pie. Cherry pie. Bread pudding. Carrot cake. But desserts are *not meant to be heated.* They are intended to be served cold. Like—out of the fridge. Heat your filet. Or mashed potatoes. Or French toast. Or scrambled eggs. But dessert? Never!

Those of you who have been with Donna and me for dinner know that if I order dessert (*if* … ha!) I will order something that will be delivered cold. I love bread pudding and so I will ask for the bread pudding to be delivered from the refrigerator. Or freezer. Waitstaff look at me as if I'm nuts. Room temperature? Yuck. Warmed? I'm gonna be sick. All desserts should be served cold.

So when it comes to desserts, it may be *de gustibus non est disputandum.* But I know I'm right.

September 30, 2018

The Chocolate Brain

DATELINE WILMETTE, IL — Chicago lawyer Scott Petersen has a problem. His brain is slowly turning into chocolate.

After years of overindulging in Oreos, chocolate chip cookies, Hershey's Kisses, Hershey bars, Easter eggs, and chocolate rabbits, frogs and sweets, Petersen's brain is slowly but surely becoming a chocolate mass. A routine physical exam turned up this unique phenomenon last Tuesday. His doctor said, "Mr. Petersen's cerebral cortex has already developed a quarter-inch layer of chocolate. I believe that his cerebellum and occipital area are now crusted with a 60% cocoa."

In a few years, Petersen's head will be filled with a commercial grade of bittersweet chocolate.

Petersen was interviewed in a local restaurant, where he was dining with his wife, Donna. "I think it's silly. I eat pizza too, and you don't hear that my brain is turning into mozzarella cheese," he said testily. Petersen then ordered a *double* Chocolate Decadence—the menu's signature dessert. For his main course.

Once Petersen's brain has become solid chocolate, his wife is expected to put him on display at a local museum on weekends. "Hey, I might as well get something out of this too," she said.

Petersen is, however, expected to continue practicing law. A solid chocolate brain is not expected to interfere with his duties or knowledge as an attorney.

September 14, 2017

8

TO YOUR HEALTH*

The Dirty Dozen

It has to be 30 years or more since I started reading about how "water-based" fruits literally *soak* in water—along with everything that is *in* the water. As apples, blueberries, strawberries and grapes grow—and become flush with their liquid nutrient—they also absorb high concentrations of the pesticides, weed killers, insecticides and fertilizers that are *dumped* on them to make them grow.

These toxic chemicals are then ingested (often unwittingly) by the masses. And the ingestion of these toxins has been linked to cancer, lower birth weights, shorter pregnancies and other maladies.

There was a time when I stuck pretty much with bananas. And then came *organic*....

I love *blueberries*. I have them on my cereal nearly every morning. But the blueberries I buy are *organic*. If organic blueberries are not available, I will break down and buy the "conventional" kind, but *only* those blueberries grown in the United States.

I am convinced that my daughter and her family should buy organic of the really (and truly) "dirty dozen": apples, peaches, blueberries, grapes, nectarines, spinach, lettuce, potatoes, green beans, strawberries, celery and cucumber.

---

* My comments here are not medical advice.

The "safe" fruits and vegetables are onions, corn, grapefruit, mushrooms, watermelon, pineapple, avocado, mango, peas, asparagus, cantaloupe and bananas.

And then there's the (pretty one-sided) debate on grass-fed beef....

July 9, 2012

Blood Type and Health

Do you know your blood type? You *should*. Thousands of years of evolution have split human blood into four basic types: A, B, O and AB. Each has a positive (+) and negative (-) Rh factor as well. Roughly 43% of us are type O; 40%, type A; 12%, type B; and 5%, type AB.

While there is *speculation* that blood type predicts broad personality traits (especially in Japanese studies), there is strong indication that different blood types have different vulnerabilities—and do better with certain diets. And certain blood types are more prone to heart disease, according to a Harvard study (https://www.hsph.harvard.edu/news/hsph-in-the-news/qi-blood-type-heart-disease-risk/). Where one blood type does well on a meat diet, others might suffer.

Type O is the oldest blood type in the world and typically goes with the most robust digestive system. O folks need animal protein for good health, have trouble with wheat and gluten, thrive on vigorous workouts and are less prone to heart disease. O negative is a universal donor.

Type A can be associated with a more fragile digestive system, which has trouble tolerating animal protein. This blood type might do well as a vegetarian. People with this blood type can be lactose-intolerant or anemic. Iron and vitamin B12 supplements may be helpful.

Type B often correlates with wheat and gluten sensitivity, though dairy is usually just fine. Chicken is an apparent red flag and can turn into a serious health issue because of an agglutinating lectin that can adversely affect the circulatory system.

Type AB is the new kid on the block, having been around for perhaps 1,000 years. AB tends toward low stomach acid (so does Type A), and diminished stomach acid can mean vulnerability to stomach cancer. For that reason, people with Type AB blood may want to avoid red meat, *especially* smoked and cured meats.

October 4, 2012

Acupuncture

I've had foot pain for a long time. It hurts to walk. I don't like—or take—pain relievers. I just try to ignore the pain (yes, I know, *not too bright*). A few years ago, I was at the train station talking to my friend Peter. He was telling me about some *knee* pain *he* was having. And he said he had tried acupuncture. *Sure*, I thought. *Acupuncture.* He said he had gone for seven or eight sessions. And the knee issues had abated. *Sure*, I thought. *Acupuncture.* He added that he'd gone into the sessions skeptical. And come out ... well ... believing that there was something to acupuncture.

We got on the train, and that was that. My feet growled at me as I walked to my office. *Acupuncture.* I chewed on the idea. And thought to myself that there was no downside. A few needles. So I called and made an appointment.

I went for six or seven sessions. The needles were placed not in my feet but in my *hands*. A couple in my knee, as I recall. Later a few were put in my ankle. And when I walked out on that last day, my foot pain was *nothing* like the first day. Truth be told, I still have occasional foot pain, but it's *not* like it was. When it returns, I've gone back for a treatment. And I walk out feeling better.

As most people know, acupuncture originated with the Chinese. Metal needles have been found dating to 100 B.C. Acupuncture is said to increase (and correct imbalances in) the flow of *qi* (energy) through various meridians in the body. Thus, a knee pain may be treated with needles in the elbow or stomach or hip. Scientific studies have shown that acupuncture can actually relieve some types of pain and post-operative nausea. And recently, acupuncture has been endorsed for certain conditions by the U.S. National Institute of Health, the National Health Service of the U.K. and the World Health Organization.

I'm still a skeptic. But an open-minded one. So if my feet ever start griping, I know what I'm going to do....

February 3, 2013

Trouble Sleeping?

Insomnia comes in many forms. Some suffer from transient (occasional) insomnia; others, acute (short duration) or chronic (long duration). But all forms of insomnia result in sleep deprivation, which can (especially after longer duration) have serious health consequences.

I fall asleep easily—and quickly—but at times I will wake up at 2 or 3 a.m. thinking about this or that. I'm familiar with the usual Rx for getting to or back to sleep: a cool room, no meal just before bedtime, easy on the alcohol, no caffeine (that includes chocolate), a glass of warm milk, no afternoon naps, regular sleep hours, exercise (but *not* right before bed) and something *boring*—or soothing—to read before turning out the lights.

However, I have three further remedies that work for me, and I've never read about them. They are:

> **Unclenching hands.** When I wake up in the middle of the night, I sometimes find that my hands are clenched. I simply unclench and lay them flat. Suddenly, I feel relaxed.
> **Deep breathing.** I will breathe in through my nose, hold the breath and then exhale. Slowly. Deeply. Through my mouth. I get exhausted doing it. After seven or eight times, it's pretty much back to dreamland.
> **A pad of paper.** Often I wake up *thinking*. So I have a pad of paper by the bed. And a flashlight. I jot down whatever random drivel comes into my brain, and then I can forget it. *Zzzzzzzzzzzzz.*

And if these remedies don't work, call me and I will start singing "Oh Shenandoah." That should do the trick.

March 19, 2012

The Lazy Face

When I'm trying to fall back to sleep in the middle of the night, the one big thing for me is *clenched hands*. If I open and relax my hands, the rest of me starts to relax.

But recently I've noticed another phenomenon that also keeps me awake. When I am lying there—thinking of work, handyman projects (as we *non*-handymen do), cooking, writing this blog—I come to realize that my eyes, while closed, are *squinting*. My face is screwed up as if I were in deep contemplation.

So I've been relaxing my shoulders and letting my jaw drop a bit to relax my *face*. I think of it as adopting a *lazy face*. And you know what? It *seems* to work. In combination with the 337 other things I do to relax while wide-awake at night, I've now added putting on the *lazy face*.

March 23, 2014

A Light Show

When we close our eyes, we are usually greeted by an assortment of exploding stars, shapes and colors. When the head hits the pillow and it's *dark*, we can see a veritable light show with our eyes closed. The phrase *seeing stars* from a bump on the head or being dizzy refers to these closed-eye light phenomena. The illuminations you see—when there is no light—are called *phosphenes*. The term comes from the Greek *phos* (light) and *phainein* (to show).

When people are deprived of light for long periods of time, phosphenes occur when eyes are *open*. Thus phosphenes have been called *the prisoner's cinema*. People who are blind will sometimes press or rub their eyes to stimulate phosphenes (which they can see).

While phosphenes have been around as long as the human condition, the term was coined by French surgeon J.B.H. Savigny in 1838. Benjamin Franklin was reported to have used an electrical stimulation to cause a closed-eye spectral effect.

Trouble sleeping? Just close your eyes and watch the unfolding kaleidoscope of phosphenes. You'll be asleep in no time.

January 3, 2016

Feeling Down?

Men's Journal (May 2014) had an interesting article on dealing with depression. When depressive episodes occur, it sometimes signals a drop in the body's levels of serotonin. Medications that counteract the effects of depression often contain tryptophan, since tryptophan provide a natural boost in serotonin.

There are, in fact, foods that are high in tryptophan, such as cashews, spinach and game meat. According to one therapeutic nutritionist, two handfuls of cashews provide 1,000 to 2,000 milligrams of tryptophan. The body converts tryptophan into serotonin, which can enhance good mood, healthy sleep and feelings of sexual desire. The high levels of Vitamin B6 in cashews also may help stabilize mood. Five ounces of cashews (157 calories per ounce) can provide a middle-aged man with his daily intake of magnesium (low levels of magnesium can trigger mild depression).

Bottom line: There's not a lot of downside to chowing down some cashews. With breakfast. Lunch. Dinner. Or as a snack. You'll feel good about it.

May 4, 2014

Anaphylaxis

A few weeks ago, my daughter, Lauren, and her husband, Trent, took our granddaughter Eve out for a treat. They went to a bakery and ordered a coconut cookie. They were assured there were no nuts in the cookie. Eve took a bite. And within minutes her face turned red. Her body began to turn red. And she began to swell. Her eyes began to swell shut. Lauren and Trent raced to a hospital ER, where Eve was whisked into a treatment room and given a shot of epinephrine. And things began to calm.

Like a good many children, Eve has a *peanut* allergy. And, now we know, a *coconut* allergy. And the allergy is serious. For a child or adult with such allergies, eating the wrong food can bring on life-threatening anaphylaxis. Anaphylaxis can be triggered by foods (such as peanuts or shellfish), biting or stinging insects, medication (such as penicillin), latex and other causes.

Anaphylaxis affects people differently. The airway is often affected. There is swelling, chest pain, low blood pressure, dizziness—and in some cases the result can be fatal. Emergency treatment is *essential*. For parents of children with allergies, an epinephrine pen—EpiPen is one brand name— is standard equipment. I carry one in my briefcase.

What you need to know about these pens is, the dosage only lasts for about 15 minutes. And then the allergic reaction resumes. We have friends who, when traveling, carry eight of the pens for their child. Enough to get them to an emergency room.

Apart from the ER or an epinephrine pen, there isn't much you can do when anaphylactic shock begins to set in. An antihistamine like Benadryl can *help*, but reaction time is usually much too slow for the sudden onset of anaphylaxis. If you have a child (or know someone) who has such allergies, the best thing is to carry an epinephrine pen—and know where the nearest ER is located.

July 3, 2014

A PSA on PSA

I have elevated PSA (*prostate specific antigen*). Past tests have been negative. But the PSA numbers remained high. My urologist at the University of Chicago suggested the 4Kscore˚ test, introduced around 2015. Instead of measuring PSA, which is helpful but not determinative (and often unreliable), the 4Kscore test looks at four *kallikreins*—enzymes that can more readily identify prostate cancer. He also recommended an MRI with a *contrast dye* this time, to highlight trouble areas.

Some men have a *genetic* propensity to higher PSA. Prostate size can affect PSA. The aging process (a lot of that going around) can elevate PSA. And then there's cancer....

It's not fun to hear about medical issues (or nonissues). But I believe it is important to my brethren (and the brethren of my sistren) to know about these two relatively new means for detecting prostate cancer.

Prior to 1988, prostate cancer was diagnosed by palpitation of lumps or hard nodules. Then a biopsy. *Or,* a man would develop chronic back pain (and then be diagnosed). In 1990 the PSA test became widely used. But elevated PSA often resulted in unnecessary biopsies—or surgery. Then came the 4Kscore and contrast-dye MRIs. I had both done, and the two tests together were highly optimistic.

Thank heaven for modern medicine.

_____

June 4, 2017

Lucretius

I was walking to the train station with a retired friend. He mentioned that he is taking a course on Lucretius, the Roman poet and philosopher (99–55 B.C.). My friend's previous course was on Cicero, and the one before that on some unpronounceable Roman chap. My friend went on talking about Lucretius and his publications on the nature of the universe and Epicureanism. Sounded pretty neat. I asked what he was taking next semester, and he was not sure. Maybe something on analytics or Euripides. It was then I stuck my chin out....

I asked my friend if he had ever had a course on first aid. He looked at me. "No." I asked if he'd ever taken a Heimlich maneuver, CPR or AED course. I got the same answer. He asked me if I had done so, and I recounted briefly the yearlong course I took to become a civil defense emergency medical responder at Augustana College and my AED review. I said that over the years, knowledge of first aid has come in handy. And on a few occasions *very* handy.

It's great taking courses on Lucretius and Cicero, though my personal bent might involve guitar lessons, drum lessons, bird study or a tutorial on doing card magic. But lemme say this—acquiring knowledge on the subject of first aid may someday prove to be more valuable than reading *De rerum natura* or *Iphigenia at Aulis*. You never know when some fast-moving southbound emergency will raise its ugly head. And there is *no one* but *you*....

_____

October 31, 2015

AED

I just learned that a good friend of mine—a lawyer—had a heart attack. He almost died. He was standing at the elevator with a bunch of other lawyers. And he collapsed. None of the lawyers knew how to use the AED unit—the automated external defibrillator—parked on the wall, since none had attended their firm-sponsored AED course. Fortunately a *staff* person who *had* taken the firm's AED course came out and helped save his life.

How many of *you* have taken training for an AED? Heimlich maneuver? CPR? First aid? The best course I ever took in college was a yearlong program on civil defense first-aid training. It has come in *very* handy over the years.

Thus, a few years ago when I looked at the AED sign on the train heading to my office, something clicked. *I oughta figure out what this "AED" thingy is.* So while having lunch at my desk, I logged on to a YouTube video, which told the story of the AED. I now have a better idea of what an AED does. And how it works. I urge you to spend four minutes to learn about the AED. And while you're at it, why not learn the Heimlich maneuver? I've done it twice—*successfully.*

Here's a "watch list" of YouTube videos for emergency preparedness:

AED
www.youtube.com/watch?v=xfvu5FCQs6o

Heimlich maneuver
www.youtube.com/watch?v=7CgtIgSyAiU&feature=kp

Baby choking
www.youtube.com/watch?v=DUSnEpheYkY

CPR (Cardio Pulmonary Resuscitation)
www.youtube.com/watch?v=cPEFskCrdhQ&feature=kp

Heavy bleeding
www.youtube.com/watch?v=OwV39oxGwZU

Rescue breathing
www.youtube.com/watch?v=Xu9WTPOCxwU

If you watch all of these videos, you will spend about 40 minutes. But it may be the most valuable 40 minutes you ever spend. Someone—maybe *you*—will be eternally grateful.

February 11, 2018

My Workbench

I have a workbench in the basement. I never use it, but I've got one. Complete with a vice, two drawers full of tools and two toolboxes sitting on top. Then there's a little drawer thingy full of nails and screws. If I am called on to change a light bulb or hang a picture, I even have a tool belt and a hard hat to wear (you can never be too careful). We handymen are *semper paratus*.

However, tools don't do much good sitting in the basement gathering dust on my workbench. *Sooo,* I keep a lot of stuff in the trunk of my car. My car is a *rolling workbench.* You never know when tools might come in handy. I have a fire ax, an E.T. (entrenching tool), a crowbar, an air pump (I mean, what good does *that* do sitting in the garage?), and a Heinz 57 variety of hammers, screwdrivers and wrenches. And I have the obligatory jumper cables and a couple of road flares.

I could probably build a house with the stuff in my trunk. Over the years, these things have been selectively (and, once, urgently) useful ("Gosh Scott, I'm sure glad you have that quarter-inch hex wrench with the double bend…."). For the most part, my rolling workbench rarely sees the light of day. But the tools are *there*. If I need them in the house. *Or* on the road.

December 7, 2017

Don't Get Tired

My friend Al reminded me that, in cold weather, it's a good idea to check car tires, since the cold will contract air pressure, and tires can flatten out.

Wisely, I did. And sure enough—my front two tires were low. *Really* low. It was night. Cold. So I drove to a gas station with one of those air pumps where you have to pop for 75 cents. I unscrewed the valve caps, had my air gauge at the ready and dropped three quarters. The machine kicked in, and I applied the hose to the tire valve. Nothing happened. The hose *and* valve were frozen.

Now this is not an issue I've dealt with before, so I went into the gas station where a lone clerk sat behind a thick glass partition. I explained the problem. "Valve's frozen," he said. *Hoookayyy…* "Stick the hose up your exhaust while the motor's running and"—he grabbed a lighter from the shelf and passed it under the window—"warm your tire valves."

"Bring back the lighter," he said.

I went out and slid the hose a couple of feet up the exhaust. And let it sit for a few minutes. And warm. I fired the lighter and warmed the tire valves. After a few minutes, I took a breath, dropped in another 75 cents and applied the hose to the tire valve. *Pffft.* It worked like a charm. *Whew!*

The tire inflated, and I brought the lighter back. I thanked the clerk (offered him a tip; he declined). "I used to drive a semi," he said. "Used to happen all the time. It's one of those little tricks you learn."

Now you *all* know the trick.

_____

December 31, 2017

Little Feet

When I was about 10 years old, I pestered my father to let me drive the family car. One Sunday, my dad let me drive home from church. Not all the way, but the last mile or so, on a road that was pretty vacant and ran in part along a cornfield. I'd sit there peering over the steering wheel—my father with one hand on the wheel, one hand on the ignition and one hand on the gear shift. From then on, I was the *Chuber* (*Church Uber*) driver on Sundays.

Sometimes, my dad would take me to an empty parking lot and let me drive. Round and round. So I *learned* to drive at a pretty early age. My father had a lot of wisdom to impart to me in my formative years (which, my wife comments, are still in progress). My dad always told me to keep my eyes moving when I was driving. Left. Right. Check the mirrors. And he always told me to watch for "little feet."

As I drive along a street, I was told to glance forward—under the cars parked along the street. Why? It's easy to see an adult standing by a car. But there's no way to spot a child unless you see the little feet peeping out below the car you are approaching. So I'm always watching for little feet.

Try it next time you're driving. Keep an eye out for little feet....

November 26, 2017

Watch for Anomalies

When my daughter was young, I taught her a phrase: "Watch for anomalies." As she was growing up, I wanted her to be keenly aware of her surroundings. To know where the exits are in a restaurant, theater or other public place. And always to be aware of what doesn't "look right." People. Places. Things. I cautioned her, if something doesn't look right, get out. Go the other way.

I have a feeling that my daughter, at the age of 12, could "case" a room as well as anyone. Though today when I say, "Watch for anomalies," she'll usually respond, "Oh, Dad..."

I picked up the expression years ago when working with police. I learned that they watched carefully for anomalies. Situations that don't look right. Things that look out of place or out of character.

Apart from teaching my granddaughters about playing the guitar, speaking Spanish, spitting, hitting a golf ball, making spaghetti carbonara, playing poker, doing magic tricks, finding pennies on the street and so on, I want to teach them *situational awareness*. And to "watch for anomalies."

November 19, 2015

Thump My What?

Humor can be *so* important in the healing process that Denise—a delightful oncology nurse in Lake County, Illinois—started a "Humor Exchange" for patients. This monthly get-together is designed to encourage people who have health issues to start *laughing*. And keep laughing.

More and more studies confirm that laughter provides a smorgasbord of physiological benefits. It increases the count of *natural killer* (NK) and T cells (lymphocytes that activate immune responses in the fight against cancer); decreases stress hormones; lowers blood pressure; works your abs; releases endorphins; and essentially makes you smile. And *snort*.

A recent conference brought up another healthy technique that sounds pretty funny. It's called *"thumping the thymus."* The thymus gland—which is responsible for T cells—lies beneath the sternum. Patting the sternum for a few minutes can make a person feel better. And it has the potential for improving immunity.

Don't take my word for it. There are articles *galore* on this subject (see for example facebook.com/notes/karen-nauman-eft/eft-tapping-the-thymus-gland-8-interesting-factoids-about-the-thymus/198886030151782). So go ahead. Thump your thymus. What've you got to lose? And while you're at it … *laugh*.

August 27, 2017

The Best Medicine

Joseph Addison, a 17th-century English writer, said, "Man is distinguished from all other creatures by the faculty of laughter." Sigmund Freud in *The Joke and Its Relation to the Unconscious* states that jokes release us from traditional inhibitions that make up the veneer of our personalities.

The earliest known smile is etched on the lips of a statue of Ebbeh—a Mesopotamian factotum who lived in 2400 B.C. (Ebbeh now resides in the Louvre.) Four centuries later, we enter Biblical times. There were no Old Testament comedians, but the word laugh (or laughter) makes its debut in Genesis. When Abraham and Sarah are told they will have a son, both fall on their faces—laughing. Perhaps that is why their son was named Isaac, which in Hebrew means He (or God) laughs.

The word laugh or its derivations appear 43 times in the Bible (six of those in the New Testament). The Quran chronicles 16 uses of the word, but most relate to the faithful laughing at the inglorious fate of unbelievers.

The Veda, Hindu texts, record the word laugh eight times. In the Buddhist tradition, the "laughing Buddha" was supposedly a real person—a wandering happy Zen monk named Pu-Tai who lived around A.D. 1000.

The first joke book was *The Philogelos* (*Laughter Lover*) from the fourth century. It was a collection of 264 jokes. One depicts a chatty barber. "How shall I cut your hair?" he asks his customer. "In silence," the man responds.

On March 14, 2005, I delivered a paper to the Chicago Literary Club titled "The Best Medicine." (You can find it at https://go.aws/2UAvgJ7.) The paper delved into this *history* of humor. But it also discussed the healing power of humor. *It works. And can help.* A great deal.

March 10, 2019

9

FUNNY PAGES

Joe Miller's Joke Book

I always wanted to be a stand-up comedian—*but I don't have the legs for it.* Comedians actually *run* in my family. *They have to if they want to survive.*

I like jokes. Humor. Comedy. *The Three Stooges* (are you kidding, Petersen?). *The Honeymooners. Seinfeld.* I like to laugh. A favorite funny movie? *Planes, Trains and Automobiles.* Or maybe it's *Airplane!* Or *Young Frankenstein.* Or *The Pink Panther.* Humor is a great medicine. One of the best.

The first book of jokes wasn't published until 1739. It was Joe Miller's joke book, then known as *Joe Miller's Jests* or *The Wit's Vade-mecum.* Joe Miller (1684–1738) was an English actor who played a large number of humorous and comedic parts. After Miller died, a chap named John Mottley (1692–1750) published Joe Miller's "jests" in 1739. It was a collection of contemporary and ancient witticisms. The first edition had 247 numbered jokes.

A famous teacher of Arithmetick who had long been married without being able to get his Wife with Child. One said to her "Madam, your Husband is an excellent Arithmetician."

"Yes, replies she, only he can't multiply." (That's number 234.)

Joe Miller was referred to by Scrooge in Charles Dickens' *A Christmas Carol* (1843). (*"Joe Miller never made such a joke as sending* [the turkey] *to Bob's will be!"*)

After I croak, perhaps someone will write *The Renaissance Hombre's Joke Book*. I have a card file *full* of them....

A (Short) Tale of Two Mice

Two very small mice were walking together in an alley when—*ooof!*—a *huge* cat jumped down from a fence—right in front of them.

"MEEEOOOWWW," said the cat as it opened its mouth and began moving toward the trembling mice. "*MEEEEOOOOOWWW!*"

Suddenly, one of the small mice stepped forward and in a large voice began, "ARF ARF ARF Grrrrrrrrr... WOOF WOOF WOOF!" Now the cat—eyes big as saucers—stared at the small rodent. "Grrr...OOOOF ARF ARF ARF! WOOOF *WOOOF!*" As quickly as he had appeared, the cat turned and sprang away, dashing down the alley."

"Wow! That was close!" said the other mouse. "Where in the world did you learn that?"

The small mouse looked at his friend and smiled. "That is one of the benefits of knowing a second language."

The Parrot

A man was looking for a present to buy his elderly mother. *What to get?* he thought. An idea came to him. His mother had lived alone for years. Maybe a pet? Not a dog or cat—too much work. So he went to the pet shop.

The owner said, "I've got just the thing. I have a parrot. Smart as a whip. Speaks seven languages. Friendly. Your mother can talk to him. Great companion. Bird likes to watch TV too." The owner named a hefty price.

The man grimaced but said, "I'll take him." He had the pet store deliver the parrot to his mother. And he called her the following week.

"Hi Mom! Hey how do you like the parrot I sent you?"

"He was delicious," the mother said.

"WHAT! Don't tell me you ate him!"

"Of course I did."

"Mom—that parrot was supposed to be a pet! He spoke seven languages."

"Well, he should have said something."

July 19, 2012

The Poor Canary

A small canary was under the weather and went to the doctor.

"Doctor," the small bird said, "I don't feel so well."

"Well, take off your feathers and let's have a look."

The doctor examined the small bird, sighed and said, "I have bad news for you. You have a canarial disease. It's chirpes. And it's untweetable."

July 30, 2013

So This Guy

So this guy goes to the doctor.

The doc says, "I've got bad news for you, and I've got worse news."

Guy says, "OK—what's the bad news?"

Doc says, "You've got 24 hours to live."

Guy says, "That's *terrible!* What's the worse news?"

Doc hesitates. "Well ... I should've told you yesterday."

June 4, 2012

The Last Brownie

A man lay on his deathbed. Perhaps a few hours to live. His hands were folded on his chest. And his eyes were closed. Suddenly, his nose began to twitch. A familiar smell. He drifted upward out of the deep recess of sleep. That smell he thought. CHOCOLATE. *Brownies* baking!

One eye flickered open. Then the other. And he slowly tilted his head. The smell of chocolate was overpowering. The kitchen was just down the hall. *I need ... one last brownie....*

With great effort, he rolled onto his side and let gravity take its course. He flopped heavily onto the floor. Slowly, laboriously, he elbowed his way toward the kitchen. After what seemed like hours, he crossed the threshold of the kitchen. And there—on the kitchen table—was a plate of warm brownies. He clawed his way forward and then slowly extended his grasp ... fingers ... reaching ... *almost there.*

Just then his wife walked into the kitchen. *"GEORGE!* You leave those brownies alone! Those are for the funeral!"

November 29, 2012

Baseball in Heaven

Two very old men lived together. They *loved* baseball. Each morning they would get the newspaper and read the stories about the day's games. They studied the box scores, statistics and players. In the afternoon, they would watch baseball games on television and occasionally go to the games when their team was in town. In the evening, they'd talk over dinner about the games, the players and statistics. And each night, they would dream— dream of baseball.

They knew their days were numbered, and so they made a pact. When one of them died, he would do his best to come back and let his friend know if there was baseball in heaven.

One cold gray morning, one old man did not arise. He had passed away in the night. He was buried, but his friend carried on. Reading, studying, watching and dreaming about baseball.

A few weeks later, the old man got up and shuffled into the kitchen. Who should be sitting at the kitchen table but—his old friend!

"My friend! How I've missed you. How are y... Is there baseball in heaven?"

The friend smiled. "I have good news, and I have bad news for you."

"Well, what's the good news? Is there baseball in heaven?"

His friend responded, "Is there! I'm on a team with Babe Ruth and Ty Cobb. We played yesterday."

The old man smiled. "What's the bad news?"

His friend looked at him. "You're pitching tomorrow."

April 12, 2012

Spunk

A 94-year-old Irishman gathered his clan together and began to speak. "You know I've been a lost and lonely man since your mother passed away. But I've met a young lass—she's 23 years old—and we've decided to get married."

The children, stunned, quickly huddled. After a few minutes, the eldest son stepped forward. "Father. We know that you've been a lost and lonely man since mother passed on. But the idea of marrying a 23-year-old girl… We are concerned that this could be fatal."

The father looked up and frowned. "Well, if she dies, she dies."

December 22, 2011

So This Guy

So there's this single guy living at home with his father and working in the family business.

Then he finds out he's going to inherit a fortune when his sickly father dies. So he decides to find a wife with whom to share his fortune.

One evening, at an investment meeting, he spots the most beautiful woman he's ever seen. She takes his breath away. "I may look like just an ordinary guy," he says to her, "but in just a few months, my father will die, and I will inherit $200 million."

Impressed, the woman asks for his business card and three days later, she becomes his stepmother.

Women are so much better at financial planning than men.

March 26, 2015

Four Husbands

The local news station was interviewing an 80-year-old lady because she had just gotten married for the fourth time. The reporter asked her questions about her life, about what it felt like to be marrying again at 80 and then about her new husband's occupation. "He's a funeral director," she answered.

"Interesting," the reporter observed.

The reporter then asked her if she wouldn't mind telling a little about her first three husbands and what they did for a living. She paused for a few moments, needing time to reflect on all those years. After a short while, a smile came to her face, and she answered proudly.

She had first married a banker when she was in her 20s, then a circus ringmaster during her 40s, a preacher in her 60s, and now—in her 80s—a funeral director.

The interviewer looked at her, quite astonished, and asked why she had married four men with such diverse careers.

She smiled and explained, "I married one for the money, two for the show, three to get ready, and four to go."

July 16, 2013

Cutting Out

So this guy sticks his head into a barbershop and asks, "How long before I can get a haircut?"

The barber looks around the shop full of customers and says, "About two hours." The guy leaves.

A few days later, the same guy sticks his head in the door and asks, "How long before I can get a haircut?" The barber looks around the shop and says, "About three hours." The guy leaves.

A week later, the same guy sticks his head in the shop and asks, "How long before I can get a haircut?" The barber looks around the shop and says, "About an hour and a half." The guy leaves.

The barber turns to his friend and says, "Hey, Bob, do me a favor, follow that guy and see where he goes. He keeps asking how long he has to wait for a haircut, but he never comes back."

A little while later, Bob returns to the shop, laughing hysterically. The barber asks, "So where does he go when he leaves?"

Bob looks up and wipes tears from his eyes and says …

"Your house!"

October 16, 2014

So This Guy

So this guy walks up to a house and rings the doorbell. A woman answers the door.

"Ma'am, I'm a painter. I will paint anything."

The woman thinks. "Why don't you paint my porch. Paint it dark brown."

So the guy goes to work, and a few hours later, he rings the doorbell.

"Ma'am, I'm all done. By the way, it wasn't a Porsche—it was a Mercedes-Benz."

March 6, 2012

Why the Black Eye?

On a Monday morning, this guy goes to work with a nasty-looking black eye.

"What happened to you?" asks his friend.

"*Geeesh…* I was in church yesterday. When we all stood up to sing a hymn, this old woman in front of me stood up. She was wearing this huge billowy dress, and the back of the dress was stuck in her belt and in her rear end. So I reached forward and pulled it out. And, she turned around and smacked me."

"Gee, that's too bad," says the friend. "You try and do a good deed and look what happens."

The next Monday the same guy comes to work—this time with the other eye all blackened. His friend sees him and says, "Wow! What happened to you?"

Guy says, "So yesterday we went to church. And we sat behind this same woman. We all stood up to sing a hymn and—just like last week—her big billowy dress was caught up in her belt and in her rear end. The guy next to me reached over and pulled it out. But I knew she didn't like that, so I just leaned forward and tucked it all back in...."

September 25, 2013

So This Little Old Lady

So this little old lady is working in a hardware store. She is dusting and cleaning and fussing. In walks a large workman wearing bib overalls and high-top boots.

She smiles. "Can I help you?"

"Lady, I need to buy a file."

She puts her hands together. "Oh my.... We have all sorts of files." She turns and points to the array of tools. "We have these. And these. And these...."

"I really need a bastard file," he says.

The old woman puts her hand to her mouth and runs to the manager. She glares sternly. "That man used a bad word in front of me. He said he wanted a 'bastard' file."

The manager smiled and said, "It's not a bad word. There are wood files and metal files, and a 'bastard' file is actually a type of file for metalworking. Why not go back and sell him the file."

So she does.

A few days later another big workman comes in. He says, "Ma'am, I need a file."

She smiles. "Would you like this bastard here?"

No, he thinks, *I'll take that SOB over there....*

May 4, 2016

Sam's Shoe Shop

An old man was sitting in his easy chair when he heard the mail fall through the slot. He got up, stretched and shuffled off to pick up the mail. There was an envelope with a return address from his old Army unit. *My old unit*, he thought. He tore open the envelope and read that there was to be a reunion. "Wear your uniform!" the letter said.

My uniform. Where is my unif... The attic! He slowly padded up to the attic, and there was his footlocker. He opened it and pulled out the pants. They fit. He then shrugged on the tunic. It fit too! But his shoes were not there. *Where could they b...* He felt in his pocket, and there was a card.

SAM'S SHOE SHOP – NEW YORK CITY

Then the old man remembered that he had dropped off his shoes for repair—50 years before.

There was a telephone number on the card, so he picked up the phone and dialed. A voice answered, "Sam's Shoe Shop. Sam here."

"Sam! Sam! I was in your shop 50 years ago and dropped off my shoes." The old man read off the claim-check number. "By any chance do you still have them?"

Sam said, "All right. Just a minute." The old man waited for several minutes, then Sam got back on.

"OK. I got 'em. They'll be ready next Thursday."

September 3, 2012

My Psychiatrist

Ever since I was a kid, I've always had a haunting fear that someone was under my bed at night. *Sooooo,* I went to a shrink.

I told him, "I've got a problem. Every time I go to bed, I think there's somebody under it. I'm scared. I think I'm going crazy."

He steepled his fingers. "Just put yourself in my hands for one year. Come talk to me three times a week, and we should be able to get rid of those fears."

"How much do you charge?" I asked.

"Eighty dollars per visit," replied the doctor.

"I'll sleep on it," I said.

Six months later, the doctor saw me on the street.

"Why didn't you come to see me about those fears you were having?" he asked.

"Well, 80 bucks a visit, three times a week, for a year, is $12,480. A bartender cured me for $10. I was so happy to have saved all that money, I went and bought me a new pickup truck."

"Is that so?" Then he offered—with a bit of an attitude—"And how, may I ask, did a bartender cure you?"

"He told me to cut the legs off the bed. Ain't nobody under there now."

It pays to get a second opinion.

July 29, 2020

Two Guys in a Plane

Two guys are in an airplane flying at 35,000 feet. Suddenly, there's a loud *BANG*. The captain comes on the intercom. "Ladies and gentlemen, we have just lost one of our four engines. We have three other engines, and it is no problem to fly. But we'll be about one hour late getting to our destination."

A little while later, another loud *BANG*. The captain comes on the intercom and says, "Folks, we have lost a second of our four engines. This plane can fly on two. But we're going to be about two hours late getting to our destination."

A few minutes later, there is another—huge—*BANG!* The captain comes on the intercom and says, "Ladies and gentlemen, I've never had this happen, but we've lost a third of our four engines. This plane is designed to fly on one engine, so we're fine. But we're going to be about three hours late getting to our destination."

So the one guy turns to the other and says, "Man… If we lose that fourth engine, we're going to be up here all day!"

March 13, 2014

Guy on a Bridge

Once I saw this guy on a bridge about to jump. I said, "Don't do it!"

He said, "Nobody loves me."

I said, "God loves you. Do you believe in God?"

He said, "Yes."

I said, "Are you a Christian or a Jew?"

He said, "A Christian."

I said, "Me too! Protestant or Catholic?"

He said, "Protestant."

I said, "Me too! What denomination?"

He said, "Baptist."

I said, "Me too! Northern Baptist or Southern Baptist?"

He said, "Northern Baptist."

I said, "Me too! Northern Conservative Baptist or Northern Liberal Baptist?"

He said, "Northern Conservative Baptist."

I said, "Me too! Northern Conservative Baptist Great Lakes Region or Northern Conservative Baptist Eastern Region?"

He said, "Northern Conservative Baptist Great Lakes Region."

I said, "Me too! Are you Baptist Great Lakes Region Council of 1879, or Northern Conservative Baptist Great Lakes Region Council of 1912?"

He said, "Northern Conservative Baptist Great Lakes Region Council of 1912."

I said, "Die, heretic!" And I pushed him off the bridge.

April 22, 2018

At the Pearly Gates

A Dane and a Swede both died at the same time. They found themselves side by side, winging their way to heaven.

The Dane looked at the Swede and said, "I hope you know that St. Peter—the guardian of the Pearly Gates—is Danish."

The Swede scoffed. "That's silly. Especially coming from a Dane. I don't believe you. That's ridiculous."

The Dane gave him a knowing smile and said, "Just wait."

Suddenly, the two landed on a cloud—right in front of a large, ornate podium. Behind it was a massive figure with long beard and flowing robes. It was St. Peter.

"Welcome to heaven," he bellowed. "Before you can enter heaven, I am required to ask you a religious question." St. Peter turned to the Dane and said, "In the parable of the loaves and the fishes, how many did Jesus feed?"

The Dane scratched his chin, looked up and said, "Five thousand." St. Peter smiled and said, "Go on in." And the Pearly Gates parted.

St. Peter looked at the Swede. "You're Swedish, aren't you?"

The Swede puffed out his chest, put his hands on his hips and said, "Yep. That I am!"

St. Peter nodded. "OK—in the parable of the loaves and the fishes ... what were the names of those who were fed?"

July 19, 2015

So This Guy

So this guy goes to the doctor. He's nervous and fidgeting. The doctor says, "Do you smoke?"

The guy answers, "Yeah—four packs a day."

The doctor responds, "Well, if you don't quit smoking, you're going to be dead in five years."

The guy says, "But Doc, I'm nervous. I gotta have something to keep me calm."

The doctor thought for a moment. "Why don't you chew toothpicks?"

So the guy quit smoking and started chewing toothpicks. Three boxes of toothpicks a day. He died five years later.

Dutch elm disease...

January 23, 2012

Lutefisk

A man had a problem with a family of skunks that lived under his porch. He tried everything to get rid of them, but nothing worked. He went to the local hardware store and asked if they had any ideas.

"Put lutefisk and pickled herring under your porch," the clerk said. "That should clear up the problem."

So the guy went to the market, bought a few pounds of lutefisk and pickled herring, and put it all under the porch. The next morning, the guy ran downstairs and looked under the porch. The skunks were gone.

But a family of Swedes had moved in....

February 27, 2012

Loons

A game warden is walking through a forest in northern Wisconsin. He spots a guy skulking through the forest. The guy is looking right and left. And he's carrying a large plastic garbage bag over his shoulder. The game warden watches for a few minutes—then steps out.

"*Excuse me!*" the warden yells. The guy jumps, and the plastic bag falls to the ground. And opens. And out slide about a dozen dead loons. The warden looks at the loons and then at the guy.

"L-l-loons! You killed *loons!* Loons are an endangered species," the warden sputters. "You're under arrest. Killing loons. That's terrible!"

The guy is contrite. Puts the loons back in the bag and begins walking to the warden's pickup truck.

"Loons. *Loons!* What the heck do you do with loons?" the warden asks.

"Oh, I eat them," the guy says. "They're delicious."

The warden looks at the guy. And thinks. "All right—I've never had a loon before. What do loons taste like?"

The guy looks at the warden, thinks for a moment and says, "Well, they're kind of a cross between a California condor and a bald eagle."

August 3, 2014

Baskin' Robins

Two large robins were sitting in a tree. It had been raining hard, and they were hungry. The pair looked down, and there on the ground were dozens of large thick worms. One bird looked at the other and gave a nod. "Let's go," he chirped.

The two flew down and began devouring worm after worm after worm. The sun came out, and it warmed. And the pair ate more and *more* worms until they finished the feast. They smacked their beaks and tried to launch. But the two had eaten so many worms that they could not get off the ground.

"Let's just sit here in the sun and rest," said the one. The other— eyes glazed over—nodded in agreement and sat back to rest in the warm sunlight.

Meanwhile, a huge alley cat was skulking through the bushes. He saw the two robins ... and slowly crept—and *pounced*. He ate both birds with a smile.

"I just love baskin' robins," he thought.

December 14, 2014

Honk if You Love Peace and Quiet

I can't take credit for these examples of lexophilia, but I can be given credit for selecting the ones that made me laugh the hardest.

I just got lost in thought. It was unfamiliar territory.
42.7% of all statistics are made up on the spot.
99% of lawyers give the rest a bad name.
I feel like I'm diagonally parked in a parallel universe.
I wonder how much deeper the ocean would be without sponges.
Remember, half the people you know are below average.
Despite the cost of living, have you noticed how popular it remains?
Atheism is a non-prophet organization.
He who laughs last thinks slowest.
The early bird may get the worm, but the second mouse gets the cheese.

I intend to live forever—so far so good.

Borrow money from pessimists; they don't expect it back.

Love may be blind, but marriage is a real eye-opener.

Experience is something you don't get until just after you need it.

Success always occurs in private and failure, in full view.

The colder the X-ray table, the more of your body is required to be on it.

The hardness of butter is directly proportional to the softness of the bread.

To succeed in politics, it is often necessary to rise above your principles.

Mondays are an awful way to spend one-seventh of your life.

A clear conscience is usually the sign of a bad memory.

Change is inevitable, except from vending machines.

Plan to be spontaneous—tomorrow.

Why are there five syllables in monosyllabic?

February 7, 2019

Centipede Jokes

A centipede went to college and made the football team. As a running back, *nothing* could stop him. In practice, he would plow through the line, knocking defenders here and there. And he would score. Every time.

When the day of the big first game arrived, the team took the field, but the centipede was nowhere to be found. At halftime, the coach walked into the locker room, and there was the centipede, sitting on the bench.

"Where the #%&*X! have you been?" the coach yelled.

"Sorry, coach," said the centipede. "I've just been putting on my shoes."

"Good thing you don't have athlete's foot," snarled the coach.

After the game, the centipede went out with his girlfriend. Smooth talker that he was, he said to her, "You've got a nice pair of legs…. You've got a nice pair of legs…. You've got a nice pair of legs…."

May 5, 2013

So This Old Guy

So this old guy goes to the golf course. "I'd love to play," he says to the pro. "But my eyes are really bad. I hit the ball pretty well, but I can't see where the ball goes."

The pro smiled. "I've got just the guy to pair you up with. Old Scott isn't much of a golfer, but he has got eyes like a hawk. I'll put you and Scott together."

So the old guy and Scott are introduced, shake hands and head for the first tee. The old guy bangs his drive about 250 yards. He turns to Scott. "Did you see where it went?"

Scott looks over. "I saw precisely where your ball went."

They get in their golf cart and start rumbling down the fairway. They drive and drive. The old guy looks over at Scott. "So where did my ball go?"

Scott rubs his chin. "Gosh, I don't remember...."

July 14, 2016

Teed Off

Golf is 65% mental and 35% mental.
~ Anonymous

The only time I ever took out a 1-iron was to kill a tarantula. And I took a 7 to do that.
~ Jim Murray

The only sure rule in golf is, he who has the fastest cart never has to play the bad lie.
~ Mickey Mantle

Sex and golf are the two things you can enjoy even if you're not good at them.
~ Kevin Costner

After all these years, it's still embarrassing for me to play on the American golf tour. Like the time I asked my caddie for a sand wedge and he came back 10 minutes later with a ham on rye.
~ *Chi-Chi Rodríguez*

Give me golf clubs, fresh air and a beautiful partner, and you can keep the clubs and the fresh air.
~ *Jack Benny*

Professional golf is the only sport where, if you win 20% of the time, you're the best.
~ *Jack Nicklaus*

The only time my prayers are never answered is on the golf course.
~ *Billy Graham*

If you watch a game, it's fun. If you play at it, it's recreation. If you work at it, it's golf.
~ *Bob Hope*

If you think it's hard to meet new people, try picking up the wrong golf ball.
~ *Jack Lemmon*

You can make a lot of money in this game. Just ask my ex-wives.
~ *Lee Trevino*

December 8, 2016

A Priest, a Lawyer and an Engineer

During the French Revolution, three noblemen—a priest, a lawyer and an engineer—were condemned to die on the guillotine. As noblemen, they were afforded one final courtesy of rank, that of choosing whether to die face *up*—or face *down*—on the guillotine.

The priest was led to the top of the steps, where the black-hooded executioner stood. "How do you wish to die, face up or face down?" asked

117

the executioner. The priest thought, looked up and said, "I wish to die face up—so I may see the heavens one last time and meet my maker face to face."

With that the priest was placed into the guillotine, and the executioner pulled the rope. The heavy blade fell swiftly—but an inch above the priest's throat, the blade screeched to a stop. It was *jammed.* Under French law, if someone was spared death on the guillotine, he was a free man. So the blade was raised, and the priest walked away—*free.*

Then the lawyer was led up the wooden steps. "How do you wish to die, face up or face down?" The lawyer quickly looked up and said, "*Ohhh,* I too want to die face up to see the heavens one last time and meet my maker face to face."

The lawyer was put into the guillotine, and the executioner pulled the cord. *Whoosh!* The thick blade sped downward—but just over the lawyer's throat, the blade came to a halt. And of course under French law, being spared death on the guillotine meant the lawyer was a free man. He hopped up and walked away.

Then the engineer was led up, and the executioner asked, "How do you wish to die, face up or face down?" The engineer looked up and said, "I too ... want ... to die ... face up to ..." He stopped and pointed. *"Heeey! I think I see your problem up there!"*

January 7, 2018

The Envelope, Please

A man was on his deathbed. He called his three best friends together—a priest, a doctor and a lawyer. "My friends," he said, "I've decided that I want to take my money with me. I'm giving each of you an envelope containing $300,000 in cash. Just before they close my coffin, I want you to throw in the envelope. I will be happy because I'm taking my money with me."

The friends solemnly agreed, and a short time later the man passed away. At the funeral, each of the friends stepped up and tossed his envelope into the coffin—just as it was being closed. Following the funeral, the three friends gathered to have a drink.

After a moment, the priest broke down and tearfully said, "I have a confession. I took $50,000 out of the envelope to give to a homeless shelter." With that, the doctor broke down and sobbed, "I have a confession. I took $100,000 to help fund the children's hospital."

The lawyer's eyes narrowed. His stoic face turned to a frown. "I am ashamed of you. Ashamed! Taking money like that. I want you to know that I put my personal check in that envelope for the full $300,000."

December 2, 2012

April Fool!

The first mention of "April Fools' Day" as being on April 1 was in Chaucer's *Canterbury Tales* in 1392 (in "The Nun's Priest's Tale").

Jonathan Swift (1665–1745) was the foremost prose satirist in the English language. And he was also a twinkle-in-the-eye practical joker who authored a doozy of an April Fools' prank, bringing the tradition to a whole new level.

In February 1708, using the name *Isaac Bickerstaff*, Swift published an article solemnly predicting that John Partridge, a local author of astrological almanacs, would die at 11 p.m. on March 29, 1708. All of London held its collective breath. When the fateful day arrived, Swift—still writing as Isaac Bickerstaff—penned a moving obituary announcing the death of Partridge at 7:05 p.m.—four hours earlier than predicted.

Of course Partridge was very much alive—and *outraged* over Swift's prediction and the false reporting of his death. Because the story of John Partridge's demise was printed on April 1, it ignited a new—and more creative—breed of April Fools' pranks.

I think I'd like to have Jonathan Swift join Aristophanes and me for a very special dinner....

August 30, 2011

Aristophanes

A few years ago, I was asked (for a biographical sketch) what famous figure I would most like to have dinner with. My answer? *Aristophanes*. Nicknamed by his contemporaries "*Old Baggy Pants*." He was my kinda guy....

This Athenian satirist was probably the world's first stand-up comedian. He was well-educated and began writing satire in his teens. He wrote more than 40 plays, of which 11 have survived. The first play penned under his own name was *The Knights* (424 B.C.). It was a scathing satire about the Athenian politician and military leader Cleon—the arrogant demagogue who succeeded Pericles.

Cleon is aptly depicted in the play as a bloated and intoxicated *lout*—whose face and toga are always smeared with wine. Aristophanes sometimes played the part of Cleon—lurching onto stage, staggering around and mumbling—because he wanted to make sure the part was played *properly*. The spoof was wonderfully popular with everyone in Athens—except for Cleon, who sent messengers to Aristophanes suggesting that he *cool it*.

In the world of literature, the satiric works of Ben Jonson and Henry Fielding were influenced by Aristophanes. Examine the comedies of Shakespeare and you will find the tongue-in-cheek humor of Aristophanes swimming beneath the surface.

If we sat down to dinner, I'd order some Greek crabcakes, *moussaka*, *spanakopita* and *pastitsio*—with a bottle or two of *agiorgitiko*. Then we'd start telling jokes....

March 14, 2019

10

SEEING THE WORLD

Shangri-La

When I go on vacation, I'm looking for a place like … well, like Shangri-La. Heck—maybe I'd like to *move* there.

When I was little, my father would sing a song that included the word *Shangri-La*. He would do a lot of humming and then belt out "Shangri-La." You hear the term every once in awhile, so I thought this might be an interesting point to explore.

Shangri-La is actually a fictional location introduced in the 1933 book *Lost Horizon* by British author James Hilton. The place is described as a mystical paradise—isolated and insulated from the rest of the world. Everyone in Shangri-La is permanently happy, and the people live beyond normal lifespans—aging slowly and joyfully.

Shangri-La is supposed to be situated on the western end of the Kunlun Mountains in China. Many villages and locales have claimed to be *the* Shangri-La, but so far there is nothing definitive. Hilton said he was inspired to invent—and write about—Shangri-La after reading articles in *National Geographic* about the travels of botanist and ethnographer Joseph Rock. But Hilton died in 1954, so he's not talking.

August 27, 2013

Arequipa

Two years ago my wife, Donna, and I were slated to go to Machu Picchu in south central Peru. Machu Picchu is the iconic home of a pre-Columbian Inca nation. However, in the week before we were to leave, Machu Picchu and the surrounding area were *inundated* with torrential rains. The Bingham Highway was washed out in parts, and nearly 2,000 visitors were stranded (and had to be helicoptered out). What to do…

The question was—do we head for Buenos Aires, or do we try to go somewhere else in Peru? We decided to go to the second most–populous (though infrequently visited) city in Peru—Arequipa. All I can say is *wow*. It was too bad that Machu Picchu was rained out, but it was oh so good to make the choice we did.

We stayed in a beautiful hotel—the Casa Andina. It is the largest hotel in Arequipa. And we stayed for three nights. Traveling around the city and seeing the sites (such as the truly *amazing* Santa Catalina Monastery, where 450 nuns lived). And trying new and unique restaurants. We dined once in the hotel (wonderful) and at a place down the street—Zig Zag Restaurant (sat upstairs). Again—*wow*.

Want an experience? Go to—or plan to get stuck in—Arequipa. Pretty special. And *yes*—I would go back.

July 23, 2012

The Footsteps of St. Paul

Donna and I recently returned from a trip to Greece and Turkey with the Catholic Theological Union—the CTU—at the University of Chicago. There were 35 of us making a pilgrimage, following in the footsteps of St. Paul.

Saul of Tarsus was born in Tarsus in the Roman province of Cilicia in about A.D. 5. Saul was a Roman citizen, but he was also a Jew and a Pharisee. As a young man, he zealously persecuted the followers of Jesus of Nazareth and vigorously attacked the early Christian church—and its members. He played an active role in the stoning of the St. Stephen. And he was involved in rounding up and silencing Christians.

However, in or about A.D. 35, while walking on a road to Damascus, Saul of Tarsus was struck down by a bright light and the voice of the Lord (Acts 9, Acts 22). For three days Saul was blind, and then he literally saw the light. He underwent a dramatic conversion and began preaching the Christian gospel to all who would listen. St. Paul went on to preach the gospel of Christianity to Jews, Christians and gentiles until his death at the hands of the Romans in A.D. 67.

The pilgrimage with CTU took us to most of the places where St. Paul wrote his iconic letters—Thessaloniki (1 and 2 Thessalonians), Philippi (Philippians), Corinth (1 and 2 Corinthians) and Ephesus (Ephesians)—as well as other places where he spent time: Antakya; Athens; Kavala.... And we visited Tarsus. Where it all began. All I can say is—*wow*—and ... St. Paul sure got around.

We did too. The trip was a bit arduous on occasion but immensely fulfilling. The only time of mild concern was when we arrived in Istanbul on the evening of Friday, May 31. Going to our hotel off Taksim Square...

June 21, 2013

Taksim Square

We arrived in Istanbul and drove in the direction of our hotel—the Crystal (No. 7, Taksim) a little after 9 p.m. The activity going on around us was disconcerting. *Hundreds* of people on the streets, wearing masks and balaclavas, and carrying signs and banners. All heading to the thousands already gathered in Taksim Square.

Our bus could not make it up the narrow street to Taksim No. 7, so we had to get off the bus and carry or pull our luggage the last block and a half. The street had barricades a la *Le Mis*.

It was about halfway up the street that the tear gas hit us. At first, I thought there was something wrong with my eyes, and I began blinking. Rapidly. Then squinting. And I realized—*tear gas*. I squinted as hard as I could, keeping just enough vision to *Sherpa* my way up the street. I looked around. Donna followed in my wake. Head down. "Let's go," I said (quite unnecessarily).

We mercifully got to the hotel. One of our number was in distress and being attended. The lobby was jammed. People. Luggage. The faint whiff of tear gas. And sweat (the day had been warm). Our hotel was at near-capacity, filled with Libyans (some with medical conditions from the revolution). And Iranians. After what seemed an age, we got our keys and went up to our room. The toilet was flooding. And the flush mechanism fell into the toilet.

I went down to the lobby. Got another room and went up to check it out. I went in. And quickly went out. The room was full of tear gas, thanks to wide-open windows. *Brilliant...*

We got a third room. Seemed to work. No tear gas or toilet leaks. We drank some water and looked at each other. *Welcome to Istanbul.* And we went to bed.

The next few days were perfection. We were able to travel around unhindered. The Blue Mosque. Hagia Sophia Museum. Topkapi Palace. Mass in one of the old Christian churches. Wow! But the evenings that weekend made the stay interesting, as the crowds gathered in protest.

June 25, 2013

Second City

In 1938, my father and his friend Bill took a driving trip to Mexico. This was an unheard-of expedition at the time for two 20-something guys from Chicago. Despite numerous car troubles (a Model A Ford), they nearly made it to Mexico City. At that point, running low on money—and enthusiasm for confronting a chronically ailing car—they chugged back north.

I have a wonderful vintage film (now on DVD) my father made on this trip. The amazing thing—it is in *color*. One of the classic images of my father is him standing next to the famed Obispado in Monterrey, Nuevo Leon. Built in the late 1780s, this church building has served as a barracks, retirement home, fortress and now—a museum.

In the late 1980s I began traveling to Monterrey on business. I have been there often—visiting two or, in a few cases, three times a year. Monterrey has become almost a *second city* for me. I know my way around (though it is challenging), and I enjoy the wonderful restaurants, sites and people.

When there, I normally stay at the Quinta Real, a beautiful hotel in the San Pedro Garza Garcia neighborhood. I have visited the Obispado—and have a wonderful picture of myself standing in the exact spot where my father stood 70 years before.

I have made good friends in Monterrey—Antonio G. and his family being chief among them. He and his family have been to my home (for Thanksgiving one year), and Donna and I have been to his. Monterrey is a great city with wonderful people. I look forward to seeing my second city again soon.

_____

December 17, 2017

The Hotel Selu

Cordoba, Spain. 1972. Donna and I had been married a few months, and we took a belated honeymoon trip—three weeks—to Spain and Portugal. Two 25-year-olds driving around with no reservations. No plans. No itinerary. Getting up each morning and going, "What shall we do today?"

Fortunately, we were in sync on pretty much everything, so the trip went swimmingly. We stayed in the state-run *paradors* for about 10 bucks a night. We dined on the "big four"—calamari, coffee, churros and chocolate. And informally followed the famed matador Diego Puerta as he wound his way through various *corridas* in Spain. The bullfighting was special since I had just read Hemingway's 1932 classic *Death in the Afternoon*. And Michener's *Iberia*.

Then—we got to Córdoba. It was late. And the parador was booked. And other hotels had no room. Finally—tired and hungry—we found a room. In the basement of the Hotel Selu. Cue the theme from *Dragnet*....

Now today, the Hotel Selu may be a four-star offering. But in 1972 it was ... *Anyway*, we checked in. There were chickens cackling outside our window. And some guy was yelling at his wife in the next room (I think the walls were made of cardboard). Donna sat down on the bed, and she began to cry. And that was *before* the rooster woke us up at 4:30 a.m....

I felt like an idiot. But mind you—I am *not* as dumb as I look. So I resolved right then there would be no more Hotel Selus in Donna's future. Over the years we've come close a few times, but so far I've stayed out of *that* kind of trouble.

February 17, 2017

14 Years Later

In 1972 Donna and I took an extended honeymoon to Spain and Portugal. In Spain, we traveled around, sightseeing and attending the corridas of famed matador Diego Puerta in Madrid, Córdoba and Sevilla. *And* we took pictures galore.

In Ayamonte, Spain, I traded three ice cream cones for a photo of three little boys ("It's OK, he's a tourist," said the woman working the open-air shop). Then there was the fishing boat, where the six crew members were quick to pose when I asked. And in Lisbon, we walked the gardens of Jerónimos Monastery. A gardener—wearing a black turtleneck and jeans—was suspended on a board over a large circular clock garden. Clipping flowers. He smiled, tipped his beret and posed. *Snap. Snap. Snap.*

Fast forward 14 years. Donna and I returned to Spain and Portugal with our 10-year-old daughter, friends Diane and David, and their son Dave. Before leaving, I had the photograph assemblage mentioned above blown up to 8-by-10s.

In Ayamonte, we went back to the *same* ice cream shop and I showed the *same* (now older) woman the photo of the three little boys. She gasped. And identified each one. She asked us to be at her store in the morning. And we were—greeted by a crowd. *And* the three little—now grown—boys. We gave each one an 8-by-10. One mother cried on seeing the photo, as she had no pictures of her son as a little boy.

The fishing boats were gone—replaced by a small office of the Guardia Civil—the national police who sport the tricorn hat. An officer identified one fisherman as the father of Ayamonte's *head* of Guardia Civil—who marched over. And began weeping when I gave him some 8-by-10s. His father had died a few years before. He handed me his card ("If you ever need help in Spain, you call me"). I still have his card.

And in Jerónimos, we found the gardener—now in a drab gray uniform. Raking leaves. And three weeks from his retirement. He saw his photograph. And his eyes filled with tears. At his request, we buzzed through two rolls of Polaroid film, taking pictures for our gardener friend—and each member of his entire gardening crew.

October 21, 2018

My Last Cigar

In his 1924 classic *Death in the Afternoon*, Ernest Hemingway constructs a dialogue between himself and another American on the subjects of bullfighting, soccer and football. The number of young men injured, paralyzed and killed playing football numbered in the thousands (today, it's the *tens* of thousands). The number of young men hurt playing soccer is minimal by comparison. And then there is bullfighting. Where humans occasionally get hurt—but rarely killed. Hemingway's point: Those who decry bullfighting rarely raise a whisper about American football.

Many years ago, in another lifetime, Donna and I spent the better part of a month following the *corrida de toros* circuit in Spain. Diego Puerta was a favorite. Madrid. Córdoba. Málaga. Sevilla. And others. It was pretty special. I still have great pictures from those Sundays. There was artistry. Tension. Spectacle. A unique smell. There was the classic music. And the *denouement*...

The last time I went to a bullfight was in Monterrey, Mexico, with my good friend Antonio G. The Plaza de Toros Monumental on the Avenida Alfonso Reyes. That was the last time, too, when I had a cigar. A gigantic Cuban. Hand-rolled. Cohiba Robusto.

If you haven't been to a bullfight, read Hemingway's classic and then go. I've read it a few times. And get yourself a big hand-rolled Cohiba Robusto....

June 9, 2019

Don't You Like Our Looks?

Some years ago, Donna and I were in Galway with some friends. We decided to go exploring with another couple. We reconnoitered the town and saw a pub called the Quays (pronounced "Keys"). It was night. Raining. The place was off the beaten path. Donna and I and our friend Ivo and his wife walked in.

The pub was dark and filled with smoke. Big men. Heavy. Bellied up to the bar. Beards. Black leather jackets. Noise. Many of the occupants turned to give us the eye. Have you ever been somewhere and gotten that feeling you just don't belong? Once inside, we looked around and got that feeling.

As we moved toward the door, a loud voice from a corner booth holding about eight people caught our attention. "What's the matter? Don't ya like our looks?" Ivo and I looked at each other, and I—respectfully—pointed out that the place was "very crowded," and there was no room for us to sit. The chap who'd called us out started to move. "Sit here. We'll make room for ya." And people began shuffling. Shifting. All watching us. I looked at my friend. He raised his eyebrows like, *Let's see where this goes.* And we moved into the group—squishing ourselves into corner seats.

They were curious about where we were from (Chicago/Edgartown, Massachusetts), why we were there (a meeting) and where all we were going (we detailed). They bought us drinks. More drinks. And refused our offer of reciprocity. After an hour or so, Morris—the chap who'd called out to us—invited us to join him and some of the others at another pub. The Tribesman. Where he was playing a horsehide drum in an Irish band. At that point, how could we say no?

We walked a few blocks. The Tribesman was packed. Morris shooed people away as he pushed his way to the small alcove stage, with us in tow. He set two small stools right in front of the band. Donna and I sat. Listened. Enchanted. Then we traded seats with our friends, who'd been standing in the back. It turned out to be one of the most memorable evenings I've ever had. It could've all turned out *verrry* differently if we'd said, "Gosh, thanks anyway." And scurried out the door.

October 27, 2018

He's a Devil

When I traveled to Portugal years ago, I sometimes had dinner in a little cafe off Rossio Square in Lisbon. One evening I was sitting in the restaurant with a cab driver, George.

George looked at me. "Scott, do some magic tricks." So I did a few effects. With that, George called over some of the waiters. "You gotta see this stuff." A gaggle of waiters began to congregate by our booth. I asked for a deck of cards—it arrived—and I began my routine. Nothing fancy but some good stuff.

It was when I poured water into my fist and made it disappear—and then reappear—that one waiter looked seriously at his colleagues. "*Ele é o diabo*" ("He's a devil"). And I suddenly realized my visage had quite possibly morphed from curiosity to danger to the human race and all that is holy.

George coughed and looked at me. My face got warm. I thought, *I better do something or I may have trouble leaving the restaurant. Sooo*, I did what any other red-blooded American magician would do. I looked up at the waiter who had branded me a *diabo* and said, "Here—I'm gonna show you how I did that."

I did. I showed the waiters how I did the tricks—*without* making them take the mandatory Magician's Oath never to reveal the secret. The waiters laughed nervously. Seemed relieved. And walked away. George gave me one of those eyes-in-the-air looks that said, *I won't ask you to do that again*. And I lived to tell the tale.

March 17, 2016

Mr. Lucky

Last month we were on a cruise in the Baltic. Wonderful experience. On the first evening, Donna and I walked from our stateroom to the elevators. To go have dinner. *Whoa!* There on the floor was a wad of greenbacks. I picked it up. I looked down the halls. *Not a soul around*. It was five 20-dollar bills. A hundred bucks.

My Boy Scout mentality compelled me to report finding "some currency" on Deck 8. I did *not* add the detail of denominations or nationality. So with this newfound stash of cash, I decided to hit the shipboard casino. The first night, I surrounded our lucky number with chips. Half hour later—I was $855 richer. My number had come up *four* times.

With this increased largesse, I visited the casino on a few additional nights, thinking that before too long I would own the ship and the Regent Cruise Line. But that didn't happen. The $855 slipped away, and I debarked in Copenhagen only 20 bucks richer than when I started. Oh—and *no one* claimed the 20s.

October 4, 2018

Carry On

Donna and I just returned from a 14-day adventure to Rome, the Amalfi Coast and Sicily. It was wonderful. But this trip was different from all other trips we've been on in one key—and defining—way. We traveled with carry-ons. No checked luggage.

Normally, when going on a trip, Donna and I will pack so as to be prepared for white-water rafting, dinner at the White House, cocktails with Giorgio Armani or a barbecue at the King Ranch.

This time, we pared down our wardrobes so much that I had little more than a toothbrush, an extra pair of shorts and a golf shirt. Even in the limited space, Donna was able to pack such that when we arrived at our destinations, opening her suitcase was like springing open the door of the clown car at the circus.

For me, this has been something of a Damascus Road conversion. I can't deny that one day I may decide to fill up three suitcases for a weekend trip to Rock Island. But I do believe that Donna and I have both turned a corner in transportational paraphernalia.

October 23, 2019

Liberia

What's the only country besides the United States to have its capital named after an American president? Answer: Liberia (Monrovia). What is the only country whose flag copies the American flag—but has only one star? Answer: Liberia. What is the only country in Africa where the U.S. dollar is the national currency? Answer: Liberia. What is the only country in Africa that has English as its national language? Answer: Liberia. What African country frowns on "African" first names? Answer: Liberia. What is the only African country to have declared independence without a revolt or incursion by another country? Answer: Liberia.

Liberia—"Land of the Free"—was settled in 1822 by the American Colonization Society. And populated by former slaves who had left the United States in search of a better life. James Monroe was a supporter of the ACS. Hence *Monrovia*.

During the 1950s, Liberia enjoyed the world's second-highest rate of economic growth. But then things began to unravel. From 1989 to 1995, a bloody civil war claimed more the 200,000 Liberian lives. Since then, there have been sporadic uprisings, though the country has been fairly stable since 2005.

Liberia offers a "flag of convenience"—the second-largest maritime registry in the world (behind Panama)—allowing maritime vessels to register under the Liberian flag for business and tax purposes. Corruption and crime are problems in Liberia. But there is now *one* 18-hole golf course in Liberia—the Seaview Golf Club in Virginia, Montserrado County. Thus Liberia is back on my bucket list.

December 16, 2016

Trips versus Vacations

I like *vacations*. I just returned home from 10 days in the Caribbean. Every morning, I slept until 8 a.m. Or later. Got up. Sat on a recliner overlooking the ocean. Sipped coffee and lingered over my cereal and fruit. Did some work on my laptop. Then, more coffee. A book. More coffee. A little exercise. *Yawn.* Stretch. And *think* about lunch.

Lunch was around 1:30 or 2 p.m. Usually a salad or something light. Bread and olive oil. Oh—and a large bowl of *pommes frites*. Looking out on the emerald waters and golden sands. Then back to the home we rented. To rest. Read. Some bridge. A little wine. And then we'd start thinking about dinner. *Yawn.*

That vacation was pretty special. It was *not* a "trip." I've been on *trips*. And let me tell you. They are *different*. Where you have to get up at 6 a.m. Wolf down some breakfast and be at the bus at 7:30. *Sharp.* And then you drive on a bus with no bathroom for two hours to a place where you hike what seems like 20 miles to see a historical site. Then hike 30 miles back to the bus. Drive another hour to where it's time for lunch. "We have to finish lunch in half an hour. *We're running late!*" Lunch is lettuce, olives, gray meat and bread. We're like Navy Seals doing their "crucible" training on Base Coronado—devouring food on the fly and racing back to the boats. *Go, go, go, go!!* More bus. Late dinner. Collapse. Alarm goes off at 6 a.m. Groundhog Day...

I've enjoyed most of the *trips* I've been on. But let me tell you something. *Vacations* are special. I'm always ready for another. Maybe next time with my Callaway X-20 irons...

March 2, 2014

11

NOTES ON CULTURE

On the Verge of Icky

The day before Thanksgiving, my wife, Donna, dumped all of the ice from the freezer into the sink. I asked *why*. She said the ice was "on the verge of icky." It was stuck together. Hence, "verge of icky."

It occurred to me that this expression would be a great title for a book—*On the Verge of Icky*. It could be a book about Illinois politics or General Petraeus or asparagus.

There are a *lot* of things that, in my opinion, are on the "verge of icky." Ultimate fighting. Dirty dishes. Certain four-legged creatures. Certain two-legged creatures. Politicians. High school (or younger-kid) contact football. Texting while driving. Mullets. Smoking. Mosquitoes. Many plaintiffs' lawyers. Spitting. Prejudice. Intolerance. Three-putting.

Actually, some of these things are *downright* icky.

December 13, 2012

Coming Attactions

Donna and I went to the movies last Saturday. We saw *Zero Dark Thirty*. The movie was excellent and moving. It was the "coming attractions" that turned me off. Every coming attraction began with loud, angry violence. And each one got worse as the "attaction" wore on.

We saw trailers for *Dead Man Down, The Call, Pain & Gain*.... All were smothered in violence, gunfire, car crashes and horror. I feel like saying, "Come on, people! Don't you know what you are doing to your children? To our society?" But I am one small drip of a voice.

February 27, 2013

A Culture of Violence

On Saturday mornings when I was growing up, I could watch one hour of television. I was not allowed to watch *Superman* (the *old* one with George Reeves) because my mother thought it was "too violent." So I usually picked *Mighty Mouse* and *Sky King*. On Saturday nights, I sometimes watched *Have Gun—Will Travel* and *Gunsmoke* with my father. In the old Westerns, if a bad guy was shot, he'd fall down. Nary a drop of blood. No coughing. No twitching. No movement. And no gloating.

In 1969 Sam Peckinpah ended that age of innocence with his iconic *The Wild Bunch*, in which blood flowed in rivers and the carnage was suffocating. I remember seeing the movie and going, *Whoa!*

Today we accept that young people can watch movies that *glorify* horror, death, murder and fear. They play (often for *hours* on end) the most violent, brutal, cruel and bloody video games. Killing. Burning. Defiling. Bombing. There are the scalding inhumanity and bloodlust of ultimate fighting and the degrading and debasing reality television shows where manipulation and back-stabbing win. Hollywood sinks lower. And lower. And the discourse is more hateful.

But—hey—don't you *dare* try to impose your values on anyone. There is no *right* or *wrong*. Don't even think of mentioning the word *God* in school or a public place. And heaven help you if you bring a Bible to school.

When you see the *horrific* violence that we as a society *wreak* upon ourselves, I have to wonder if this new casual acceptance of violence and debasement of traditional values doesn't invite it.

February 27, 2018

The NRA

When I was a kid, my father sent me down to the local creek to shoot rats. Big Norway rats. I used a BB gun or a single-shot .22 loaded with CB shorts.

When I was 14, I was on staff at a Boy Scout camp in Wisconsin. I got on the school bus for the ride up north with my knapsack and my Stevens Model 416 .22-caliber, bolt-action rifle. Plus two boxes of ammunition. Art T. brought *pistols* to camp, since he was on a pistol team back home. We arrived on Sunday, put our guns under our bunks and on Monday checked them in at the rifle range for the duration of the summer. No one *ever* thought of doing something violent or hurtful to another person. Many of the boys were junior members of the NRA. I was for a couple years. But never since.

I believe that folks who want guns for hunting, target-shooting or protection should have them. But I object to semi-automatic weapons, bump stocks, massive clips or military-style weapons. They are not necessary. Nor are they contemplated by the Second Amendment. The NRA has changed.

The current NRA seems to care little about the gun violence that suffocates our nation. Instead, it preaches the same sermon that most weapons should be legal. With little limitation. Easy on the background checks. As we all know, *some* NRA members crave *automatic* weapons. And even more treacherous devices.

But one should at least *understand* the NRA's position, since there are those on the other side who believe that by confiscating *all* weapons, violence will come to an end. And then there are some who proclaim that even those who are mentally ill and prone to violence cannot be forced to take meds or have institutional treatment *unless the individual agrees*. Toxic agendas. Toxic results.

With such extreme positions—competing for legitimacy—it is tough to find common ground. And common sense. We *need* to do something. But sanity and compromise seem to have gone out the window.

February 22, 2018

Illegal Weapons

I used to have an illegal weapon. And every once in a while I *used* it. Know what it was? It was a switchblade knife.

Now mind you, my switchblade knife was old and decrepit and had a blade that was maybe 2 inches long. And it opened with the speed of a snoozing turtle (*sh-sh-sh-sh-clunk*). And it was *d-u-l-l*. I used it when I was in the garage cutting up boxes for recycling (*take that, box!*). I never had any nefarious designs on anyone with my switchblade. But technically, it was illegal. And if I still had it, it would still be illegal. Even though my victims were cardboard boxes.

I have my old Boy Scout knives, which are so sharp that I can shave with them. They seem to be far more dangerous. But a switchblade? *Outrageous.* Illinois remains one of the few states where it is illegal to have a switchblade knife. Maybe we should *tax* them! Now *that's* the spirit.

May 24, 2015

Ultimate Fighting

Who watches ultimate fighting? The *Sports Business Journal* pegs the median age for those who watch ultimate fighting as men—49 years old. But when I ask *who* watches ultimate fighting, I'm more interested in what kind of human being enjoys watching men trying to kill each other.

In "Decline and Fall" (keep reading, it's coming), I speak of Edward Gibbon's classic work *The History of the Decline and Fall of the Roman Empire.* The reasons for Rome's destruction are scarily similar to things happening today in America. One reason for the empire's unraveling was the blood lust of Romans in the brutal gladiator games.

Is ultimate fighting any different? For some *aficionados,* the more brutal and bloody the match, the better. Yet read the statistics on ultimate fighting "warriors" who have died in the ring (or shortly after leaving it). These guys are dropping like flies (or becoming vegetables). Bump someone on the street too hard and you can be charged with assault and battery.

Extinguish a human life in the ultimate fighting ring and you become a legend.

Who watches ultimate fighting? I scratch my head on this one.

January 20, 2019

They Dwell Among Us

I've seen silly emails circulated with this title. I always delete them as I've felt the stories are so far-fetched as to be unbelievable. Until Monday.

Scout's honor. I was on the train on Monday. Heading home after a long day. The train was crowded with a few folks standing in the aisles. A woman sat down next to me. She took an orange Visa credit card from her purse and—holding it in her hand—pulled out her cell phone and dialed a number. And then in a voice loud enough to be heard three or four rows away, she said she had a question on her credit card. She needed details on the last dozen or so transactions. And she repeated the card number into the receiver.

Then (as if that weren't enough) after a pause, she repeated a family name and a calendar date (presumably security codes). *Then* (of course) she read off the three-digit security code on the back of the card ("*Ummm, lemme see ... two three eight ... yes, THREE eight*").

For the next 15 minutes, with phone shouldered to her ear, she proceeded to go back and forth on the telephone in this highly public place about questioned purchases (one charge was—I kid you not—9 cents).

We do not need—or want—educational tests or intelligence tests for a person to vote. But *maybe* there is something to having a Stupid Test. This woman would be the poster girl. Then again, we have no Stupid Test to serve in Congress. Or in the White House.

By the way, I just bought a great bunch of new books online, some shoes for Donna, a new Martin guitar. Then I booked us a trip to Europe, and I ... oops. *Never mind....*

August 16, 2013

Tribes

I am troubled by the animosity that we see on both sides of our political spectrum. I'm sure many of you are too. So what do we do about it?

Rather than promote *political* labels, it may be more productive to work toward consensus on *issues*. I *want* to help the poor. I *hate* inequality. And prejudice. I *want* to eliminate hunger in America and everywhere. I *yearn* for peace among nations. All Americans need health insurance. I *want* to improve education in America's poorest schools. Our country needs a strong economy where *all* will benefit. We need freedom of speech on campuses—*and* in politics. All sides should have a voice. America has a right to control its border, but a fair and compassionate policy for admitting immigrants is needed.

I love my family—and want my grandchildren to grow up healthy, happy, safe, wise, educated and with a religious faith. And to abide by the principles of faith, hope and charity—for *all* of humanity. And you know what? I want that for *your* children and grandchildren too. So what am I—a Democrat or Republican?

Yes, there are one or two hot-button issues on which neither side will bend (and some refuse to discuss). Yet I like to think that most folks are on the same page on the issues above. While we may differ on how best to address them, *that* is where civil discourse, compromise and conciliation come into play. To solve these issues. And to bring our tribes together as one.

November 8, 2018

Incentive

I get up in the morning. Exercise. Go to work. I pay my mortgage. Pay my bills. Donate to charities. I take care of the house. Take the dog out. Put dirty laundry down the chute and put the garbage on the curb. I drive carefully and obey the law. I pay my taxes and (usually) don't grouse. I love my wife and family. I go to church on Sunday. I try to eat right. And I try to be nice to and respectful of *all* people—those I know and those I don't.

So—big question—*why on earth do I do this?* Why do *you?* The answer—to me—is the single most important word in the English language. *Incentive.* I have *incentive* to do all of these things. To earn a few bucks. Keep a nice house. Eat right. Be respectful to everybody. Drive carefully. *Yada yada…*

I'm concerned that we are losing that sense of motivation. It is being replaced by a sense of entitlement. A sense of expectation. Something for … *nothing.* Incentive is waning. Maybe it's a bit old-fashioned. On January 20, 1961, President John F. Kennedy admonished, "My fellow Americans: ask not what your country can do for you—ask what you can do for your country." There was loud applause. Nods of approval. Media approbation.

Today though, more and more people are asking what their country can do for them. *Gimme, gimme, gimme.* With no strings attached. Some politicians encourage it. According to the Tax Policy Center, 40.4% of all Americans *paid no income tax* in 2013. In 2017, that number rose to 42%. A continued rise in that number could reach a tipping point. And become unsustainable.

What's *your* take? More importantly—*what's the answer?*

May 6, 2018

Why People Are Late

Each morning I get up, check my email and lurch down the stairs. I make the coffee, get the newspaper, make my breakfast, chow down my cereal and sip two cups of coffee while reading the paper and watching *Squawk Box.*

All the while, I keep a weather eye on the clock. Why? *Because I have to catch a train.* If I miss the train, I miss the train. The train waits for no one. I'm left standing. And I'm late. Therefore I always allot myself precisely 14 minutes to walk from my house to the train station. And I catch my train. I am on time. *Ta-daaa…*

I don't like waiting. Drumming my fingers. And I don't want people waiting for *me.* If I say I will be there at 5:45 p.m., I will be there a few minutes early. Sure, there's a reasonable "fudge factor," but generally, I feel one should live up to time obligations.

I have a theory. People who do not need to catch a train or a bus or an airplane for work (or link life to the clock on some other time-sensitive obligation) have less incentive to be on time. Hence ... there may be a higher incidence of running late. Think about it. Test my theory.

April 28, 2019

Sticks and Stones

When we put bits into the mouths of horses to make them obey us, we can turn the whole animal. Although ships are so large and are driven by strong winds, they are steered by a small rudder.... Likewise, the tongue is a small part of the body, but it makes great boasts. Consider what a great forest is set on fire by a small spark. The tongue also is a fire, a world of evil among the parts of the body. It corrupts the whole body, sets the whole course of one's life on fire, and is itself set on fire by hell.... Animals have been tamed by mankind, but no human being can tame the tongue. It is a restless evil, full of deadly poison.
~ James 3:3–6

There are times—especially when discussing politics—that I would like to be honest. But I usually don't take the bait. Because some people will not listen to reason. Or logic. And furthermore, words—once said—cannot be retrieved.

My father always counseled, "Think before you speak." His words were as biblical as they were prophetic. I may not always succeed, but I do try and keep a hand on the tiller of my tongue. Usually, I succeed.

September 24, 2015

Did You Ever Use a Bad Word?

Did you ever use a racial, religious, ethnic, body-shaming, gender or other epithet when you were in third grade? Eighth? Twelfth? Did you ever call someone a *name*? Or use such a term in a joke? Or while talking with others? If you say *no*—I'm not sure I would believe you.

Either way, it leads to the vexing question of whether men and women should be judged by the worst thing they ever said (or did) when they were children. Or teenagers. Yet that seems to be the demand of some self-righteous souls who are quick to condemn others for things that happened in their adolescence.

As time goes on, and the maturation process continues, we *learn*. I am not the boy I was when I was 16. I was probably guilty of using bad words when I was 9 years old. Or 18. (You want to see what happened to me when I used a slur when I was 12 years old? Read "A Lifebuoy Lesson.") But the *child* of then is not the *me* of today.

Yet the current demand for adolescent accountability begs two serious questions: What if at the time (50 years ago), such commentary was viewed differently? Is it appropriate to judge people for words and deeds in the past by the moral compass of today? Then there is the question of whether there should be *forgiveness* for words or deeds done in one's adolescence—when one's current life does not reflect the "bad words" spoken in ages past.

We forgive criminals when they get out of prison. Christians seem to forgive St. Paul for once being Saul of Tarsus. Why not forgive those who use bad words in adolescence? How about forgiving those older folks who are contrite and repentant about stupid comments?

I have grown up. As just maybe you have too. While you and I said and did stupid things when we were 12 years old—or 18—we are not the same person today. This notion of maturation is even Biblical (1 Corinthians 13:11): *When I was a child, I talked like a child, I thought like a child, I reasoned like a child. When I became a man, I put the ways of childhood behind me.*

So tell me—should *your* sons or daughters be condemned *forever* and denied occupation—because of some ill-chosen words or acts of stupidity when they were in grade school, high school or college? How about an ill-tempered word in adulthood? If you believe they—and others—should be condemned, then *you*—who are without sin—pick up the first rock. And let 'em have it.

February 10, 2019

Mulligans

When I'm with my buds on the golf course and we tee off on the first hole, a *mulligan* is frequently offered for an errant tee shot. We call it a *breakfast ball*. It's a do-over. Even if we're playing for a few coins, it's, "Hit another—nobody saw that first one."

Wouldn't it be nice if in life we had do-overs? Mulligans? For errant words or deeds? We do in a way, though the granting of a do-over often lies in the province of the *recipient* of the errant words or deeds. It's called *forgiveness*. I'm sure we all have things we'd like to do over. Words. Deeds. And we're all grateful for the granting of forgiveness (or lack of ill consequence).

"I'm sorry."

"It's OK. No worries."

But today, the poison of political correctness can sink careers. Free speech is being crushed. Do-overs? For the wrong word? *Forget* it. Accusations are often enough to destroy a life.

I've *said* some dumb things and *done* some even dumber ones that I'd like to call back. But in the words of the great poet Omar Khayyam:

> *The Moving Finger writes; and having writ,*
> *Moves on. Nor all your Piety nor Wit*
> *Shall lure it back to cancel half a Line,*
> *Nor all your Tears wash out a Word of it.*

The "moving finger" business is probably a good reason to think twice before we act—or speak. And knowing of our own fallibility—and frailty—is a reason to consider granting mulligans to others.

June 7, 2018

Tort Reform

When you go to the hospital emergency room, the first person you see after checking in is a triage nurse or physician's assistant who will determine the nature and severity of your injury or illness. And then you will be treated accordingly.

In criminal law, there is a triage system to determine the merit of criminal cases. It's called a *grand jury* or a *preliminary hearing.* If a case does not have merit, a judge will throw it out (or a grand jury will vote down taking the matter further).

But for civil cases, there is regrettably no triage system for determining their merit. The result? Many of America's civil cases have little or no merit. Yet you hear plaintiff's lawyers squealing like stuck pigs whenever someone talks about limiting their right to bring lawsuits.

In his *Apology* (399 B.C.), Plato explains how any case that one wanted to bring needed a threshold approval—one-fifth of the 501 jurors of Athens. There was a triage system for new civil cases—2,500 years ago.

One of the biggest costs to America's health care system is *lawyers.* If not for *lawyers,* doctors would not perform needless procedures and order unnecessary testing. If not for *lawyers,* damage claims might be held within reason. It is because of *lawyers* that tort reform and damage caps need to be put squarely on the table (especially if our ailing health care "system" is to survive). Maybe losers should pay.

If there is pushback from the *lawyers,* it may be Dick the Butcher (Shakespeare's *Henry VI*) was onto something. "The first thing we do ..." You know the rest.

_____

December 19, 2013

Freshness Dates

How did my generation (and those before) ever survive without freshness dates? Those dates that counsel that food is "best by" or a store must "sell by" or you have to "use by" a certain date. *How did I live?* I will tell you how....

My father would take a sniff of a carton of milk that had been in the refrigerator since before I was born—and say, "It's OK. Drink it." And I would. I remember going to my grandmother's apartment once. She made me a peanut butter and jelly sandwich. I took a bite and started chewing. I looked at the sandwich and then at my grandmother. Mouth open. About to heave the whole thing onto the table. She picked up the peanut butter. Waved it under her nose. And made a face. "It's rancid," she said (I swear, those were her words). "OK—spit it out." And I did.

My cousin Wayne came over to our house one day. I was perhaps 7 or 8. He went into the fridge and pulled out the orange juice. Poured a glass. "*Yuck!*" he said. "This stuff is baaad." My father took a whiff and said, "It's just a little over the hill." *Over the hill*, as in enough botulism to wipe out the entire State of Pennsylvania. I'd been drinking it sporadically for the last few weeks. Or months.

I'm sure my experience is not unlike those of many of my generation. We've become a nation of wimps. Allowing the *freshness date* to dictate whether a food is good. Or not. What about letting the old sniffer make that determination? But for the fact that I have granddaughters (who will never know the meaning of the word *rancid* or *over the hill* except as it applies to me), I might be using the "sniff test" to determine what's good. And what is—*yuck*. Then again…

May 5, 2019

Idiot Casual

Donna and I have been traveling. Vacation. So we went to a couple of nice restaurants where *smart casual* (or *business casual*) is the norm. Our first dinner was on the top floor of a swanky hotel. I wore dark slacks, a button-down shirt and a sports coat. Donna was in her LBD (little black dress). Smart casual. Donna was—for sure. But I was so far out of style that I … Lemme explain.

The women—older and younger—in this wonderful restaurant all wore dresses. A few strapless. Low heels (a few high). Shawls. Smart. Elegant. But the men for the most part looked as if they were homeless. Jeans. T-shirts. Untucked shirts. One guy wore (are you ready?) a white V-neck *T-shirt*. And ripped jeans. I watched a few of these guys to see if they would snort corn niblets out their noses. One character wore his hat. *Backwards*. Though he finally did take it off.

Some people say that the human species is actually *devolving* rather than *evolving*. If you want evidence of that (at least as to the male of the species), I'll give you the names of a few fancy restaurants. And you can judge for yourself.

February 23, 2017

The Peril of Pockets

Every morning, I stuff the same things in the four pockets of my slacks and in the vest pocket of my shirt. Every evening, when I get home from work, I unload these things—putting them in the same spot—on the desk of my home office. Next morning, the stuff is there—pocket-ready.

Over the years of shoving a wallet in my back left pocket, the fabric on some of my pants has become worn. And faded. In fact, on a few of my pants, the faint outline of the words *Prince Gardner* can be seen. My back right pocket bears the faded outline of a scrambled set of keys.

Last week, I tossed some dirty clothes down the laundry chute to the basement. The chute is in a closet that also serves as a repository for clothes destined for donation to a local church. As I tossed the clothes down the chute, I noticed—there on top of some old T-shirts was my favorite pair of dark-blue Bonobo slacks with the white outline of a wallet on the back pocket.

I picked them up, shook them off and decided to put them on. I asked Donna why my Bonobos were in the donations closet. "I put them there," she said. "You can't wear those. Look at them." I looked. They appeared brand-new to me. The outline of a wallet and scrambled keys added character.

Later I went down to the kitchen and told Donna there were a couple of her outfits that appeared worn, so I'd placed them in the closet for donation to the church. I got the *look*. "That is *very* different," she said. The emphatic *very* signaled that I was on *very* thin ice.

I *think* I know now what happened to my black jeans, my ripped chinos, my "I'm the Boss" sweatshirt and my green bib overalls....

January 11, 2018

Facials for Men

I wouldn't *think* of having a facial. I'm a *man. Grrr... Snort-snort.* But I will confess—I had one a few years ago.

I'm still in the dark as to how or why this happened, but one Christmas, Lauren and Donna presented me with an envelope. Inside was a coupon for a *facial.* I remember looking up and saying something like, "I can't have a facial. I'm a man." *Grrr... Snort-snort.* But the two of them looked at each other and giggled. They must have thought it would be a stitch to see my reaction. Or maybe they thought my face was in serious need of help. Either way, I agreed. And had a *facial.*

So I went into this spa place, and I was sitting there. With a bunch of *women.* Yes—of course I was self-conscious. But I'm a *man....* *Grrr... Snort-sn...* Anyway. They called my name—"MR. PETERSEN"—loud enough for guys in the sporting goods shop next door to hear. I was led into a darkened room, and the female "therapist" smilingly had me place my head over a steam thingy. Then she put a towel over my head and told me to "be still." *Hoookayyy...* I was "still" for a while.

When she came back, she had me lie back and started squeezing heaven knows what out of my cheeks, nose and forehead. Then she wrapped my face in a towel that smelled of something unmanly. After an hour or so, there was a freezing *cold* towel, and I was done. I puffed out my chest and strutted out of the room, through the waiting room and out the door. And exhaled.

I'm sure I'll never have another facial, though I can say without a blink, "Yeah, I've had a facial. Wasn't bad...." *Grrr... Snort-snort.*

February 14, 2019

Names

Adam and Eve. The first names of the first people. These names are still—after millennia—clearly in vogue. (I can attest to the latter. It's the name of my first granddaughter.)

I saw an article that talked about the most popular *girls'* names of 2015. The top 10 were:

1. Emma
2. Olivia
3. Ava
4. Sophia
5. Mia

6. Isabella
7. Charlotte
8. Amelia
9. Harper
10. Abigail

How quickly time passes. I remember the "top 10" girls' names of my relatives: Laverne, Mildred, Edna, Lois, Myrna, Hilma, Lillian, Greta, Ruth and Bernice. All are fine names, to be sure. But today, I haven't seen many girls being named from this cadre of examples.

And *then* we move to the girls' names of generations *long* past: Hortense, Mona, Gertrude, Fannie, Faye, Mabel, Beulah, Maude, Beatrice, Myrtle, Ethel.… Good names as well, but I don't see Hortense or Fannie making a comeback anytime soon.

And funny thing—I don't see the name Bambi on *anyone's* list.

November 20, 2016

Burning Leaves

For millennia, folks have been burning garbage and "stuff" with relative impunity. The smoke was often choking. And sometimes toxic. Now there are limitations on such activity.

But … I remember, when I was a kid, my father—and other men in the neighborhood—raking *leaves* in the fall. And ushering them out to the street—at the curb—and lighting them up. Saturdays and Sundays in October were the optimal days for raking, gathering and burning leaves.

The distinct smell of burning leaves was overpowering. And—from my recollection—not so unpleasant. *Everyone* burned their leaves. I mean, what were families supposed to do with them? My dad would stand—smoking his pipe—and talking with the other men. As the leaves burned…

It would be nice if, for one day in the fall, everyone could spoon some dead leaves out to the street. And burn them. Like the *good old days*. (Did I really say that?) I don't need a *bad for the environment* speech. Or *think of what it does to your lungs*. Or *aren't there regulations?*

Just think about sharing an indelible olfactory moment of an autumn afternoon long ago.

September 11, 2016

We'll Be Over in an Hour

Maybe it's a Scandinavian thing. Or generational. But when I was a kid, I remember well my parents saying—usually on weekends—often on Sunday after Church—"Let's go see the Lynches." Or Roland and Elaine. Or, "Let's stop over at Lor and Bill's."

And we would get in the car, drive for half an hour and literally drop in on friends or relatives *unannounced*. Often around dinner time. The hosts would hurriedly throw some chicken breasts or burgers on the grill. My parents and their friends would talk. Smile. I would be bored out of my gourd. And we'd drive home.

On days when we didn't drive off to see someone, I'd be outside playing baseball, see a car pull into our driveway and mentally go *uh-oh*. And know that my Sunday afternoon was shot.

If it was my cousin Jack, I knew I'd be able to play cowboys and Indians, or sit in a parked car with Jack at the wheel making sounds like a motorboat. My cousin Larry could always be counted on to play with soldiers. But today—no one just *drops in* on anyone. Unless it is a dire emergency.

Today, plans are made weeks—months—in advance. "Wanna have dinner on Friday?" "Oh, mercy no. We can make it on a Tuesday in about eight weeks." Was that a simpler time 60-plus years ago? You betcha. Maybe I should reestablish the *drop-in* trend. Gotta start somewhere.

All right. Listen up. And *be prepared*. We may be stopping over on Sunday afternoon. I like my burgers medium-well. With sharp cheddar. Onion roll. Grey Poupon. Sweet potato fries. And cabernet...

October 30, 2014

12

ON FAITH

Our Neighbor's Faith

Back in 1977 my wife, Donna, and I joined a Lutheran Church in Northfield, Illinois. For the next year, the pastor asked if I would help coordinate and present the adult forum (up to that point a Bible study averaging a few people each Sunday). I reluctantly agreed—on the condition that *I* decide on the program. The pastor reluctantly agreed—on the condition that he know what kind of program I contemplated.

For the ensuing September–May, the adult forum series of our church was titled "Our Neighbor's Faith." Each week (or two) we would focus on a different religious faith (Donna spoke on being an Episcopalian). I had two Mormon couples, a Jewish rabbi, a Jesuit priest, two Jehovah's Witness couples, a Salvation Army officer and so on.

By the time the year ended, average weekly attendance was 30 to 40 people. Talk about interesting! We had an *abbondanza* of questions, comments and pointed observations. For some of the visitors, I had to draw the line between proselytizing and informing. I declined to take on programs for the following year, and the church got a professor from the Lutheran School of Theology to present instead. "Our Neighbor's Faith" was a tough show to top.☺

I continue to be interested (*fascinated* is a better word) in religion, since it continues to unite—and divide—so many of us.

March 14, 2013

Peace

Pax vobiscum. As-salamu alaikum. Shalom. Shanti. Aloha. Peace be with you....

It's interesting how most faith traditions include a blessing to others—extending *peace*. And asking for *peace* in return. In my church, there is a time when we *share* the peace. *Peace* be with you. And also with you.

The Prince of *Peace* has been around for more than 2,000 years (going back to the prophesy in Isaiah 9:6). Plato encouraged moderation and a sense of limits that bring *peace*. There is a Nobel *Peace* Prize. There's a *peace* symbol. The Paris *Peace* Conference of 1919 ended "the war to end all wars." There's a *Peace* Corps and the United Nations has "peacekeeping" missions.

With all the *peace* being promoted around the world, you would think that peace would be bubbling over. But no. Families suffer discord. As do school boards. City councils. Communities. Counties. States. Washington, D.C. Other countries. The world. Pain. Anger. Hatred. Violence. Just how serious are we about being *peaceful*? Seems as if everyone *wants* peace. But nobody wants to *give* it.

So ... what's the answer? Perhaps peace begins at home. Or in the workplace. We need peace in the political arena. That's for sure. I believe charity of heart can help. Along with an understanding that good people can have differing views on different subjects.

Peace is like a bridge. It's always under construction, and has been for several millennium. Will it ever be completed? That's the 64 dollar question. While we wait and wonder...

Peace be with you.

January 12, 2017

The Sikhs

The terrible shooting at the Sikh Temple of Wisconsin prompted me to revisit what I have learned about the Sikh religion. A brief overview.

First of all, contrary to common misperception, Sikhs are *not* Muslim. The Sikh religion began in the 15th century and today is found mainly in the Punjab area of India. The three tenets of the religion are equality of humankind, universal brotherhood of man and one supreme God. Sounds pretty good to me.... The religion is founded in belief in the teachings of 10 gurus or teachers.

Traditionally, all Sikh men have *Singh* as a surname, middle name or title, while Sikh women are given the surname *Kaur*. There is a belief in reincarnation and an emphasis on ethics, morality and values. Sikhs abstain from alcohol, drugs and tobacco, and they do not believe in "miracles."

There are five articles of faith, all beginning with the letter *k*: *kesh*, uncut hair wrapped in a turban; *kanga*, a wooden comb; *katchera*, cotton underwear (a reminder of purity); *kara*, an iron bracelet symbolizing eternity; and *kirpan*, a curved sword. It's the *kesh* and turban that sometimes get Sikhs confused with Muslims.

The Hindu greeting in Sanskrit is *namaste* ("The divine in me recognizes the divine in you"). In the Punjabi language—and among Sikhs—one says *sat sri akal* ("God is the ultimate truth"). Both phrases are offered with hands together. And both sound pretty ecumenical to me.

August 8, 2012

Adam(s)?

I just finished the book *The Lonely Man of Faith* by Rabbi Joseph Soloveitchik. This wonderful book examines two separate and quite divergent characterizations of Adam set forth in the Old Testament book of Genesis. The two Adams are different indeed.

In Genesis 1, Adam I (and Eve) are *created* in God's image. Adam is charged to take dominion over fish, fowl, cattle and all of the earth, to multiply, replenish the earth and subdue it.

In Genesis 2, Adam II is *formed* from dust, has life breathed into his nostrils—and is ordered to tend the garden. Eve was later formed from Adam's rib.

I was drawn to this book by David Brooks' thought-provoking 5-minute TED Talk on the personality differences between Adam I and Adam II. Brooks does not reference Genesis, but he does discuss Soloveitchik's work. Brooks offers that Adam I is motivated by his *resume* virtues. Adam

II is driven by *eulogy* virtues. And guess which virtues Brooks finds of superior importance.

Until I heard that talk, I was unaware of the sharp differences of Adam in Genesis. Rabbi Soloveitchik's book—apart from using words that require a dictionary close at hand—is a fascinating and inspirational read.

March 30, 2017

The Old Testament

I just finished reading the Old Testament (also called the *Tanakh*). Took me about 15 months (between other books). What a journey. Powerful. Occasionally inscrutable. Sometimes scary. But also encouraging. I did not come upon any Old Testament comedians, though the word *laugh* does appear 96 times in 93 verses....

There was a lot to relish in this literary endeavor. Here are a few favorite verses.

"Whatsoever thy hand findeth to do, do it with all thy might." (Ecclesiastes 9:10) I keep this on a 3-by-5 card.

"Then I heard the voice of the Lord saying, 'Whom shall I send? Who will go for us?' and I said, 'Here am I. Send me.'" (Isaiah 6:8) This one too.

Isaiah 9:5–6 provides the refrain from Handel's *Messiah*. And Isaiah 40:1–2 gives the opening lines of Handel's masterpiece.

Isaiah 40:4–5 contains famous lines used in Martin Luther King's "I Have a Dream" speech.

Then there is Psalm 17:8, which I quoted in my father-of-the-bride speech at my daughter's wedding: "She will always be the apple of my eye and in the shadow of my wings."

And of course there's Proverbs 17:28: "Even a fool when he holdeth his peace is counted wise. And he that shutteth his lips is deemed a man of understanding."

This passage tracks my father's not entirely Biblical counsel when I was young: "Better to keep your mouth shut and have people think you're a fool than to open your mouth and have them *know* you're a fool."

June 11, 2012

The New Testament

I just finished reading the *New* Testament. Again. Quite a trip. The Gospels are interesting and inspiring, as they have been forever. But there are some verses I just had to write down. Because sometimes one needs special inspiration.

1 Timothy 5:23 gives sage counsel: "Drink no longer water but a little wine for thy stomach's sake...." So who doesn't feel obliged to have a nice cab now and then?

1 Timothy 4:8 admonishes that "bodily training is of some value." So I (sigh) feel the push to go to the fitness center a few times a week.

Which leads to the whole reason for a personal trainer. I mean, it's right there in Hebrews 12:12: "Therefore lift your drooping hands and strengthen your weak knees."

But seriously, there is one chapter I discovered on a gray day in 1969. 1 Corinthians 3. For me, much of Christianity seems to distill in these 23 verses. ("If you think you are wise by this world's standards, you need to become a fool to be truly wise.") The words are old friends. I find peace. Calm. And faith.

November 11, 2013

The Quran

In preparation for our trip to the Middle East, I read the Quran. All 114 *suras* (chapters). The Quran is *intended* to be read in Arabic (26:195), but my copy was in English. *Whew.*

The Quran has an Old Testament attitude (some of it is pretty dark) with frequent repetition of theme. Yet there are numerous theological similarities with Judeo-Christian texts. The cast of characters, the prophets named and the stories told are similar. The commands (believe, do good works, give charity, pray) are comparable. There are parallels in God's (or Allah's) warning to his people about heaven and hell.

At the risk of oversimplification, I discerned three fundamental differences between Islam and Christianity, the Quran and the Bible.

First, the Quran does not say that Isa—Jesus—is the son of God (so no Father, Son and Holy Spirit). Instead, God simply said, "Be," and Isa was conceived (19:35).

Second, Mohammed is said to have written the Quran over 23 years, after receiving the word of God through the Archangel Gabriel.

Third, the Quran—and thus Muslims—consider Islam to be a "perfection" of Judaism and Christianity. They deem Islam the *true* religion.

Notwithstanding, Jews, Christians and another group, the Sabians, are considered *Ahl al-Kitab*—People of the Book—and thus related in the faith. Whether you call Him God, Jehovah or Allah; whether you worship on Friday, Saturday or Sunday; the three Abrahamic religions have similar roots and much in common.

June 21, 2015

Jesus in Islam

When the angel said: O Maryam, surely Allah gives you good news with a Word from Him whose name is the Messiah, Isa son of Maryam, worthy of regard in this world and the hereafter and of those who are made near to Allah.
~ Quran, Sura 3:45

His name is Isa Ibn Maryam. He was born of a virgin, Maryam. She gave birth to Isa by the miraculous will of God. Devout Muslims believe that Isa—Jesus—is a messenger of God who was sent to guide the children of Israel with the Holy Gospel. Most Muslims accept that Isa will return on the Day of Judgment to restore justice and to defeat the *al-Masih ad-Dajjal* (Antichrist).

Jesus—Isa—is revered in Islam as *al-Masih* (the Messiah) and is mentioned nearly a hundred times in the Quran. Mary—Maryam—is the only woman mentioned by name in the Quran and has her own sura, the 19th.

One of the concerns among Muslims is that a great many cannot read. So they get their information, including information about the Quran, from imams, *madrassahs* and politicians. Who often have a political agenda. And you know what happens then....

July 31, 2014

Islam, Judaism and Christianity

Islam, Judaism and Christianity all trace their lineage to a common ancestor—Abraham. And before that, Adam and Eve. Abraham had two sons: Isaac (by Sarah) and Ishmael (by Hagar). Isaac begat the line of David from which Jewish and Christian traditions derive. Ishmael was the forefather of Muhammad—the Messenger of Islam. God promises in Genesis 21:18 to make a "great nation" of Ishmael.

Common heritage, beliefs and commands. Yet many in each religious tradition view the differences as irreconcilable. Islam has 72 insular sects. Christianity has its own islands of belief, and Judaism has various divisions. Despite common origin, there is distrust, misunderstanding and even violence—*all in the name of religion*. And, according to a 2011 Report on Terrorism from the U.S. National Counterterrorism Center, between 82% and 97% of all violence by Islamic terrorist groups *is directed at Muslims*.

I mentioned earlier the Archangel Gabriel—the divine messenger. Gabriel comes into Judaism, Christianity, Islam, Mormonism and Bahaism. Each faith urges peace: Peace be with you. *Pax vobiscum. Shalom. As-salamu alaikum.* You tell me: Is a divine being—call it God, Allah or Jehovah—trying to give us mere mortals an ecumenical message?

March 18, 2018

Ahl al-Kitab

What does it mean, in the Muslim faith, to be *Ahl al-Kitab*—People of the Book?

Again, People of the Book refers to those who share Abrahamic roots and believe in one God. Now about the Book: Islam accepts the Old Testament (the *Tanakh*) as the word of God. Muslims consider the Quran to be the *completion* of these Scriptures.

The Quran offers tolerance toward the *Ahl al-Kitab*, called the "Family of Imran" in sura 3. In sura 5:69, the faithful are advised, "Verily! Those who believe and those who are Jews, Christians and Sabians, whoever believes in God and the Last Day and do righteous good deeds shall have their reward." Then there is sura 5:82: "You will find the nearest in friendship to be those who say 'we are Christians.' This is because there are priests and monks among them and they do not behave proudly."

Every religious tradition has its own interpretation of Biblical text. The Old and New Testaments *and* the Quran have been selectively interpreted over the centuries to justify various faith traditions and practices. And to trivialize (or demonize) others. It would be nice if we could recognize the shared heritage of our respective faiths as a way to foster cooperative and ecumenical headway into some of the world's most pressing, agonizing— and *dangerous*—problems.

March 24, 2018

Gabriel

In Protestant and Roman Catholic faith traditions, there are three archangels: Michael, Raphael and Gabriel. Of the three, Gabriel is the one who curiously keeps popping up—in Christianity and in other faiths as well. Gabriel is not just a divine messenger from God; he is an *uber* messenger.

In the Old Testament book of Daniel, Gabriel is the holy messenger who offers an explanation of Daniel's visions. In the New Testament, it is Gabriel who foretells the birth of John the Baptist and Jesus. It is Gabriel who visits Mary to deliver the good news of her new role.

In the Mormon faith, Gabriel ministered to Joseph Smith. In his earthly life, Gabriel is believed to have been Noah. Some say Gabriel continues to serve as a divine messenger and visited Earth as recently as 1954.

In Islam, Gabriel (Jibril) revealed the Quran to Muhammed. And Gabriel is referenced in the holy texts of the Baha'i faith, Bahá'u'lláh's mystical work *The Seven Valleys*.

With Gabriel's positive and influential involvement in so many religious traditions, one has to wonder why we have so much religious strife, so much focus on differences in faiths. Perhaps we aren't getting Gabriel's message....

January 30, 2012

Anti-Semitism

I recently read the book *Anti-Semitism: Here and Now* by Deborah Lipstadt. Read it. *Please.*

Most of us are aware of anti-Semites of the "alt-right." It is a small collection of jerks who wave their despicable flags. But there is a growing anti-Semitism on the left—especially in American colleges and universities. And that is troubling. It is pointless to ask those on the left why we do not boycott human rights abuses in China, Russia, Syria, Saudi Arabia, North Korea, Sudan, Zimbabwe.... It is *Israel* that is in the crosshairs. And because many Israelis are Jewish, it is their *faith* that takes the heat.

There are glowing embers of discrimination in Europe. It is dangerous for a man to wear a *kippah* (skullcap) in public. Synagogues are guarded by police. And Jews feel concerns for safety from the moment they arise in the morning. Anti-Semitism. Making a comeback. Or did it ever leave?

In a *Washington Post* review, Harvard professor Randy Rosenthal comments on and quotes Lipstadt's work: "And so if we think ourselves to be liberal, or progressive, or simply decent, 'we must insist that anti-Semitism be treated with the same seriousness as racism, sexism, homophobia, and Islamophobia.'"

I hope you say amen.

June 1, 2019

The Seder

Years ago, I was asked to teach Sunday school at our church. A September to May obligation. I said, "Sure" and was promptly given the sixth grade class. We had a textbook that I was to use religiously (no pun intended).

But I have to confess that from the beginning I often ad-libbed. *Uh-oh, he's going rogue....*

While I stayed with the basics of the curriculum, I took liberty to discuss relevant questions within the context of the day's chapter. And occasionally, I would bring in people and things to enhance the one-hour class. The most memorable improv was when I conducted a Seder at the time of Passover.

I enlisted the help of two Jewish friends for guidance. One gave me the blue *Haggadah* (the order of the Seder), which was in English and in Hebrew. (I still have it.) And both tutored me in this solemn ritual. They wanted to make sure I had the protocol down to a *tav* (or *t*).

Donna helped prepare the (almost) kosher meal. And I set the table in the sixth grade area. Plates, platters and potables (no wine). Then the students began to arrive. They looked around like—*Whoa!* Mr. Petersen is off the grid. They sat down—and I began with an explanation of Passover. And the Seder. And its significance. And a Passover prayer.

The hour went quickly. Elijah made his obligatory appearance. The food was consumed. And I did the cleanup. I guess I did OK, because the next year I was asked to continue teaching sixth grade Sunday school. I did so until finally one year I said *no mas*.

Some 20 years later, the Sunday school Seder was long forgotten. Until we saw some old friends from church. And their son Eric. He walked right up to me. "Hello, Mr. Petersen!" And he immediately began to bubble about the Seder being the most memorable time of his Sunday school career. Gosh. Kinda made me wish I hadn't said *no mas*.

May 4, 2017

The Talmud: Part I

I am a Christian. But since Jesus was Jewish, I thought it would be good to learn more about Christianity's Judaic heritage. I've read the Torah, the *Tanakh* and the rest of the Bible cover to cover (more than once), but I'd never dug into the Talmud. *Sooo...*

A few months ago, I drove past a store that offered a large selection of Judaica. It was the book section that enticed me to stop. I asked the gentleman at the counter for the best book (I confessed to being an Episcopalian) to learn about the Talmud. He nodded and handed me *The Essential Talmud* by Rabbi Adin Steinsaltz. All I can say is—*wow*. The book was captivating. And hard to put down.

While the *Tanakh* (Old Testament) is the cornerstone of Judaism, the Talmud is the pillar—the most important book in Jewish culture. The Talmud is an assemblage of commentary, questions and answers—about the Torah, the *Tanakh,* culture, social order and … *everything.*

The Talmud *invites* questions. None of which is considered inappropriate. Questions about the Torah are encouraged. Discussed. Debated. Resolved. And discussed again. One is not supposed to just *read* the Talmud but to *study* it. And to become a scholar of the Talmud. (This is quite unlike Islam, which mandates that questions about the Quran are *haram*—forbidden.)

Rabbi Steinsaltz's book includes chapters on the sabbath, marriage, divorce, civil and criminal law, dietary laws, ethics, prayer, scholarship, women and so on. And on. It is a truly enlightening read.

January 31, 2019

The Talmud: Part II

Unlike Rabbi Steinsaltz's compendium, the Talmud is more than just a single book. It is volume upon volume. More than 6,200 pages comprising at least 63 tractates, or treatises. It is not authored by one or two people. It has been penned by hundreds of hands and collective minds.

The Talmud is divided into two parts: the Mishnah (circa A.D. 200), the written version of Jewish oral law, and the Gemara (A.D. 500–present), rabbinic commentaries on it.

Originally, Jewish scholarship was passed down from generation to generation in oral narration. Then—with the destruction of the second temple in A.D. 70—there was a move to memorialize this oral tradition. And so it began. The Talmud is written in Hebrew script, but the language is Aramaic—the language of Jesus. Arguably, the Talmud is no longer open for further edits. However, it continues to be open to discussion, commentary and footnote. Thus, in a way, the Talmud will never be completed.

What are the topics discussed? For example, when the Third Commandment says, "Remember the Sabbath Day, to make it holy," just what does "remember" mean? That admonition (along with so many others in the Old Testament) has prompted extensive discussion and debate about the meaning of certain words, statements and commands.

I may never become a Talmudic scholar, but I am glad I took the time to read Rabbi Steinsaltz's book. And further investigate this important chapter of our Judeo-Christian heritage.

February 3, 2019

Betting on Belief

Parents are normally wiser than their children in making decisions. A child may want to eat only chocolate cupcakes for each meal. Yet the parent knows better. What's to say that we as adults don't have a grander force that "knows better"?

In 1660, French philosopher Blaise Pascal offered "Pascal's Wager" on belief. Briefly:

If you believe in God, and there is no God—no problem.
If you don't believe in God, and there is no God—no problem.
If you believe in God, and God exists—peace now and eternal.
If you don't believe in God, and God exists—big problem.

Isaac Newton summed it up thus: "In the absence of any other proof, the thumb alone would convince me of God's existence." For me, I just open my eyes in the morning. And I think ... *wow.*

13

HISTORICAL PERSPECTIVES

Here's a Toast To ...

When Benjamin Franklin was the emissary to France, the British Ambassador led off with a toast to his king. "To George the Third, who, like the sun in its meridian, spreads luster throughout and enlightens the world."

Not to be outdone, the French minister declared, "To the illustrious Louis XVI, who, like the moon, sheds his benevolent rays on and influences the globe."

Finally, Franklin rose and lifted his glass and offered, "To George Washington, commander of the American armies, who, like Joshua of old, commanded the sun and moon to stand still, and both obeyed."

Here's looking at you, kid. Cheers!

July 29, 2011

The Rosetta Stone

From before the fall of the Roman Empire (A.D. 408) until 1799, no one was able to decipher ancient Egyptian hieroglyphs. On July 15, 1799, all of that changed.

Soldiers in Napoleon's army, while rebuilding a fort near the Egyptian port city of *el-Rashid*, stumbled across a stone marker made of black granite. What made this marker unique was that it had writing on it—in two languages but in three scripts: ancient Greek, Egyptian Demotic script and ancient Egyptian hieroglyphics.

Viewed as a curiosity by the French, the stone was acquired by the British in 1801. (That would be shortly after the British defeated the French in Egypt.) The next year the Rosetta stone was ensconced at the British Museum. Over the next 25 years, the Rosetta stone was translated—and the secrets of (and "key" to) Egyptian hieroglyphs were revealed.

The Rosetta stone was carved around 196 B.C., during the reign of Ptolemy V. It takes its name from the town where it was found—Rosetta (*Rashid*). To this day it stands as one of the most amazing "finds" in world history. Whenever someone uses the term, it most likely refer to a "key" ("The spectrum of hydrogen atoms has proven to be the Rosetta stone of modern physics....").

Someone ought to write a book about it. Or at least a blog post.

_____

June 13, 2019

Cremona

Cremona is a city of 75,000 in the Lombardy region of northern Italy. The city is known for many things, but it is famous for one—*violins*. Beginning in the 16th century, Cremona was home to three legendary luthier families: Amati, Stradivari and Guarneri. While many associate the names Guarneri and Amati with fine violins, everyone knows the name *Stradivarius*.

When I was young, I read a lot about treasure—the Lost Dutchman gold mine, the Oak Island mystery, the San Saba River treasure, Padre Island doubloons and so on. I avidly read books like J. Frank Dobie's *Coronado's Children*. And I always longed to go hunting for these treasures, or rarities like a Gutenberg Bible or a Stradivarius violin. I've come close to a Gutenberg, but the Stradivarius has escaped me.

During his lifetime, Antonio Stradivari (1644–1737) made about 1,100 instruments. A few hundred survive, and those that do are rare and valuable. Why? Because the sound is near perfection. Antonio created his works of musical art with spruce tops, willow blocks and maple for the backs, ribs and neck. The technique has been duplicated but the sound never replicated. There's a theory that the coatings on the wood made the difference. So far, the exact recipe remains a mystery.

I still think of taking a sabbatical someday—and heading off in search of a Gutenberg Bible or a Stradivarius violin. Or maybe the Lost Dutchman Mine.

April 9, 2012

There Is This Girl....

There is this girl. Her name is Lisa. She is captivating, and I've admired her for a *long* time. My wife, Donna, is vaguely aware of my interest in Lisa, but she's let it go. I have gone on websites to read about Lisa. And there was one occasion, some years ago, when our paths actually crossed. It was in Paris. There she was. And I stood. Watching her. For quite a while. From about 30 feet away. Lisa's last name is Gherardini.

I guess I'm not the only guy in the world who has had a special interest in Lisa. You see, Lisa Gherardini is—the *Mona Lisa*.

Lisa, the young wife of Francesco del Gioconda, was painted by Leonardo da Vinci (1452–1519) between 1503 and 1506. However, Leonardo—who claimed he never completed a single work—continued to refine Lisa after he moved to France. He may have applied the final touches of paint in 1516 or 1517.

After Leonardo's death, the painting was purchased by Francis I of France. Louis XIV moved Lisa to the Palace of Versailles—and after the Revolution, Lisa was placed in the Louvre. In 1911, Lisa was stolen by a Louvre employee, Vincenzo Peruggia, who felt that Lisa should be returned to Italy. Peruggia's theft was discovered two years later when he tried to sell Lisa to the Uffizi Gallery in Florence. There have been several attempts to deface Lisa, but she continues smiling seductively—now behind layers of bulletproof glass.

The aesthetics of Leonardo's painting are nuanced. Lisa is sitting upright with hands folded in a reserved attitude. There is an imaginary landscape behind her, an early example of an *aerial perspective*.

Lisa is considered the most famous painting in the world. And the most valuable (with an estimated worth of at least $850 million in 2019). I can't wait to cross paths with her again.

July 10, 2016

Shakespeare

William Shakespeare was born on April 23, 1564, and died on April 23, 1616. In his 52 years, he is alleged to have written some of the world's greatest plays, tragedies, dramas, comedies and poetry. As for me, I don't buy it.

The Shakespeare Oxford Society is a 501(c)(3) dedicated to getting to the bottom of who *actually* wrote the works of Shakespeare. The society leans toward Edward de Vere, the 17th Earl of Oxford. DeVere was born on April 12, 1550, and died on June 24, 1604. It was de Vere who likely wrote the works of "William Shakespeare," despite the fact that several plays were arguably (but disputably) written after de Vere's death.

The personal details of historical William Shakespeare do not ring true for one endowed with the *amazing* literary gift ascribed to the Bard. There was actually doubt about his authorship dating back to when the plays were first written(!). De Vere was in the mix of speculation from the beginning.

As a collector of historic manuscript material, there is another—significant—factor in this disputed attribution. For a man who allegedly wrote thousands of pages of glorious literature, there is not one sentence of handwritten text penned by "Shakespeare" (or de Vere for that matter). In fact, there are only six known examples of Shakespeare's signatures—and those are on legal documents.

I'm sure I would enjoy a hunt for the handwritten copies used for setting the type of Shakespeare's works. I'm sure there are manuscripts out there. Somewhere. Waiting. Perhaps waiting for me....

Maybe I need a sabbatical.

August 30, 2012

Decline and Fall

Between 1776 and 1788, English historian (and Member of Parliament) Edward Gibbon published his classic six-volume work *The History of the Decline and Fall of the Roman Empire.* It is interesting to examine the causes of the decline—and fall—of the grand empire, which expired in about A.D. 476—not with a bang but with a whimper. The reasons?

Ongoing wars and heavy military spending

Failing economy and high inflation—and high unemployment among the working classes

Declining morals, ethics and values

Rising demand for blood and violence in entertainment (think gladiator "games")

Growing antagonism between the emperor and the senate

Heightening political corruption

Increasing hero worship of athletes and actors

Diluting of the Roman language

Look at America. Frankly, look at the world. Each of these qualities is present. In abundance. George Santayana in *The Life of Reason* commented, "Those who cannot remember the past are doomed to repeat it." Is anyone surprised? Is it too late?

March 29, 2018

The Vikings

From about 790 until the Norman Conquest in 1066, the Vikings sailed the world. They were warriors, raiders, traders, merchants and discoverers. They discovered America *long* before that Columbus fellow, and they sailed their longships wherever the wind would carry them.

The Vikings came from the Scandinavian countries—Denmark, Sweden and Norway. French Normans were descended from Danish and Norwegian Vikings who were made feudal overlords in northern France. The Vikings who raided—and *remained behind* in Ireland (often because they had met young women) were given the name "Doyle," from the Celtic Ó Dubhghaill, which means "son of the dark [or evil] foreigner." (Next time you're watching *The French Connection*, just think ... "Popeye" Doyle was descended from Danish Vikings.)

As Christianity spread through Scandinavia, the Viking raids diminished. By the end of the 11th century, the great Viking age came to an end.

My father's great-grandparents were from Lyngby, Denmark, just north of Copenhagen. They were caretakers of the local cemetery. As they dug graves, they uncovered various artifacts from the Viking age. I have at home two beautiful stone ax heads they found—displayed on a shelf. Great paperweights but still sharp ... and ready to use.

December 16, 2011

The Year With No Summer

There was really an entire year *without a season of summer*. No, I'm not talking about the year 2019 in Chicago (although it seemed that way). I'm talking about *1816*.

It is well-documented that the year 1816 had no summer. Severe climate abnormalities caused temperatures to drop for the entire summer season across the Northern Hemisphere. The ones who suffered most were those in New England, Canada's Atlantic seaboard and parts of Western Europe.

This climatic anomaly was characterized by a persistent "dry fog" that dimmed the sunlight such that sunspots were visible to the naked eye. Neither wind nor rainfall dispersed the "fog." Lake and river ice continued unabated in the northern climes of America—*in August.*

Evidence suggests that this anomaly of nature was prompted by the massive eruption of Mount Tambora in the Dutch East Indies (Indonesia). The weather had a dramatic negative effect on crops—and thus the supply of food. The *Columbian Register* (New Haven, Connecticut) reported:

It is now the middle of July and we have not yet had what could properly be called summer. Easterly winds have prevailed ... the sun has been obscured ... the sky overcast with clouds, the air ... damp and uncomfortable, and frequently so chilling as to render the fireside a desirable retreat.

I'd like 1816 to remain *alone* in the history books. But hearken! I'm writing this in June, and the seven-day outlook has *snow* in the forecast.

June 27, 2019

Fort Reno

In August 1865, the terrible pain of the Civil War was still white hot. Thousands of Confederate soldiers remained in Union prison camps. Cities in the South still smoldered, and the dead of both sides—perhaps 620,000 of them (2% of America's population)—were still being buried. Eight hundred miles west, Red Cloud, an Oglala Lakota chief, began "causing trouble" along the Bozeman Trail by objecting—with violence—to the incursion of troops.

So in August 1865, along the Powder River in Wyoming, Fort Connor was built. (Later that year, it was renamed Fort Reno.) To staff the fort, the United States offered some Confederate prisoners the option of swearing allegiance to the United States and then going off to fight American Indians in Wyoming. Many signed on.

This contingent of newly minted soldiers was called *galvanized Yankees*. They went out to Wyoming, took care of business and came home—to help rebuild the South. Fort Reno was abandoned in 1868 and became a part of the meandering Powder River.

In 1969, while I was hoofing around Wyoming, I was in Lysite (population perhaps 20) along the Powder River. There I met with a Mr. Skiles, a rancher. He took me to the site of Fort Reno and pointed the way through perhaps a mile of high grass. I waded through the brush and finally arrived at a place where nothing but a few brick foundations remained. I pulled out my trusty metal detector and went to work.

After a few hours, I had found some heavily rusted artifacts: nails, a few horse bridle parts and two really neat pieces—the top of a cooking pot and … a perfect ax head formed by one piece of folded steel. The ax head had been perhaps a foot beneath the surface, in a position where it *leaned* against the brick foundation.

I've got these pieces at home. One on my desk. Pretty special to think about those pieces being used by some chaps 150 years ago. No one much remembers galvanized Yankees or Fort Reno. But I sure do.

April 23, 2015

Isandlwana

January 22, 1879, was the first major encounter in the Anglo-Zulu War between the British and the Zulu kingdom in South Africa. The battle took place in a remote area of the Natal province called Isandlwana.

Isandlwana is remembered as the worst single defeat in British military history by an indigenous force. Surrounded and attacked by nearly 20,000 Zulu warriors, nearly all of the 1,800 British defenders were massacred. Armed mainly with *assegais* (slender, stabbing spears), the Zulus completely overwhelmed the British.

The reasons for the defeat? The British, led by the inept Lord Chelmsford, arrived at Isandlwana with about 10,000 troops. But they refused to *laager* (circle the wagons) or entrench (as was normally required). Why? Chelmsford severely underestimated Zulu capabilities.

Shortly after arrival at Isandlwana, Chelmsford marched off with nearly all of his troops "looking for Zulus." Meanwhile, the entire Zulu nation was just over a hill. Waiting. Watching. A similarly inept Col. Anthony Durnford took charge of the remaining soldiers. Durnford—with a bare 1,800 men—set a sparsely defended perimeter *nearly a mile* out from the camp. And when the 20,000 Zulus attacked, they quickly knifed through the perimeter and set upon the camp.

Durnford never gave the order to "strike the tents" (in other words, pull down the center pole of the hundreds of tents to open a clear view of the terrain). Thus the battle raged around canvas tents. And there is rumor that an idiot quartermaster refused to pass out ammunition ("I have no orders to give out ammunition") even though the Zulus were pouring through the lines and the encampment.

It is clear that the British underestimated the Zulu capabilities. And this gave rise to the major military disaster where only a hundred or so

British soldiers (barely) escaped with their lives. The few who escaped raced in all directions. Many raced in the direction of Rorke's Drift.

January 21, 2018

Rorke's Drift

Following the dreadful defeat of British troops at Isandlwana, a small British outpost/hospital called Rorke's Drift—a bare dozen miles from the site of the massacre—quickly mobilized. They hastily built walls and fortifications with mealie bags between a series of buildings and a cattle kraal. The 150 defenders settled down to wait. They didn't wait long.

By late afternoon, about 4,000 Zulus arrived, fresh from *the washing of the spears*—the rite of cutting open their dead enemies so their spirits could escape (hence the title of a magnificent book by Donald R. Morris on the history of the Zulu campaign). The Zulus descended on the small outpost. And attacked.

As at the Battle of Isandlwana, the Zulus configured their attack like the head of a water buffalo—the horns surrounding the enemy and the head and chest crushing forward. The battle raged through the night and into the morning. The defenders fell back into smaller and smaller redoubts. The 150 defenders poured a withering fire at the Zulus, who surged a bare foot or two beneath the mealie bag walls.

Come morning, the small garrison still held—suffering a few score casualties. Zulu casualties ran into the hundreds. And the Zulus fell back as British reinforcements were detected in the distance. The defenders— the 24th Foot Regiment—won more Victoria Crosses (11) than any other regiment in British military history. And 85 years later, a Hollywood offering captured with historic accuracy this pivotal battle of Rorke's Drift.

That movie was *Zulu*.

January 25, 2018

Zulu

In 1964 I was in my first year of college. Two afternoons a week, I worked as a lifeguard at a local YMCA (thanks to my lifesaving merit badge). One day after work, I noticed that a new movie was playing at the theater across the street. I had time. I had interest. So I went in. Alone. To watch *Zulu. Wow!*

The movie *Zulu* debuted in 1964, and it was Michael Caine's first starring role. He played Lt. Gonville Bromhead—one of two commanding officers (with Stanley Baker as Lt. John Chard) of the small garrison that defended Rorke's Drift. None other than Mangosuthu Buthelezi, the former prime minister of Zululand and noted South African politician, played his ancestor King Cetshwayo kaMpande—the leader of the Zulu nation in 1879.

Names and characters are based on actual participants in the battle. While the movie is historically accurate, there are some *Hollywoodizations*—limited pretty much to personalities, not events. Nonetheless, *Zulu* is one of the most captivating action movies I have ever seen.

In 2008, while in South Africa, I couldn't resist. I chartered a four-seater, flew to Isandlwana and walked the battlefield. The place was barren, remote and silent—except for lonely white cairns scattered over the landscape. The stones served as markers for the 1,500 who lay buried beneath them.

Then I went to Rorke's Drift. The interesting thing? There was hardly a soul at either place. A Zulu guide spoke eloquently of the British defense at Rorke's Drift. But he spoke more eloquently of the Zulu courage—and military savvy—that nearly drove the British from South Africa.

January 28, 2018

Lawrence of Arabia

Having visited Wadi Rum in Jordan (and enduring a sandstorm), Donna and I put *Lawrence of Arabia* at the top of our Netflix list. And we watched. All 3 hours and 36 minutes. *Wow!* Hard to believe the movie was filmed in 1962. The cast was a who's who of Hollywood—Anthony Quayle, Alec

Guinness, Claude Rains, Jose Ferrer, Jack Hawkins—and introduced Omar Sharif and Peter O'Toole. The story is historically accurate, though it doesn't tell all of it.

Thomas Edward Lawrence (1888–1935) was a British archeologist, army officer and diplomat. He is best known for his liaison role during the Sinai and Palestine campaign in World War I and the Arab Revolt against the Ottoman Turks (1916–1918). He was born out of wedlock to Sir Thomas Chapman and Sarah Junner, a governess. Chapman left his first wife and family to live with Sarah under the name *Mr. and Mrs. Lawrence.* And had five sons.

The movie begins with Lawrence's motorcycle accident—trying to avoid two bicyclists (which is what happened). The scene jumps back to Lawrence as a soldier working in the army's Cairo office during World War I.

What you *don't* learn is that Lawrence was an archeologist who, in 1909, spent three months in Syria mapping crusader castles. From 1910 to 1914, he spent a great deal of time on digs in the Middle East—learning Arabic. His language skills made him a natural to send to Cairo (in the intelligence unit) when the war began. Because of his fluency and keen knowledge of the area, he was tasked to liaise with the Arabs. And he did, in the manner that legends—and movies—are made.

After the war, he returned to London, where he basked in but then shunned the publicity. In 1922 he tried to enlist in the Royal Air Force under the name John Hume Ross, but his true identity was discovered. He then changed his name to T.E. Shaw. He ended his formal military career in 1928 after a three-year posting at a remote base in India. He did, however, continue an enlistment with the RAF until 1935.

Lawrence wrote two books on his experiences: *Seven Pillars of Wisdom* (1926) and *Revolt in the Desert* (1927). Both are on my to-read list. If you want some armchair adventure, get the movie. It's *fascinating.* And the music is stirring. Director David Lean blacks out the screen for the beginning, middle and end while the music plays. There's nothing wrong with your television....

July 2, 2015

Lady Be Good

I'm not talking about the 1924 Broadway show that featured music and lyrics by George and Ira Gershwin. I'm talking about a B-24D Liberator that vanished after a bombing run over Naples during World War II. That fateful day was April 4, 1943.

When I was a kid, my parents subscribed to *Life* magazine—the news journal that was published weekly from 1883 to 1972. I couldn't *wait* to get my hands on *Life* when it walked in the door. Simple kid that I was, I loved the pictures. And the armchair adventure. And I remember with clarity a day in 1960 when I learned that a mysterious B-24 Liberator that had been spotted a year before deep in the Sahara had been identified as the *Lady Be Good*.

On the day it disappeared, the *Lady Be Good* was staffed by a crew of nine newbies—just one week off the boat. Their first mission was a big one. A night bombing run over Naples harbor.

The *Lady Be Good* took off with 25 other bombers from Soluch Field in Libya. Near Benghazi. Most of the bombers returned to base within a few hours—because of high winds. But the noble *Lady* pressed on. And ended up dumping her bombs in the Mediterranean. Then the *Lady* with its nine souls began the return trip—alone.

In the black of night, the plane overflew the base and continued on. Deep into the Libyan Desert. The pilot apparently believed the desert below was the ocean. So they continued. Until they ran out of fuel. And the crew bailed out....

In February 1960, the U.S. Army visited the plane and conducted a formal search for the remains of the crew. Eight of the nine were found. And in August 1994, the remnants of the plane were removed from the site. Only one member of the crew—Staff Sgt. Vernon L. Moore of New Boston, Ohio—was never found. His body still rests where it fell.

September 15, 2016

The Rock Island Line

In 1845, the Chicago and Rock Island Railroad began with a charter penned in the city of Rock Island, Illinois. For 130 years, the Rock Island Line hummed and drummed across the landscape of America. Until 1975, when a federal judge in Chicago ordered the famed railroad into bankruptcy.

On December 10, 1977, a one-day auction was held in the old LaSalle Street Station in Chicago. Tables, chairs, paintings, rolling stock and office supplies were sold off from the old railroad. There were also several hundred "tote" boxes full of archives of the railroad. All were filthy, and all were sealed. Any bid was on the contents. Sight unseen. The local news touted that perhaps the boxes contained a letter of Abraham Lincoln or Stephen Douglas, both of whom worked for the railroad.

I was drawn like a moth to flame—and I bought 45 boxes of "stuff" at $3.50 a box. I crammed the boxes into the trunk and interior of our Plymouth Valiant. And drove home. Donna thought I was nuts. Until I opened the boxes.

There were *hundreds* of letters of U.S. congressmen, senators, vice presidents and members of the Supreme Court. There were Chicago mayors, and aldermen like "Bathhouse John" Coughlin and "Hinky Dink" Kenna. Original letters of Clarence Darrow. It was a trove of major value. And I ended up selling most of the material to the University of Iowa. For *many* times what I paid for it. Then I went on a three-year quest to acquire the *rest* of the defunct railroad's archives.

After scores (hundreds?) of phone calls over three years, the squeaky wheel got the oil. A gusher. I was told the rest of the Rock Island Railroad archives were housed in a 10-story, 100,000-square-foot building at Polk and LaSalle streets. No one had been in the building for several years. "I'll buy it," I said. And did. I bought the entire contents of the building for $500. They handed me the keys, and it was mine. The only hitch—I had to get it out in four weeks.

Within a few hours, I had the contents sold—to the universities of Iowa and Oklahoma. Iowa had first choice, and Oklahoma got the remainder. I walked alone through the 10 floors. File cabinets. Boxes of files. Empty desks. Coffee cups ringed with dried coffee. A mausoleum. Over the next few weeks, I orchestrated eight 48-foot over-the-road tractor trailers. Loading up the goodies. I looked back, walked out and locked the door.

I still have a few things from the RI. A ceremonial spike. A slice of track. Oh and yes—a few old letters. In 1998, I delivered a paper to the Chicago Literary Club. Telling the whole story. It's online at http://chilit.org.

The Rock Island Line was a mighty good road, as the song goes. And it was sure good to me.

May 15, 2014

Sidewalks

Sidewalks. We walk on them. They serve their purpose—providing a durable and predictable path from point A to point B.

When I walk to and from the train station, I keep an eye on *where* I'm walking—looking for cracks or holes in the sidewalk. Or those slightly elevated slabs. That habit has helped me avoid trips and twisted ankles (*and* find money, jewelry, wallets and such). While I walk, I also take note of the stamped impressions identifying the contractor—and the year the sidewalk was laid down.

One stony sidewalk near my home bears the weathered yet clear date: 1912. *Wow!* More than a century. As I walk from the train station to my office in downtown Chicago, I pass two such markings that go back decades. One is 1935—six years before the United States entered World War II. Another is 1947—the year I was born.

I think of my trips downtown with my parents. Years ago. I'm sure I walked here. Then. My parents and grandparents and even great-grandparents probably walked on these same sidewalks. And here I am today—sharing the same space. Walking with purpose. On the sidewalk.

September 24, 2012

Edward Everett Hale

Edward Everett Hale (1822–1909) was a prominent Boston theologian and author. He penned the classic narrative *The Man Without a Country* (1863), the story of an American Army lieutenant who renounces his country during a trial for treason. The lieutenant is sentenced to life at sea—never again to hear news about or the word *America*. The story was designed as an allegory about the pains of the Civil War.

From 1901 to 1909, Hale was the chaplain of the United States Senate. While the Rev. Hale was serving as chaplain, he was asked if he prayed for the senators. "No," he said. "I look at the senators and I pray for the country." Given the current chaos, perhaps we might all profit by extending similar petitions.

As a collector and dealer of historic autograph material, I long focused on Edward Everett Hale. Over the years, I acquired nearly 400 of Hale's original letters and signed first editions. How I started collecting Hale's original letters is a story in itself. Among the letters were perhaps a dozen small cards—each carefully handwritten—with Hale's favorite advice:

To look up and not down,
To look forward and not back,
To look out and not in,—and
To lend a hand.

I couldn't agree more.

June 3, 2018

175

14

READ, WATCH AND LISTEN

Dearie

I just finished Bob Spitz's delightful biography of Julia Child—*Dearie*. You may scratch your head when I say it was hard to put down. It was. What a read! And what an *amazing* story of success.

Julia Carolyn McWilliams was born in 1912 in Pasadena, California. She attended Smith College and worked for several years as a copywriter in New York. When World War II came along, 6-foot-2-inch Julia was too tall for the WACs or WAVEs, so she joined the OSS (Office of Strategic Services, a predecessor of the CIA).

She was posted to Asia, where in 1944 she met Paul Child, a low-level career diplomat. They were married in 1946, and Julia followed Paul as he was transferred to Paris. Bored, she took up cooking and attended *Le Cordon Bleu*, the legendary culinary institute. At the age of 39, she began teaching cooking to American women—in her small Paris flat. And with two colleagues, she began writing a cookbook directed to American housewives. After nearly 10 years of writing, her book *Mastering the Art of French Cooking* was published by Knopf. Julia's star began to soar.

In 1962, she appeared on Boston's WGBH television, on a book review program. Instead of sitting and talking, Julia arrived with food and paraphernalia (including a one-burner tabletop stove). Much to the consternation of the directors, she *insisted* on cooking an omelet. *On camera!* The producers feared no one would ever watch the show again. Of course, Julia's appearance had the opposite effect. Her success spawned her own show—*The French Chef*—and Julia Child became a household name.

In 2004, she passed away at the age of 92. Her kitchen was moved to the Smithsonian, where it is on permanent display. *Bon appétit!*

October 1, 2012

At Home

In her classic work *You Just Don't Understand*, Deborah Tannen speaks of how men talk to *report* and women talk for *rapport*. Well, speaking of books, I just finished one that—guys—you will *love*. It's *At Home* by Bill Bryson. It contains so many facts and factoids that I want to read it again. Just to absorb more stuff to *report* on.

It may sound boring, but *At Home* takes you through the house, room by room, and explains just about everything. Why did the kitchen develop? Why is it called a *living room*? What is the importance of ice? How did bathing come into fashion? (Quick answer: It didn't for a *looonnng* long time.) Why are there bedrooms? Bathrooms? Why glass windows?

Bryson devotes infinite—fascinating—detail to these and hundreds of other blips and tidbits of information. From architecture and electricity to hygiene, food preservation, and the daily life of eating, sleeping and trying to get more comfortable.

Guys, you can carry this book to cocktail parties and, when other guys start spouting facts, you can pull this baby out and *wow* 'em.

May 11, 2014

The Road to Abilene

It's a hot, dry, sun-drenched afternoon in Coleman, Texas. A family is playing dominoes on a steamy porch. The father-in-law looks up and suggests that they get in the car and take a drive to Abilene, 53 miles away. One by one, the family members nod acquiescence.

They pile into the car. The drive is hot. Dusty. And long. The family arrives in Abilene. They go to a diner where the food is as bad as the drive.

They get back in the car and take the same hot, dusty, long drive back to Coleman. They arrive home *exhausted*.

One by one, the family members admit they never really *wanted* to go to Abilene. They *agreed* to go because they thought the *others* wanted to go. Thus, everyone decided to do something *no one* wanted to do.

This scenario was first introduced by Jerry B. Harvey in a 1974 article "The Abilene Paradox: The Management of Agreement." Harvey suggests that individuals are normally averse to acting contrary to the inclinations of a group. Social conformity and social influence—*peer pressure*—drive agreement. The reservations one might have with a decision or direction is subsumed by the feeling that these concerns must be *out of step* with those of the group. And so reluctant silence. Grudging acquiescence. And, frequently, poor decisions.

We see this in families. Businesses. Organizations. And politics.

March 23, 2016

Haiku

A *haiku* is a short form of Japanese poetry characterized by three qualities:

1. There are three stanzas of five, seven and five syllables.
2. There are two well-defined images (with a *kireji* or "cutting word" between them).
3. The subject is usually drawn from the natural world (often seasonal).

The most famous composer of *haiku* poetry was Matsuo Basho (1644–1694). He was the grand poet of the Edo period, and his poetry has achieved international renown. His works frequently appear on Japanese monuments and at traditional Japanese sites. Probably the best-known example of *haiku* is Basho's "The Old Pond":

Fu-ru-i-ke ya
Ka-wa zu to-bi-ko-mu
Mi-zu no o-to

The translation?

Old pond
A frog leaps in
Splash

A *haiku* can be a poignant teaching tool for students, since it requires structure, thought, concentration and result. And so I offer:

"The Winter Squirrel," by Renaissance Hombre
A squirrel sits still
His tail begins to move
And away he goes

Move over, Mr. Basho.

February 7, 2012

Charlie Russell

If anyone has received a greeting card or letter from me, it may have included a hand-drawn cartoon. You can thank Charlie Russell for the artistic addition.

Charles Marion Russell (1864–1926) was an American artist who painted iconic scenes of the Old West. Charlie was born in St. Louis. At age 16, he moved to Montana, where he got a job working on a sheep ranch. Charlie chronicled the bitter winter of 1886–1887 in a series of watercolor paintings.

He was working on the O-H Ranch in the Judith Basin of Montana when the foreman received a letter from the ranch owner, asking how his cattle had fared during the winter. Instead of writing back, the foreman sent the owner a postcard-sized watercolor painted by Charlie. The image was that of a gaunt steer surrounded by wolves, on a gray winter day. The owner showed the drawing to friends and displayed it in a shop window in Helena. And Charlie began to get work—as an *artist*.

In 1897, Charlie and his new bride moved to Great Falls, Montana, where he remained for the duration. Charlie was a *prolific* painter, with more than 4,000 works (oil, watercolor, drawings and occasional sculptures) to his credit. Today, the works of Charlie Russell go for big bucks. *The Hold Up* sold for $5.2 million in 2008.

Four decades ago, while visiting Charlie's studio in Great Falls, I learned that he had adorned many of his letters with drawings. And I got a bright idea.…

November 16, 2017

Busy Beavers

I'm an easy sell for books recommended by friends. My Boy Scout pal Bob mentioned that he enjoyed reading *Lily Pond* by Hope Ryden. The book, published in 1997, chronicles Ryden's *four-year* stint observing a family of beavers in Harriman State Park in New York. The book sounded a bit mundane, but given my friend's recommendation, I found a used copy on Amazon. When I read the preface by Jane Goodall, I thought, this could be good. And it was.

We are introduced to the species *Castor canadensis* by meeting a family of beavers (each had a name). After some preliminary introductions, Ryden offers a brief history of the aggressive beaver pelt trade two centuries ago. Beaver pelts made beaver hats and other adornments—and thus beaver trapping (with steel-jawed leg traps) was uncontrolled.

Beavers were near extinction by the early 1800s. As of 1800, the beaver population of the Adirondacks had been reduced by more than 99%. And then things slowly got better. Beavers were given protection. Fast forward to the mid-1980s, when Ryden began her four-year surveillance.

Winter. Summer. Spring. Fall. Ryden observed the growing family of beavers. She knew them by name—and they knew her. We see the circle of life. Joy. Sadness. And the occasional humans who try to poach, hurt or destroy.

If I had it to do over again, I'd probably read *Lily Pond* in the winter. A more quiet time. By a fireplace. The book is gentle. Compelling. And thought-provoking. When I finished the book, I actually felt like I was part of the family.

June 1, 2017

I Am Always Right

I am *always* right. On *everything*. I am *never* wrong. My views and opinions are always—*always*—correct. On politics, religion, social issues, economics, the law, ethnic issues, people, movies and golf courses. If you disagree with me, *you* are wrong. You may be uneducated (some of the most well-*schooled* people are *hopelessly* uneducated) or just stupid. So if you want to know the right path, the right opinion, the right way to believe—just give me a call or send me an email. Because I have a *righteous mind*.

The Righteous Mind is a wonderful book by Jonathan Haidt. It is a *New York Times* bestseller that explores why people are fundamentally intuitive—and irrational. The book suggests that our views (whether political, social, religious or whatever) are hardwired into us. You were never designed to listen to reason—only to respond with your preconceived notions and (often false) beliefs.

When you ask people moral questions and time their responses, you see that they reach conclusions quickly. And they produce reasons—later—only to justify what they have already decided. We often acquire morality (theories on right and wrong—and "justice") the way we acquire food preferences. If it tastes good, we stick with it.

Haidt's comments often sound cynical and yet if you follow the narration, you learn (if you don't have a closed mind) that Haidt is really seeking enlightenment. He *wants* you to open your mind to the moral intuitions of other people.

If you don't want to read this book, spend 20 minutes to watch a TED Talk—an *interview* with Haidt—titled "Can a Divided America Heal?" You can find it at www.ted.com/talks/jonathan_haidt_can_a_divided_america_heal.

I *want* my grandchildren—and their grandchildren—to grow up in an America that has civil discourse. And respectful disagreement. I believe you do too. And if you want to know what's right—and what's wrong—just let me know. I can tell you. And will. *I* have a *righteous mind*.

December 23, 2015

Carlos

Who remembers *Carlos?* I'm talking Ilich Ramírez Sánchez, better known as Carlos the Jackal.

Carlos was born in Venezuela in 1949. Despite his mother's desire for him to have a Christian name, his father, José, named him after Vladimir *Ilyich* Lenin. (Two siblings were named *Vladimir* and *Lenin*.) Young Carlos joined the youth movement of the Communist Party in Caracas, but his parents soon divorced, and his mother moved the family to London. It was there that Carlos began to *really* move. In the wrong direction...

The Carlos of whom I speak is *Carlos the Jackal*. Carlos volunteered for the Popular Front for the Liberation of Palestine (PFLP) and was given extensive guerrilla training. Carlos gained a reputation as a killer. And he became an assassin for the PFLP. He was involved in *many* killings, bombings and attacks. In 1975, he was detained in Yugoslavia, flown to Baghdad and settled in Aden, where he founded his own "Organization of Armed Struggle." Carlos connected with the Stasi (East German police) and planned numerous attacks from a safe house in East Berlin.

Carlos was finally arrested in 1994 by operatives of the French DST (*Direction de la Surveillance du Territoire*). He was tried and convicted of numerous offenses and sentenced to life in prison. Today Carlos the Jackal is incarcerated in Clairvaux Prison, where he converted to Islam, married his lawyer and published a series of works including *Revolutionary Islam,* which explains and defends violence in class conflict.

So why "the Jackal"? Carlos got the nickname when a copy of Frederick Forsyth's 1971 classic *The Day of the Jackal* was found near his things. (Turned out the book belonged to someone else. But the name stuck.)

It's a great book. Made into a terrific movie (1973). Four stars...

February 5, 2018

How Children Succeed

I recommend a wonderful book: *How Children Succeed*, by Paul Tough, a journalist and former editor of the *New York* Times *Magazine.* Tough addresses the controversial question of *why* there is an achievement gap between students who are underprivileged—and those who aren't.

Most educators believe that academic success relates to *cognitive* skills—the kind of intelligence that can be measured on IQ tests. However, more and more, there is an understanding that *non*cognitive skills (curiosity, socialization, character, self-control, self-confidence and "grit") are better predictors of academic achievement. A student's success has to do less with "smarts" than with personality traits such as the ability to stay focused and to control impulses.

Noncognitive skills—such as persistence and curiosity—have been found to predict future success. College graduates who participated in New York's KIPP (Knowledge is Power Program) were not so much the academic stars but more the ones who plugged away at problems and resolved to improve. *Grit.*

Are we surprised that children who grow up in abusive or dysfunctional environments statistically have more trouble concentrating, sitting still or rebounding from disappointments? *There is a neurological/medical reason for this.* The part of the brain most affected by early stress is the prefrontal cortex, which regulates thoughts and behavior. When this region is damaged (a condition that often occurs in children living in the pressures of poverty), it is tougher to suppress unproductive instincts. Studies show that early nurturing from parents combats the biochemical effects of stress. The prefrontal cortex then becomes more responsive to intervention and development of *essential* noncognitive skills.

While some view throwing money at the problem as a solution, *psychological intervention* is probably a better remedy. KIPP provides "character" report cards—designed to show students that such traits can improve with time. The motto? "Work hard. Be nice."

November 17, 2013

Malcolm Gladwell

One of the most meaningful (not just "the best") nonfiction authors I have read is Malcolm Gladwell (born 1963). Gladwell is a staff writer for *The New Yorker*. In 2005 *Time* magazine named him among the 100 most influential people. He is the author of half a dozen books (the list keeps growing). And oh my—what spectacular books! All are internationally acclaimed bestsellers and have sold millions of copies. On the list:

The Tipping Point: How Little Things Can Make a Big Difference (2000)
When an idea, trend or social idea suddenly "tips" and begins spreading like a wildfire

Blink: The Power of Thinking without Thinking (2005)
Why decisions made on gut reaction happen and why some decision-makers are usually right and others hopelessly inept

Outliers: The Story of Success (2008)
What makes high achievers different? Usually long hours and hard work—and being in the right place at the right time

What the Dog Saw and Other Adventures (2009)
A potpourri of fascinating knowledge (What is the difference between panicking and choking? What do football players teach us about hiring teachers?)

David and Goliath: Underdogs, Misfits, and the Art of Battling Giants (2013)
Why and how underdogs succeed

Talking to Strangers: What We Should Know about People We Don't Know (2019)
Why our interactions with strangers often go wrong

These works should be on everyone's "to read" shelf. I'd start with *Outliers* simply because it's easy—and nourishing—to read about how ordinary people achieve tremendous levels of success. They're all worth a read. And for me, a reread.

March 3, 2019

Louis L'Amour

In 1981 there was a center-column article in the *Wall Street Journal* about an author who wrote about the Old West—Louis L'Amour. Having spent some formative time out West when I was young, I read the article with considerable interest. A few weeks later, I was walking near my house with my 5-year-old daughter. We happened on a garage sale and went in. In rummaging through the books, I found a battered paperback copy of *Shalako* by Louis L'Amour. *Hmmm...* Louis L'Amour. For one thin dime, I bought the book. And read it. And was hooked.

In the ensuing years, I read all 100-plus of his novels. I think I still have them all—in a box—in the attic. Some I've read twice. What drew me to Louis L'Amour (1908–1988) was more than the tales of the Old West. It was his inimitable style. The good guys were good. Good men. Tough yet compassionate. The women were *always* good. Nurturing. And sweet. But mess with them, and they'd carve you up one side and down the other. And the bad guys were very *very* bad. And I relished when the bad guys got their just reward. Which they usually did.

Some of L'Amour's books have become movies. Ironically, *Shalako*—my first read—had been a 1968 movie starring Sean Connery, Brigitte Bardot and Honor Blackman. I've never seen the movie. It's still on my list.

If you're looking for a light—meaningful—read, give Louis a try. You won't be disappointed.

October 14, 2018

The Cemetery of the Books

Years ago, in another life (and over the course of several years), I traveled to Spain and Portugal with some frequency. I would normally come back with suitcases chock-full of handwritten manuscripts. Many dated to the 1400s. There were the garrison records for Gibraltar (all from the 1680s and 1690s), the thousand-page manuscript history of the church in Santiago de Compostela (1540–1822, northwest Spain), the Jesuit activities in Goa (India) dating to the early 1500s and so on. As we all say when time marches on—those were the days.

In Lisbon, during one visit, I found it. I found a genuine cemetery of the books. This was a term made popular by Carlos Ruiz Zafon in his must-read book *The Shadow of the Wind*. The cemetery of the books in Lisbon was a three- or four-story warehouse, packed with manuscripts, rare books and manuscript books. It was not a museum or archive. It was literally a cemetery of rarities. Which one could buy for a song.

Few people knew about this place. And somehow I had stumbled upon it. For those who are squeamish, stop reading here. The books and manuscripts I would pull off the shelves were literally crawling with lice. Crawling with insects. Vermin scooted in the corners and along the walls. But oh my—the things that were there.

I would load up a suitcase or two with books and manuscripts—carefully wrapping them in plastic bags—and bring them home. Once home, I would put the plastic bags in a large freezer for a month or two (the recommended Rx for dealing with the creepy-crawlers) and later leaf through what I had found. And then dispose of the items.

But on one sad trip to Lisbon, I went to the cemetery and—it was no more. It had burned to the ground a month or two before. I still have an item or two or three left from these forays. But I am sad that the cemetery of books is no more. If it were still there, I'd likely be flitting off to Lisbon every few months....

August 24, 2014

The Gutenberg Bible

No book has received as much attention or acclaim as the Gutenberg Bible—Europe's first example of mass-produced printing using "movable type." The Gutenberg Bible was first produced by Johannes Gutenberg in the 1450s with the financial backing of Johann Fust. The Bible was completed in an "edition" of about 180 two-volume sets (Old Testament and New Testament) with most on paper and the rest on vellum. Today only 49 full or partial copies are known to survive.

I first became interested in the Gutenberg Bible when I acquired the rare book room of the Boca Grande (Florida) Library in 1984. The one rarity it would not sell was a page from an original Gutenberg Bible. (The last Gutenberg Bible—Old Testament volume only—sold in 1987 for $4.9 million. Today, one might fetch $30 million. Individual leaves sell well into five figures.)

While it is speculated that the remainder of Gutenberg's Bibles have been destroyed over the centuries, I have my own theory. I believe that *somewhere* there is a copy—or two—of the Gutenberg Bible. Lying undiscovered, layered with dust, laced with cobwebs and swarming with dust mites.

My daughter has suggested that I take a sabbatical to hunt for this treasure, much as I did in the '80s, when I traveled to Spain and Portugal every few months on the hunt for manuscript rarities. I may still do this. If and when I find a Gutenberg Bible, I may then go on a quest—to seek out the yet-undiscovered ships' logs from that 1492 voyage of the *Nina*, the *Pinta* and the *Santa Maria*....

October 26, 2017

Henri Nouwen

One of the great inspirational or spiritual writers of all time was Henri Nouwen (1932–1996). Nouwen was born in Holland. At an early age, he felt a call to the priesthood. He was ordained as a diocesan priest in 1957 and studied at the Menninger Clinic in Topeka, Kansas. From there he went on to teach at Notre Dame, the Divinity School at Yale University *and* Harvard University. He died suddenly—and all too early—in 1996.

For several months in the 1970s, Nouwen lived in a Trappist community at the Abbey of the Genesee in New York. In the early '80s, he lived in Peru among the desperately poor. After a time of contemplation, he left the seemingly bright world of academia to work with mentally handicapped adults at L'Arche Daybreak in Toronto. It was at L'Arche, he said, that he felt his greatest fulfillment.

Nouwen was a prolific writer, and in 2003 a *Christian Century* survey rated his works No. 1 among Catholic and mainline Christian clergy. *Wow!* Spiritual. Inspirational. Moving. And somewhat melancholy—knowing that Nouwen died at such a young age. *Return of the Prodigal Son* is one of his most famous—and probably my favorite. I was given a copy by my friend and priest the Rev. Bob. If you have to pick one of Nouwen's books to read—this is the one.

July 12, 2012

Hakuna Matata

It's in the Bible: "Cast your cares on the Lord and He will sustain you; He will never let the righteous fall." (Psalm 55:22). And Proverbs 12:25: "An anxious heart weighs a man down, but a kind word cheers him up." And then there's John 14:27: "Do not let your hearts be troubled and do not be afraid." This is good counsel for all. The message? *Don't worry.*

Numerous sages have offered comment on the subject of worry.

> "Do not anticipate trouble, or worry about what may never happen. Keep in the sunlight."
> ~ *Benjamin Franklin*

> "Drag your thoughts away from your troubles ... by the ears, by the heels, or any other way you can manage it."
> ~ *Mark Twain*

> "Sorrow looks back. Worry looks around. Faith looks up."
> ~ *Ralph Waldo Emerson*

> "You're only here for a short visit. Don't hurry, don't worry. And be sure to smell the flowers along the way."
> ~ *Walter Hagen*

While there is wisdom in these quotations, there may be a better way to convey the message. I can think of no better way than *hakuna matata* (Swahili for *there are no problems*). "Hakuna Matata" is a song title in Disney's *The Lion King*. My granddaughters associate me with *Pumbaa* (which means *silly* in Swahili), the odoriferous warthog who "sings" the song.

189

But listen to his message. Watch for 3 minutes and 49 seconds (go to https://www.youtube.com/watch?v=nbY_aP-alkw). You'll smile. I *promise*.

October 11, 2018

Pardon My Blooper!

When I was (very) young, I would listen to—and *howl* at—a series of records my parents had. The *Pardon My Blooper!* series, compiled by Kermit Schafer (1914–1979), was a collection of "unintended indiscretions before microphone and camera."

Schafer was a broadcast producer and writer who began collecting on-air bloopers early on. (Bloopers came to prominence in 1931 when veteran radio announcer Harry von Zell introduced the president of the United States as "Hoobert Heever.")

Schafer began cataloging such bloopers, then synthesizing them into a series of records—seven altogether. He was criticized for recreating a few famous bloopers, but for the most part, what listeners heard live is what you can hear today on those albums.

May 12, 2013

Sukiyaki

Way back when, I had a half-year course in Japanese. We learned basic conversation, the *hiragana* (Japanese cursive characters), a bit of *katakana* (the angular part of Japanese writing) and snippets of *kanji* (adopted from Chinese characters). I don't have much use for the language anymore, except for one thing—*singing*.

When my granddaughters spend the night, I always *sing.* "Oh Shenandoah," which I sang to my daughter. And I inevitably launch into the famous Kyu Sakamoto song "Sukiyaki" ("*Ue o Muite Arukō*"). I remember that tune vividly from my junior prom in 1963. So when my granddaughters are closing their eyes, I'm warbling to them in Japanese.

The song title means *"I look up as I walk."* It is about a man who walks whistling—while looking up. So his tears will not fall. *Sukiyaki* was released in Japan in 1961 and the United States in 1963.

The singer, Kyu Sakimoto (1941–1985) was an instant phenom. For nearly a year, Kyu was on a world tour, performing and appearing on television (including in the United States). Sadly, on August 12, 1985, he died in the crash of Japan Airlines Flight 123—the deadliest single-aircraft accident in history. He left behind his wife and two young daughters.

You can hear Kyu Sakamoto's beautiful recording of this song—at www.youtube.com/watch?v=C35DrtPlUbc.

November 12, 2017

Stevie Ray Vaughan

I play guitar. Have for years. I often stick in a CD and play along (or try to) with Buddy Guy, Eddie Campbell, B.B. King, Eric Clapton, Bonnie Raitt and so many others. Lead or rhythm. But the chap I'd like to play like is Stevie Ray Vaughan (1954–1990). He was *amazing.* I'd give my left arm to … no—*wait a minute….*

Stevie Ray was born and raised in Dallas. At age 7, he received a gift—a plastic guitar from a Sears catalog. He liked music. He tried to play drums. Then sax. But the guitar idea stuck. He got a real guitar and learned to play by listening to the greats like Muddy Waters and Jimi Hendrix. Stevie Ray's first public performance was at age 11 in a local Dallas talent contest. And he realized—this is where it's at.

"SRV," as he was known, dropped out of high school and moved to Austin to pursue his passion—music. In 1977, the band Double Trouble was born. And it *soared*—with SRV at the helm. But SRV developed an alcohol and cocaine habit while touring with Double Trouble. His performance contracts called for two fifths of Crown Royal and a fifth of Smirnoff vodka in his dressing room. His cocaine use jumped to 7 grams a day (together with the booze). After a long stay in rehab, he returned to performing. Stevie was spiritual, ascetic and sober. And he went into high gear on producing some of his best music.

Then on August 27, 1990, Double Trouble opened for Eric Clapton at the Alpine Valley Music Theater in East Troy, Wisconsin. After the show, the musicians boarded four helicopters bound for Chicago. SRV's helicopter took off after midnight and crashed into a 1,000-foot ski hill. Killing all aboard. It was *everyone's* loss—another day when the music died.

June 22, 2014

15

SPORTS ROUNDUP

Swing Thoughts

I like to golf. I'm okay at it. Not great. I play two or three times a week—and I have a 17 index that's moving down. My attitude on any given day can affect my game. The reason is that golf is 65% mental. And 35% mental.

Upon addressing the ball ("hello, ball"), I employ an instructive word I learned from a John Jacobs Golf School in Litchfield Park, Arizona. The word is "GASP." GASP stands for "grip," "aim," "stance" and "posture." These are not swing thoughts. These are the preliminary steps you take to get *ready* to strike the ball.

Once I have my grip, aim, stance and posture lined up, a mantra from Captain Chesley Sullenberger's miraculous landing on the Hudson River comes to mind. As the plane begins its descent to the river, the flight attendants are calling over the intercom, "HEAD DOWN. STAY DOWN."

And that is my single swing thought. If I can remember it…

August 8, 2020

5 Feet From Glory

I love golf. I practice. I play. I watch (especially when Tiger is in the hunt). And when I do play, I secretly like stepping up to the par 3s because I know there is a chance....

I had a brush with glory. A 205-yard par 3. Wind against. And I popped my Pro V1 less than a foot from the pin. Twelve inches ... 304.8 millimeters.

Every time I tee it up on a par 3, I take just a tad more time. A bit more analysis on club selection. And more care on the implementation of all 49 of my swing thoughts. Or is it 50? Sometimes my ball ends up off the green, though often it's *somewhere* on the green. Sometimes it's a few feet away from glory.

I have friends who have had holes-in-one. But so far I remain untouched. Maybe one day. Probably on a Saturday when there is a special event. And the club is jammed with people. Of course I will have to buy drinks for everyone. Be just my luck.

June 25, 2012

A Harbinger of Spring?

It was about minus 7 on the thermometer (minus 20 wind chill) when I got up one January morning. I had coffee, some cereal, and drove off in shorts and a jacket—in the dark—to the local fitness center. I groaned through a couple of situps and a few minutes on the bike, and came home for some jelly doughnuts.

I pulled into the driveway and walked back to the curb to get our recycling bin. The gray fingers of dawn were struggling to come alive. As I pulled the bin up the driveway, I saw something on the lawn. I walked over and picked it up. It was a golf ball. A Titleist range ball. Brand new. How it got there, I have not a clue. I had never found a golf ball on my lawn before.

I gazed up at the sky. A faint shade of blue. Then at the ball. And I concluded that this find had to be a harbinger of spring. I mean why wait for a %#&*!@ groundhog?

When I walked into the house, Donna was at the kitchen table, finishing breakfast. "I found something," I said. "Hold out your hand." And she did. Donna has known me long enough to know that I'm not going to drop a worm or cricket or mouse in her palm—so she accepted the ball from my closed fist.

"A harbinger of spring," I said, smiling. She inspected the ball and peered out at the thermometer.

"Fat chance," she said.

January 21, 2016

Shortsworthy

I play golf during the summer and in the shoulder seasons. And my preference is to wear *shorts*. In the summer, that's an easy sell. Looking around the golf course on a hot summer day, very few (other than the pros) will be wearing long pants. You'd have to be incredibly shy—or have a sun issue—to play golf in long pants when it's 80 degrees.

However, once Labor Day arrives and the temperature begins its inexorable slide down the thermometer, some chaps pull out the long pants. Even when it's 60 degrees. But not me.

I can't count the number of times someone has said, as I walk into the locker room on a chilly Saturday morning, "You're wearing *shorts!?!?*" Posed as a *question,* the answer would be obvious—from my knobby, scarred legs. Yes. I am—indeed—wearing *shorts*. But when presented as a *statement,* it might just suggest that I meet someone's definition of *knucklehead.*

Hey, I'm comfy in shorts. But I also figure if a 98-pound cocktail waitress can—and maybe has to—wear a miniskirt when it's 10 below zero, *I* can wear *shorts* to golf on a day when the weatherman says it's going to be 59 degrees and sunny. Such weather is, in my opinion, *shortsworthy.*

November 17, 2016

The Chicago Cubs Are Lutheran

Donna and I saw a live radio broadcast of *A Prairie Home Companion* at Ravinia. On more than one occasion. In his show, host Garrison Keillor always discussed the goings-on in Lake Wobegon. He also inevitably got around to talking about Chicago, the North Shore, Illinois politics and such.

One time in particular he talked about the Chicago Cubs. And he came to the divine conclusion that the Chicago Cubs' failures over the last hundred years are because they are (are you ready?) a *Lutheran* team. He went on. And on. And the audience loved it. And collectively thought, "Gosh maybe it's true...."

In 1914, Wrigley Field (then known as Weeghman Park) was built on the grounds of the old Chicago Lutheran Theological Seminary. Because Lutherans (who are in abundance in Lake Wobegon) are devoted to "service to others," this mantra has seeped from the ground and stuck. On the Cubs.

So since 1914 the Chicago Cubs have been the living embodiment of Lutheran theology—in service to others. Devoted to ending other teams' losing streaks. Ending their rivals' batting slumps. Lowering opposing pitchers' ERAs. And so on.

The Chicago Cubs' century of failure in World Series wins at Wrigley Field is not because of the Billy Goat curse. Not because of poor management. Not because of poor players. It is because—they are *Lutheran*.

Having grown up as a Lutheran, I kinda see where he's coming from.

June 26, 2014

Hank

My favorite baseball player as a kid was Hank Sauer, left fielder for the (then) hapless Chicago Cubs. I tried—*desperately*—to get his autograph. My dad would take me to Wrigley Field, and I'd gallop down the steps to troll for autographs. I remember one day Hank was walking a few feet away. I screamed at him "Hank! Hank! Mister Sauer!" He looked at me like I was a 9-year-old lunatic. And walked on...

Some years ago, I published an article that talked about Hank and how I was never able to get his autograph. Someone read the article and sent me a note that Hank was living in Milbrea, California. The address was included. *Sooo...*

I sent him a letter—including a copy of the article. And I mentioned that I was his biggest fan in the world. A few weeks later, I arrived at my office one morning, and there was a package on my desk. In the corner was a return-address sticker shaped like a baseball. Between the stitching, it said *Hank Sauer.* My eyes filled with tears, and I opened the package. Inside was a large album full of original pictures of Hank (a few signed), original baseball cards and ... a priceless handwritten sentiment: "To Scott—my best Chicago fan."

Hank passed away in August 2001. But I will always relish the fact that I "hit the high note" in my autograph-collecting career. It wasn't a George Washington letter. Or Henry VIII. *I got Hank Sauer....*

July 11, 2019

The 1,000-Pound Man

The heaviest person in the world weighs 1,076 pounds. He is about 5 feet, 8 inches tall. The regulation National Hockey League goal is 6 feet by 4 feet. You see where I'm going?

I have long felt that the Chicago Blackhawks could win the Stanley Cup every year by simply recruiting the largest people in the world to be the goalies. You upholster them in padding, mask and protective gear, give them a stick, stuff them into the goal and let them take a nap. Every shot on goal would simply bounce off the goalie. Defense would become a thing of the past. The goalie would go into the history books, and the Blackhawks would win the Stanley Cup every year.

The only hitch would be that other teams might start recruiting similarly endowed goalies. Games would typically end 0-0. Shootouts in overtime could go on for *years....*

October 5, 2017

How High Can You Jump?

I have the aerodynamics of a sofa. "How high can you jump?" never resonated with me, since the answer was never one I wished to share (I can barely get off the ground).

In the 1900 Olympics, no high jumper could hope to succeed unless he did a scissors kick to launch himself over the bar. It was thought no one would ever jump higher—that is until 1920, when the track and field world was stunned by a high jumper who *dove* over the bar. That added nearly 2 feet to the world record. It was thought that no one would ever jump higher—that is, until 1968, when a young man from Oregon revolutionized high jumping at the Mexico City Olympics by going over the bar backward! Today, high jumpers who cannot master the "Fosbury flop" may as well take their gym bag and go home.

So how high can you jump? What do you do to challenge yourself? Improve yourself? Motivate yourself—and others? What goals do you set? And reach? I like to think that the sky is the limit.

W.N. Murray, who was on the Scottish Himalayan Expedition, said, "Whatever you can do or dream you can, begin it. Boldness has genius, power and magic in it."

August 11, 2011

The All Blacks

Rugby was first introduced in New Zealand in 1870. The Kiwi team adopted the name "the Originals." But in 1905—during a tour of the British Isles—the team became known as the "All Blacks," maybe because of their uniforms. And the name stuck.

The All Blacks are the greatest rugby team in the world. Since the introduction of World Rugby Rankings in 2003, All Blacks have held the No. 1 ranking longer than all other teams—*combined*. And they have been the World Rugby Team of the Year *10 times* since the award was created in 2001. And that just takes us up to 2017.

Before each international match, the All Blacks perform a *haka*—a Māori challenge to the opposition. I can't explain it. *Please*—spend 2½ minutes and go to your web browser and enter "greatest haka ever."

I'm teaching my granddaughters the haka. Words, too. I'm gonna start doing the haka on Saturday mornings on the first tee when I play golf. Wearing my All Blacks hat.

Ka mate! Ka mate! Ka ora! Ka ora! Whiti te ra!

May 7, 2017

Bowling

My father used to go bowling when I was a kid. And sometimes take me along. He'd want me to watch—and learn—but I'd go play the pinball machines over by the exit. Ready to make a fast getaway. My dad's team members all wore the same color short-sleeved shirt (gray) with the team name and their names stitched in pink: *Pete, Dave, Carl, Al* and so on. I still have my father's bowling shirt in the closet. Or attic. Somewhere.

Does anyone *bowl* anymore? And if so, for what purpose? You throw a big heavy ball—trying to knock down *pins*. You spend time in the *alley*. And then you're in the gutter. You do well and you get a *strike*. (like what unions do) Three strikes and you have a *turkey* (like Thanksgiving dinner). Next best is a *spare* (like a spare tire, which you want to avoid around your midsection). And if you do poorly, and don't knock any pins down, people avoid looking at you (like, *this dude is really bad*).

I haven't bowled in *years*. I may never again. The last attempt was a neighborhood gathering 35 years ago. "Let's all go bowling," Donna said. "Oh, let's go." So I smiled, drove to the bowling alley, rented the shoes (have you ever *smelled* the shoes they rent at bowling alleys?) and then didn't bowl. I drank some beer and looked at the pinball machines.

I had the shoes on. And a Hawaiian shirt. I guess I *looked* like a bowler. But my feet haven't been the same since. I can't understand. You aim a big, heavy black ball. And then roll it. Trying to hit some far-off target. Makes no sense whatsoever.

I'm gonna go golfing.

April 5, 2018

Par Tube

My father was a pretty good golfer. He played on weekends and in weekday, 9-hole leagues.

Back in the day, golf grips were leather-wound. The constant abrasion of tossing in and pulling out the different clubs would cause grips to unravel. And thus one would have to pay to have clubs regripped every couple years (or try to play while squeezing the unraveled pieces).

Around 1950, my father had an idea. He bought some paper tubes to put in his golf bag. Each club had its own tube—to slide in and out. Voila! No more abrasion! And thereby no need to have grips reattached!

Within weeks, friends and strangers were asking where he got the tubes in his bag. So my dad went out and bought 2,000 paper tubes—and a rubber stamp that said PAR TUBE. He hand-stamped each tube with the red-ink logo and offered a local sporting goods store the new "golf tubes." The owner said he would take the tubes on consignment, but if they didn't sell—he said my father would have to eat them.

Within weeks, the sporting goods store called and needed more tubes. And the Par Tube was born. A distributor began selling them to other sporting goods stores. And my father began to moonlight. Tannery by day, Par Tube by night...

In the mid-1950s, the owner of Chicago Paper Tube & Can Company (the tube maker) called my father. The owner, Mr. Lyons, wanted to retire, and he offered to sell the company to my father. And my Dad—who had 20 years' service at Chicago Rawhide—made a switch. He invested every penny he had, to buy and run a business he knew nothing about. And he made it grow. And he made it glow....

August 12 2020

Act Your Age

Every once in awhile, I hear the admonition "act your age." Or sometimes it's, "How old are you?" So I take the lampshade off my head or take out my novelty buck teeth and act contrite.

I just finished (for the second time) Bob Rotella's classic book *Golf is Not a Game of Perfect*. Among other things, Dr. Bob talks about golf and *age*. He mentions Paul Runyan (1908–2002), the great PGA champ and master golf instructor. Paul was active in golf (and other things) well into his 80s. According to Rotella, Paul and his wife Bernice embodied the old Satchel Paige aphorism about age. Someone once asked Satchel (who was in his 40s before segregation ended and he made it to the major leagues) if he could still pitch at his "advanced age." Paige replied, "How old would you be if you didn't know how old you was?" *Wow...*

I'd seen that quote before, but this time when I read it, it resonated a wee bit more. I don't feel my age. I don't feel much different than I did when I was 25 or so. Apart from a few aches and pains. For many, age is a state of mind. As Bernard Baruch, the great financier, once said, "I will never be an old man. To me, old age is always 15 years older than I am."

Amen.

July 20, 2013

It Ain't Perfect

As I've noted, golf is 65% mental and 35% mental. Having played "at" the game for a long time, I believe it. The game of golf doesn't happen on the fairway or on the green. It takes place between the ears.

I just finished reading (for the third time) Bob Rotella's classic *Golf is Not a Game of Perfect*. I like to feel that I have been steeped in the mental nuance of the game to the point I should be on the PGA Tour. Well, maybe the Hooters Tour. Or the Old Guys with Bad Breath Tour. But so far, I'm in a holding pattern. With a 16-plus index and an inconsistent short game. And long game. And putting game.

Rotella is a master, though, at providing positive reinforcement. At each reading, I have a pen in hand. Making marginal notes. Writing on 3-by-5 cards. Scribbling Rotella's wisdom on the blank pages fore and aft. You would think that with such diligence, my game would be ... never mind.

Dr. Bob's mantra is to concentrate on the short game. Pick the smallest possible target. Visualize the ball going into the hole Negative thinking will almost guarantee failure. If I were to distill this (really wonderful) tome into one word, it would be "confidence." Confidence in club selection. Setup. Swing. And result.

It didn't work today. Maybe I need to read the book again.

September 10, 2017

The Albatross

I'd love to have a hole-in-one. But what sticks in the back of my mind is the rarest of golf shots—an *albatross*. A double eagle.

A double eagle is 3 under par on any given hole. It is a hole-in-one—an ace—on a par 4 and a 2 on a par 5. They are a rarity—even on the PGA Tour. The first double eagle on record was scored by Tom Morris Jr. (1870 British Open at Prestwick). The longest albatross was scored by Andy Bean on a 663-yard par 5 (No. 18; Kapalua) in 1991. The longest double eagle/ace was by Bret Melson on a 448-yard par 4 (Oahu, Hawaii) in 2007.

Double eagles are not child's play. Yet the youngest golfer to score one was a 10-year-old girl. Line Toft Hansen scored one in 2010 on a 419-yard par 5 in a Danish juniors competition. (Two even younger golfers scored double eagles, but they were playing age-appropriate yardage tees.)

In tournament play, 834 doubles have been scored since the first in 1870. The only Tour player to have scored two in major tournaments was Jeff Maggert (1994 Masters and 2001 British Open).

The first golfer known to have scored a hole-in-one and a double eagle in one round was coach John Wooden of UCLA. He did it in 1939 (Erskine Park Golf Course, South Bend, Indiana, a good trivia question).

I've read that the odds of a double eagle are a million to one (judging by the score of my last round, I should've had one). A hole-in-one is a mere 40,000-1. (If you want to watch a few double eagles on the PGA Tour, check out www.youtube.com/watch?v=WKNs2jvmUYA.)

I'd love that hole-in-one. But I'd love a double eagle even more. Maybe if I play from the ladies tees...

June 14, 2018

A Hole in One—Almost

Watching Tiger Woods at the 2019 Masters was amazing. Tiger's success gives me renewed hope that I—Mr. 15 Index—can one day achieve *my* dream: a hole-in-one.

I've never had one, but I've come close. On August 7, 2011, I came the closest ever—about 8 inches from the cup. Evanston Golf Club, 17th hole. Playing about 215 yards. A little wind against. I pulled out my 3-wood and spanked my Pro V1 just like Tiger. The ball took off high and perfectly straight. I watched. It seemed like ages. The ball landed, bounced. And disappeared.

"Wow! Great shot," said the caddie.

"That could be in the hole," said my friend Norm.

The flagstick was obscured by a fairway bunker, so we couldn't see the result. So we walked. My heart racing. As the pin came into view, I saw that the ball resting—*inches* from the hole. An angry-looking divot splayed grass and turf where the ball had slammed into the green. I marked and cleaned my ball and thought briefly, *"What if I 3-putt?"* But I knocked down the putt for a 2. Birdie.

A hole-in-one is rare, and I *almost* had one. But *almost* doesn't count. It either is or isn't. Suffice it to say, I'm *still* looking for the elusive ace. One day. Hey—if *Tiger* can do it…

April 18, 2019

The Death March

I go to the local fitness center a few times a week. When I come home, I get the question, "How was your workout?" And my response—for the longest time—was, "Fine." And that was it.

But my workouts vary. Sometimes it's a quick in and out. Other times, I'll be there for a while—punishing my body. Grunting, groaning, lumbering and lurching through all manner of cardio, weights, stretches and contortions. So one day when I got home and Donna asked, "How was your workout?" I responded, "I did the *Puppy Dog.*"

I got the look. "What's that?" Donna asked.

"I was only able to work out for 45 minutes."

"Oh."

Later that week, I went home, got the question and responded, "I did the *Gorilla*." Nearly 90 minutes of exercise. I soon identified four distinct categories of workout:

The Puppy Dog—less than 45 minutes
The Regular—an hour
The Gorilla—an hour to an hour and a half
The Death March—pushing two hours

Death March workouts are rare, but they happen. However, while on vacation a few weeks ago, I came up with a fifth category: *Death by Workout*. This is where I try to kill myself working out. As long as I don't succeed...

_____

March 25, 2017

Scott's Knees: A Play in One Act

I go to the local fitness center. And try to exercise. My body isn't always happy. This is probably a good way to describe what's going on.

Right Knee: What the *heck* is he *doing* to us?

Left Knee: He's a nut. He's pushing me to the limit. I've had enough. *Enough!*

Right Knee: Who is it that's pushing him?

Left Knee: He's got a "personal trainer."

Heart: (*enters*) Hey guys, cool it. I'm OK with this. I really feel for you, but knock it off. You've caused enough trouble.

Left Knee: But Boss ... (*thinking*) It's the *feet*. It's *their* fault.

Feet: (*from offstage*) Huh? Whuh?

Heart: Take it easy guys. I'll talk to—

Brain: *Ahem!* (*enters; hold for applause*) Is there a problem here?

Heart: No, we're just kinda talking. Sir.

Left Knee: (*filling with fluid from fright*) Yeah… I mean yes. I mean yes, *sir*.

Brain: (*angrily*) I *want* him to exercise, you two troublemakers. And don't give him any problems. Remember—you can be *replaced. Capisce?*

Left Knee: OK, OK… Sir.

Brain: Right knee?

Right Knee: Yessir. I'll be good. Promise.

Brain: OK. 'Nuf said. And Heart—you keep pumping and keep those two weaklings happy.

Heart: (*pumping vigorously*) Will do. Sir!

Brain: Thank you. Now if you don't mind, I have got work to do. I have to help cook dinner. (*exits*)

Curtain

November 7, 2013

16

THIS AND THAT

My Favorite Day

A few years ago, I had breakfast with a client at Lou Mitchell's restaurant, a classic diner in downtown Chicago. It was winter. Freezing. Snowing. Out of the blue, my client asked me, "What's your favorite day in the year?" *Hmmm…* I had to think about it, though not for long.

"Thanksgiving," I said, "because I leave work early on Wednesday, Thursday is a family day and I eat until I keel over, I get Friday off—and I still have the weekend to recover." My friend nodded solemnly and was silent. "*Sooo*," I asked, "what's your favorite day?"

He responded immediately, "December 22."

Now I may not be the brightest light in the box, but I do have a handle on the major holidays—and even a few minor ones. December 22 did *not* ring a bell. "Why, pray tell, do you like December 22?" I asked. "Because," he said, "that is the winter solstice. When days start getting longer."

The winter solstice nearly always occurs on December 21 or 22 in the Northern Hemisphere and June 20 or 21 in the Southern Hemisphere. After that, the sun begins to stay out longer.

Many festivals and celebrations surround the winter solstice. For me, with the dog days of winter still ahead, it's the *I wish I were somewhere warm* festival.…

November 16, 2011

December 31, 1999

Does anyone remember the approach of the new millennium? I'm talking New Year's Eve 1999. Do you recall the media warnings that power grids might shut down. Telephone service was apt to be interrupted. Computers could crash. And the world might come to an end. All because the shift from December 31, 1999, to January 1, 2000, to a new millennium, would cause these catastrophic "issues" with computer networks.

As an Eagle Scout—and with my penchant to "be prepared"—in the week before this possible cataclysm, I went out and bought a few gallons of bottled water, some cans of Chef Boyardee, soup and tuna. I squirreled away a couple thousand dollars in $20 and $50 bills. *And* we had a few bottles of cabernet sauvignon—all just in case.

As the clock ticked toward the advent of the New Year, Donna and I hunkered down in bed and watched a movie. I figured, *hey*, when ya got no control, ya got no problem.

So as the nudge from 11:59:59 p.m. to 12:00:01 a.m. occurred (in Africa, Europe, New York and Chicago) and the new year went off without a hitch, we turned off the lights and went to sleep. Over the next year or so, we ate the canned pasta, consumed the soup, spent the dollars, and drank the cab (which was dutifully replenished).

Fast forward to the fall of 2018. I went down to the basement and there, in the back of the closet behind some flower pots, was a dusty gallon bottle of water. Left over from that fateful night. No, we're not drinking it. But it is being used to water plants in the house. Eighteen-year-old water. Be a shame to waste it.

December 27, 2018

Shampoo

There are any number of things we can all do (that cost nothing) to save water and energy *and* cut down on pollution. Little things like …

When taking a shower, turn on the water, get wet—then *turn off the water* and soap down. Then rinse. You'll actually get *cleaner*, and you'll save *gallons* of water that otherwise simply pour down the drain. Just think if *everyone* did this.

Speaking of showers, here's another thought that saves money and helps the environment. Shampoo. A few years ago, I was in the shower, and there was no shampoo. I had an empty container from which I could squeeze *nada. Grrr...* So I unscrewed the top, held the container under the water, swirled the liquid in the bottle and—*voila*—shampoo. It was a little watery, but it worked every bit as well as the thick, gloppy stuff. It actually lasted for a few more days.

Today, when the shampoo bottle is making that distinctive *pffft* sound as I squeeze it, I unscrew the top, let water drain in, screw the top back on, give it a shake, and I have shampoo for another week or two.

Try it. You'll like it. So will your wallet. And the sewer system.

April 11, 2013

Happy 90th Birthday

My wife, Donna, is the one in our family who normally initiates birthday (or greeting) cards. She buys them at the card store (selecting the *perfect* card for the occasion). She addresses the envelope, fills out the card with a touching message, includes a check for kids' special birthdays, then seals, stamps and sends it off. At *most*, she will ask me to sign the card or draw and color one of my artistic creations.

There are times, though, when *I* will send off a birthday card on my own (cue the trumpets). When I do, the card doesn't show a puppy dog. Or a mountain scene. Or offer a *best wishes on this special birthday* message. I have a supply of "Happy 90th Birthday," "Happy 95th Birthday" and one or two "Happy 100th Birthday" cards stuffed in my drawer.

I usually have no clue whose birthday is when. But if Donna reminds me that it's someone's birthday, I may groan. Go up to my desk. Rummage around a bit. And dash off a "Happy 90th Birthday" card to one of my fraternity brothers or golfing buds (who have a sense of humor).

These days the "90th Birthday" business is (so far) 15 to 20 years off. But if I want to add *pizzazz* to the card, I may draw a line through "90th" and scribble "Ooops—91st." Something to look forward to.

June 28, 2018

Shuji Shuriken

Kenjutsu is the overarching term for all schools of Japanese swordsmanship. Swords. Very important to the martial arts in Japan. And to the samurai class.

The study of kenjutsu has been a subculture in Japan since feudal times. For practice, swordsmen used the *bokuto* (solid wood stick) or *shinai* (bamboo pole). For battle, they used the real McCoy. And only the most disciplined of swordsmen could repeat and internalize the magic words of the Shuji Shuriken—"the cutting of the nine ideographs." Only the most devout of Japanese swordsmen could give life to these nine words:

U = being
Mu = nonbeing
Suigetsu = moonlight on the water
Jo = inner security
Shin = master of the mind
Sen = thought precedes action
Kara = empty; the void; virtue
Shinmyoken = where the tip of the sword settles
Zero = where the way has no power

It was not enough merely to think or speak the words. The words and their meaning had to be summoned from deep within. The thought was, if you get through the first one while meditating and contemplating, you're doing pretty well.

June 9, 2016

Word Quirks

Did you know ...

In the English language, only three words have all the vowels (except *y*) in consecutive order: abstemious (abstaining), arsenious (derived from arsenic) and facetious. (And no, I'm not being facetious.)

Only word is derived from the Malaysian language: amok (as in, to run amok).

Only one word has three consecutive double letters: bookkeeper.

Only three words are palindromes (same backward and forward): racecar, kayak and level.

Only one word ends in *mt*: dreamt.

The longest word that doesn't repeat a letter: uncopyrightable.

The longest word you can type on the top row of a typewriter: typewriter.

The longest word typed with left-hand keys: stewardesses.

The longest word typed with right-hand keys: lollipop.

The longest word without vowels *a, e, i, o* or *u*: rhythms.

The longest one-syllable word: screeched.

The most-used letter in the English language: *e*.

The least-used letter: *q*.

November 9, 2011

'Polish' Jokes

What happens if you eat *yeast* and *shoe polish* for dinner? In the morning you will rise and shine!

This is my only polish joke. If you know any good polish jokes, I'd like to hear. *Wait a minute.* You thought I was going to tell a ... oh *nooo*. Not me. I was telling a *polish* joke.

Polish is one of those words that have two different pronunciations and yet a single spelling. It is a *heteronym*. Other examples of heteronyms are:

Abuse. I don't *abuse* my body with substance *abuse.*
Contest. I will *contest* the results of the *contest.*

Excuse. I will *excuse* you if you have a good *excuse.*

Tear. I would shed a *tear* if I *tear* my paycheck.

There are many such examples: lead, alternate, close, permit, duplicate, insult, august, produce, bow, graduate, bass, invalid, sow, resume, dove, moderate, wound, minute, record, rebel, transplant, object, use, desert and so many others.

I had better *wind* this up before I run out of *wind....*

February 28, 2013

Ghoti

You know how to pronounce words of the English language, right? OK, pronounce this: *ghoti.*

No, it's not "GOH-tee." Nor is it "Gah-TEE." Or even "Gah-hoe-tee." It is pronounced ... are you ready?

FISH.

Ghoti is a contrived word, crafted to point out the idiosyncrasies in English spelling. It's often attributed to George Bernard Shaw, but a published reference from 1874 credits William Ollier Jr. Now—are you ready to learn why *ghoti* is pronounced *fish*? Phoneme by phoneme:

gh, as in *enough*

o, as in *women*

ti, as in *nation*

Ta-daaa! FISH.

James Joyce subtly references the word in his book *Finnegan's Wake* ("Gee each owe tea eye smells fish"). And in the Klingon language of *Star Trek*, *ghoti* means *fish*.

Sooo, if you're ever captured by Klingons, you know how to ask for food. I wonder how they say, "I prefer salmon...."

January 14, 2018

Talk Like a Pirate Day

September 19 is International Talk Like a Pirate Day. Do you know about this special day?

In 1995 two guys from Albany, Oregon (John "Ol' Chumbucket" Baur and Mark "Cap'n Slappy" Summers), proclaimed September 19 as the day everyone in the world should "talk like a pirate." The whole idea stemmed from a racquetball injury. One of them reacted with an "*aaarrr...*" as he lay on the floor in pain—and along came an idea. For seven years, it remained an inside joke, but in 2002 they sent a letter about their "holiday" to humorist Dave Barry. Barry liked the idea, pushed it in a few columns, and the rest is history.

Actor Robert Newton (who starred as Long John Silver in the 1950 Disney film *Treasure Island*) is considered the patron saint of Talk Like a Pirate Day. So remember, on September 19, when anyone says anything to you, tilt your head, give them the eye and say, "Avast you scurvy lubber. Prepare to be boarded...."

August 16, 2018

So You Think You're Glib?

Can you talk for one minute—60 seconds—nonstop? Yeah, I can too. I'm a lawyer. However, can you talk for 60 seconds, nonstop without saying a word that contains the letter *a*? Think about it. Try it.... This is a good one for kids.

I'm sure there are combinations of words and sentences that will accomplish this objective (Hebrew and Arabic contain no vowels, hence no *a*). For me though, the easiest way to do this is to go, "one, two, three, four, five, six, seven, eight, nine, ten, eleven, twelve" and on up to one hundred. The first *a* you will encounter is "hundred *a*nd one."

It'll take you about 60 seconds to get up to the number 75. *Ta-daaa!*

March 24, 2019

Alfred E. Neuman for President

As a kid, I was allowed to read *Walt Disney Comics and Stories* (the Mickey Mouse and Donald Duck offerings). Bugs Bunny and Woody Woodpecker comics were OK too. But *Mad* Magazine was strictly *verboten*. I think my parents were afraid I was going to emulate—and turn out like—Alfred E. Neuman, the cover boy for *Mad*.

It made me all the more desirous of sneaking copies home and hiding them under my bed in the small—locked—toolbox where I hid enough Black Cat firecrackers, M-80s and cherry bombs to take out Tehran. I found *Mad Magazine* (launched in 1952) hysterical! Still do. The satire is *classic*.

Alfred E. Neuman made his *Mad Magazine* debut in 1956. His famous motto? "What, me worry?" That same year, there was a write-in campaign to have Alfred E. Neuman elected president. His campaign slogan was "You could do worse … and always have."

In some election cycles, I've been tempted to vote for Alfred E. Neuman. He's often smarter than the candidates. And he doesn't have the baggage. Or I could vote for my dog Daisy. Daisy is loyal, has integrity, doesn't bite and is housetrained. It's really a toss-up. Seriously.

April 16, 2016

Five Riddles

Remember "what's black and white and red [phonetic] all over?" Answer: a newspaper. That's an oldie. These are goodies. Riddle me this:

1. A murderer is condemned to death. He has to choose between three rooms. The first is full of raging fires, the second is full of assassins with loaded guns, and the third is full of lions that haven't eaten in three years. Which room is safest for him?
2. A woman shoots her husband. Then she holds him under water for 5 minutes. Finally, she hangs him. But 5 minutes later, they both go out and enjoy a wonderful dinner together. How can this be?

3. What's black when you buy it, red when you use it and gray when you throw it away ?

4. Can you name three consecutive days without using the words Wednesday, Friday or Sunday?

5. This is an unusual paragraph. I'm curious as to just how quickly you can find out what is so unusual about it. It looks so ordinary and plain that you would think nothing was wrong with it. In fact, nothing *is* wrong with it! It is highly unusual, though. Study it and think about it. You still may not find anything odd. But if you work at it a bit, you might find out. Try to do so without any coaching!

Answers

1. The third room. Lions that haven't eaten in three years are dead. (That one was easy, right?)

2. The woman is a photographer. She *shot* a picture of her husband, *held it under water* 5 minutes to develop it, and *hung* it up to dry.

3. Charcoal, as used in barbecuing.

4. Sure you can name three consecutive days—yesterday, today and tomorrow!

5. The letter *e*, the most common in the English language, appears not once in that paragraph.

June 29, 2014

The Four Bank Robbers

This is a great magical effect that anyone can do. As a perspiring magician, I've gotten a lot of mileage out of this one.

The Effect: You ask for a deck of cards (or provide your own). You remove the four jacks and announce that the jacks are bank robbers. They are going to rob the "bank" (the remainder of the deck) and scoot with the loot by helicopter. After removing the jacks, show them—fanned—and give the deck to a spectator to "make sure" there are no jacks left in the deck. There are none. The spectator returns the deck to you.

You announce that the jacks will search the bank for safe deposit boxes, cash, negotiable instruments and bonds. As you are saying this "patter," close the fan—face down—and insert one jack on the bottom of the deck (the "first floor"), a second jack a third of the way up (the "second floor"), a third jack close to the top (the "third floor") and the fourth jack on top (the "top floor"). Set the deck on the table. Then—here comes the helicopter! Move your hand as if flying toward the "bank." The jacks *race* to the top floor to catch the copter. As the helicopter arrives, slowly turn over the top four cards and there are the four jacks.

The Secret: When you take the four jacks out of the deck, take *three extra cards* and place them *behind* the Jacks. As you take them, square them up carefully. Handing the cards to a spectator gives you time and distraction to do so. Keep them neatly squared as you insert the *extra* cards, one at a time, into the deck. When you're done, you have all four jacks, tightly grouped, ready to quickly but carefully place on top.

April 27, 2012

Torn and Restored Paper

This is a cool effect, and I've gotten a lot of mileage from it over the years.

The Effect: Say you're sitting in a restaurant. You take a cocktail napkin and shred it to pieces. You ball it up—and slowly begin to open a *fully restored* cocktail napkin. Your hands remain above the table at all times.

The Trick: Before you start, surreptitiously take your own cocktail napkin, put it in your lap, open it, ball it up and hide it in your hand, under your thumb. Now you're ready to go. Announce that you have a trick that will amaze and astound.

Ask for a cocktail napkin and open it. All the while, keep the balled-up napkin hidden under your thumb. (No one will see it because it's small, and if it shows at all, it will blend with the other napkin.) Shred the napkin and ball it up with the whole napkin. Put them together and hold the two in front of everyone's eyes. The audience will "see" only one balled-up napkin—though you know the whole napkin is on the side facing you, and the torn one is on the side facing everyone else.

Reverse the two balls and slowly begin to open the whole napkin. (If you drop any pieces, pick them up and slip them in with the ball of torn paper.) Once the napkin is open, you can drop the torn ball into your lap or on the floor. Then take a bow.

You *must* practice a dozen times or so (in front of a mirror) before attempting to wow the crowd. And (raise your right hand) you mustn't tell anyone how it's done.

Magicians actually run in my family. They have to if they want to survive....

December 19, 2011

1,089

You will have people asking, "How in the world did you do that?"

Let's say you are sitting with some friends. Or better yet, children or grandchildren. You volunteer to predict a four-digit number. And you write it down on a card and turn it over.

Ask someone to write down three single-digit numbers without repeating a number. Then have them reverse the numbers and subtract the smaller from the larger. (If you get 99, add a zero in front.)

Take that number and reverse it. Then add those two numbers together. The total will be 1,089—the number you wrote down on the card. In a few instances, when you subtract, the total will be 099. Just reverse the digits again and add 990 to 099. *Ta-dahhh.* . . . 1,089.

Whatever the first three numbers are, the end result is always 1,089. And no, I don't know how it works. Unless I take off my socks and shoes. And even then...

August 2, 2020

Happy Socks

Over the years, my feet have become increasingly *un*happy. I won't bore you with the pathology of my paws; suffice it to say I have grumpy feet.

But I walk. I wear shoes. And I wear *socks*. The colors of my socks, however, have remained lackluster. That is, until last Christmas.

My granddaughters presented me with six pairs of colorful Happy Socks. Eve and Elin are aware that Popi's feet need help. So they concluded that Happy Socks may be just the ticket.

Happy Socks is a brand started in 2008 by two Swedes—Viktor Tell and Mikael Söderlindh. They wanted to build a brand that would be a "breath of fresh air" for one's attire. In looking at my sock-drawer upgrade—they have succeeded. My Happy Socks are a symphony of color and help put my feet into a more neutral—if not happy—mood. According to the London *Evening Standard*, Happy Socks are known for their "bold, colourful designs [which] tread precariously close to garish."

I now wear Happy Socks almost all the time. Next time I wear my tux, I will likely be wearing socks that look like a Jackson Pollock painting.

April 2, 2017

Pajamas

Do men wear pajamas? It's not a topic that I think about much. The *Wall Street Journal* asked that question in an article dated August 12, 2015. The consensus was that some men do, but they're hard to find. This tracks an ABC News poll of 1,501 American adults, which found that only 13% of men wore actual pajamas.

I can see that, after getting home from work, putting on a pair of pajamas might provide a demarcation between the workday and personal time. It's time to wind down, unlax, kick back. When I get home from work, I don a pair of jeans that are standing up in the corner waiting for me (I don't think they've been washed in years). And a T-shirt. Slippers.

For me, I haven't had had a pair of pj's since I was in high school. It's usually been a pair of boxers or gym shorts and a maybe a T-shirt in winter. Or nothing. Depending on the circumstances.

I have no context on whether guys who are reading this wear real pajamas. Maybe you don't want to admit it, or maybe you want to shout it from the rooftops. But I wouldn't lose sleep over it.

December 4, 2016

Mizar and Alcor

When I was on the staff of Camp Napowan—the Boy Scout camp in Wild Rose, Wisconsin—I worked in the nature area. Camp Napowan was in the middle of nowhere, blessed with no light pollution, with a clear and amazing view of stars, planets and nebulae.

One of the merit badges I taught was astronomy. Twice a week, at around 10 p.m.—when the sun's last wisps of light had dipped below the horizon, and darkness ruled—I would gather those working on their astronomy merit badge to gaze at the stars above.

To get the evening off on the right foot, I often started with the middle star of the handle of the Big Dipper (part of Ursa Major). "Look carefully," I would say. "What do you see?" After a few seconds, the Scouts would begin to say that there were actually *two* stars—not one.

Two thousand years ago, Arabs would use that middle star of Ursa Major as a test of sight. Why? Because there actually *are* two stars: Mizar and its fainter companion, Alcor—Arabic for *horse* and *rider*. If you could see them, you were thought to have great vision. In Japanese mythology, Alcor was the "lifespan" star. Those who could not see *jumyōboshi* would pass away by year's end. (A popular Japanese *manga* comic says if you *do* see the star, you will pass away by year's end.)

If you have a chance to go to someplace where, after the sun goes down, the lights don't shine, take a look for Alcor. Bring binoculars too. You've gotta see this.

July 26, 2011

Polaris

I am as constant as the northern star, of whose true-fixed and resting quality there is no fellow in the firmament.
~ Shakespeare, *Julius Caesar*, Act 3, Scene 1

Polaris. The North Star. Probably the most important celestial guidepost in the galaxy (at least if you live on Earth). Why Polaris?

First, it never moves. Day or night, winter or summer, when you are in the Northern Hemisphere, Polaris will *always* be in the same spot. Every star and galaxy revolves around Polaris (again, from our perspective here on Earth).

Second, the degree of altitude above the horizon gives you near-accurate north latitude. Chicago is 42 degrees north latitude. Polaris is 42 degrees above the horizon. Fort Worth is 33 degrees north latitude. Polaris is 33 degrees above the horizon. And so on.

Finally, when you draw a straight line from Polaris to the ground, you have true north. True north varies from magnetic north by a few miles to a few degrees, depending on where you are. This variance is called *declination*.

To find Polaris, one need only find the Big Dipper (part of Ursa Major). Go to the two vertical stars at the far end of the dipper and draw a straight line up, five times the distance between those stars (Merak and Dubhe). There's Polaris (a bright second-magnitude star), the tail star of the Little Dipper (Ursa Minor).

Polaris sits 433 light-years from earth. It is a double star (or "multiple" star), consisting of several stars that appear to be one. Just think, if you could transport yourself to Polaris and look back with a powerful telescope, you would see the Earth—as it was 433 years ago.

January 22, 2017

The Tree

There is a tree in the front yard of my house. An elm. An *old* elm. It is the patriarch (or matriarch) of the neighborhood. Maybe the town. Or state. Every other year we pay to have it injected with a Dutch elm vaccination. I've always wanted to know how old it is—without cutting it down and counting the rings.

I did some research on the subject. There is a metric to determine the age of these magnificent gifts of God.

At a height of around 4 feet, measure the circumference in inches and divide by *pi* (3.14). This gives you the *diameter*. For an elm, multiply the diameter by 4.0 to get the approximate age. For other tree species, the multiples are:

× 2.0   aspen or cottonwood

× 3.0   silver maple, pin oak or linden

× 3.5   river birch

× 4.0   elm or red oak

× 4.5   walnut or red maple

× 5.0   sugar maple, white birch, white oak or cherry

× 7.0   dogwood, ironwood or redbud

In the case of our grand elm, the circumference is 140 inches (I used a long string to wrap around the trunk and then did the measurement). The circumference divided by *pi* equals a diameter of 44.5 inches. Multiply 44.5 by 4.0. That gives you 178 years.

Our tree was born in or around 1842. I hope it will be around for years to come.

July 23, 2020

Facial Recognition Software

Donna and I were at O'Hare airport last weekend, off to Florida for a few days. At the airport, I walked by thousands of people. And I didn't recognize a soul. One or two prompted a second glance—*is that ... no.* And then—from a hundred feet away—I went, *that's JT.* And it was. A golfing pal.

We chatted (we were on the same flight) and boarded. We arrived at the West Palm Airport and again saw a veritable sea of people as we shuffled toward the exit. All shapes, sizes and attire. But not one person did I recognize. All had the same standard equipment. Face. Nose. Eyes. Ears. Hair. But all were different (some *really* different).

After getting our luggage and walking outside, I spotted our friends Bob and Carol driving up in a car. I find it pretty awesome that we humans all have a *facial recognition software* hard-wired into our brains. We can pick out someone we haven't seen in 10 years in a crowd of thousands. We can detect an old friend from across the room (*well, look who's here!*).

These faces—and what we perceive to be an evolution of them—is reposed with clarity and order in the gray matter between our ears. Some people change dramatically and become unrecognizable. But most retain some of the remembered characteristics from years past. I remember seeing Jon, an old friend from Boy Scout camp, at O'Hare. I hadn't seen him in years, but I knew him in an instant. It's amazing how our brains work.

Now where did I leave my keys...

October 29, 2017

Locard's Exchange Principle

A crime. No leads. Police and investigators pick through the scene. Ask questions. Examine the scene again. Look. Study. Listen. Sniff. Search. And solve. Often thanks to Dr. Edmond Locard (1877–1966), a pioneer in forensic science.

Dr. Locard (known as the French Sherlock Holmes) developed a basic principle of forensics that "every contact leaves a trace." In 1953 writer Paul Kirk described Locard's Exchange Principle thus: "Wherever he steps, whatever he touches, whatever he leaves ... will bear mute witness against him." In other words, the occasion of every crime leaves behind traces of the criminal. And thus a means for solving the case.

Locard's Exchange Principle applies to life in general. As we wander through our daily lives, wherever we stand, sit or set foot, we leave behind a part of us. Whomever we talk to, cross paths with or acknowledge, we leave a trace. Of our presence. The trace can be positive or negative. A sharing of concern, love or sympathy. Or it might be anger, distraction or inattention. But as we move on this journey, whether we like it or not, there is a forensic trail. That bears witness. The traces we leave behind as we shuffle from one day to the next may not mean much to us. But they could mean everything to someone else.

September 24, 2017

17

FOR INSPIRATION

The Lottery of Birth

I'm lucky. You probably are too. Born into a relatively stable environment. To decent parents. With an education. Job. Family. Friends. A religious tradition. You can travel. And if you get sick, there are doctors to take care of you. The twinkling spark that suddenly became *you* arrived *just* in the right place. At the right time. It was a lottery. Of *birth*.

What if that spark had come to life a hundred years ago? Or a thousand? Many born in those times just *endured*. Day by day. Struggling with the things we take for granted today. Yet even now there are those who are born into a life of abysmal poverty, suffocating hunger and crippling disease. Raised in countries ravaged by violence, hatred and injustice. Where every single day may be an arduous, painful and frightening saga. Do you ever think, "That could've been me"?

I'm still at a point of wondering what we can do as a nation or as individuals to somehow make things just a little better. Whatever one's persuasion, we can all profit by the Franciscan prayer that ends, "May God bless you with enough foolishness to believe that you can make a difference in the world, so that you can do what others claim cannot be done."

Today is the first day of the rest of your life. What are *you* going to do with what's left of it?

April 9, 2015

Be a Thermostat

As we go through life, we leave trails. All sorts of them. Big and wide. Small and narrow. Through our jobs. Families. Friends. Pastimes. But some trails are unseen. Hidden. Trails we don't even know we leave. Small acts of kindness or charity (or hurt or disrespect) may mean nothing to you. But they may mean *everything* to someone else.

Trails. You just never know when you're going to leave one. We have the choice to go through life as a *thermostat* (to make change) or a *thermometer* (to sit back and accept what comes). We can make things happen. Or *wait* for things to happen.

Somehow I think that most or all of those reading this are thermostats. Leave a trail. Make it a *good* one.

April 26, 2014

It's All About the Dash

I read an interview in *Men's Journal* with Julius "Dr. J" Erving. He was asked, "What's the best advice you ever got?" He responded that it was learning one simple lesson: "Life is all about the dash." The *dash*?

Dr. J explained that in the cemetery, every tombstone has two numbers: the year you were born and the year you die. And there's a *dash* in between. *That*, Dr. J said, is what it's all about. "What you've done with your life and how you lived it are in that dash."

At some point, we are all going to have two numbers. And a *dash*. As I've said, some people are thermostats. And some are thermometers. Thermometers sit back and just tell you the score. Thermostats are out on the playing field. Scoring points. Making a difference.

The dash on your tombstone can be a thermometer. Or a *thermostat*. What's in *your* dash?

March 23, 2017

Batteries I Have Known

Ever notice when you put fresh batteries into a flashlight, the dry-cell kind start out strong. Bright. Over time they get dimmer. And dimmer. And gradually flicker out.

Lithium-cell batteries, on the other hand, pour out 100% power until—like a light switch—they go out. Most of the folks I know are powered by lithium cells. They are productive, active and moving. All the time. Regardless of age. Pouring out energy, activity and contribution.

Cemeteries are full of unused potential and squandered talent. Imagine if each plot had a light shining above, reflecting the occupant's productive time on earth. How many would be crisp beams of lithium-cell brightness? How many would be fading dry-cell lights?

How many would be dark?

May 12, 2016

I Can See

A few years ago, my wife, Donna and I were on a tour of Vietnam. Always on the scout for autograph and manuscript material, we stopped in antique shop after "old stuff" shop. In Hanoi we found a place called 54 Traditions. The shop is run by Dr. Mark Rapoport, an American pediatrician who served in Vietnam during the war. He opened 54 Traditions in 2001, stocking it with his collection of textiles, jewelry, art and tools from Vietnam. I bought a few nice goodies. But what made an impression was *Mark*.

During the war, he worked as a medical intern in a hospital. When he was visiting an outlying village, he met a very old woman who was unable to see something written on a piece of paper. He handed her his reading glasses. Tears filled her eyes. She could *see. Clearly*. Mark was so touched by the experience that he gave the woman his glasses. She said she could now embroider again.

Mark went out and bought a few extra pairs of reading glasses. And gave them away to others who could not read or see "close up." Since then he has given away *thousands* of reading glasses. And he helped inspire the

Reading Glass Project—an organization dedicated to providing glasses to those in developing countries who are dealing with age-related presbyopia (what gives us trouble reading, threading a needle or doing visually detailed tasks as we get older).

The Reading Glass Project *sells* glasses for $2 (a lot cheaper than at the pharmacy). But it urges us—when we visit developing countries—to bring along some reading glasses to give to those without.

The motto of this group is "Be more than a tourist. Be a hero." And see the difference you can make.

May 28, 2016

Listen to the Crickets

Earlier this week, my daughter, Lauren, was driving with her little girls, Eve and Elin. The windows were down. As they approached a train crossing gate, Eve yelled to Lauren, "SLOW DOWN!" Lauren turned and dutifully slowed down. And stopped the car by the crossing gate. And looked back at Eve.

Eve said, "Listen, mommy. Listen to the crickets." And through the open windows came a heavenly choir of chirping crickets—or "hot bugs," as I used to call them—singing in the trees. And Eve wanted "listen" to the chorus of crickets singing. It took a 4-year-old to appreciate this music of nature.

When I heard this story, my eyes got a bit misty. I know we are often told to "stop and smell the flowers." But I'd never really thought of stopping to listen to the crickets.

There are five traditionally recognized senses: taste, touch, smell, sight and sound. I love the *smell* of a campfire. The *taste* of spaghetti carbonara, the *sight* of a golf ball (*my* golf ball) gliding toward the green and the *feel* of hot sand under my feet. But I sometimes forget about slowing down to truly enjoy the world's *auditory* offerings. Like listening to crickets.

June 26, 2016

Thank You, Captain

One of my favorite stories relates to Napoleon, the grand emperor of the French Republic. (The story comes from *Billy Sunday, the Man and His Message* by William T. Ellis. Check it out.)

Napoleon was at a parade of troops outside Paris. His marshals, his staff and his officers were all present. As Napoleon was reviewing the troops, a small animal ran from a bush, startling his horse. The horse bucked. Reared up. And Napoleon fell backward in his saddle, clinging precariously to the reins. No one moved. *Except* for a young private who sprinted from the lines. His rifle clattered to the ground. His hat flew off. The private grabbed the reins of the emperor's horse, unceremoniously shoved Napoleon back into the saddle and snapped to attention.

Napoleon looked around. At his marshals. His generals. His officers. And then down at the young private. In a booming voice, Napoleon said, "Thank you, Captain."

Flustered, the young man asked, "Of what regiment, sir?"

Napoleon laughed. "Of my personal guard."

The example of this courageous young private can be an inspiration for all of us.

May 28, 2012

John Wooden

Every once in a while a person comes along who cuts a wide swath. And makes a big difference in the lives of others. To me, John Wooden (1910–2010) was one of those special people.

Wooden was the winningest basketball coach (UCLA) in NCAA history, winning 10 national titles in a 12-year period. Coach Wooden was known for short, simple, inspirational messages that helped players succeed in basketball and, more importantly, in life. These are a few examples of Wooden wisdom:

Make each day your masterpiece.

Never cease trying to be the best you can be. That is in your power.

Young people need role models, not critics.

Never mistake activity for achievement.

Today is the only day. Yesterday is gone.

Don't measure yourself by what you have accomplished, but by what you should have accomplished with your ability.

The main ingredient of stardom is the rest of the team.

You can't live a perfect day without doing something for someone who will never be able to repay you.

Seek opportunities to show you care. The smallest gestures often make the biggest difference.

Interestingly, Coach Wooden never mentioned *winning* to his players. He always stressed *effort*. Doing one's best was key.

—————————————

August 31, 2017

Never Give In

Calvin Coolidge has a famous quote that ends, "Persistence and determination are omnipotent. The slogan 'press on' has solved and always will solve the problems of the human race."

Winston Churchill brought these inspirational words to a new level in 1941. During the dark days of World War II, Churchill was invited to give the commencement address at Harrow School. Known for wit, wisdom and tenacity, he *addressed* the young graduates. But he *spoke* to the *nation*.

Churchill's brief comments concluded with an admonition to all: "Never give in. Never give in. Never, never, never, never—in nothing, great or small, large or petty—never give in, except to convictions of honor and good sense."

It's easy to give up. Back down. Throw in the towel. But with the words of Churchill and Coolidge, how can we look in the mirror and say, "I can't"? William Manchester's trilogy *The Last Lion* chronicles the life of Churchill. It is my favorite biography. I recommend it to you. It might take a while to read (it's nearly 3,000 pages), but don't give up. Press on. Keep reading.

Never, never give in....

April 29, 2018

Courage

In *Iberia,* James Michener facetiously observed this of Spaniards: "Any nation that can eat churros and chocolate for breakfast is not required to demonstrate its courage in other ways." I *love* Michener's writing, but courage is not a joke. To me, courage is shown by many special people. These days, it is defined in one word: *Malala.*

Malala Yousafzai was born in 1997 in the Swat Valley in Northern Pakistan. She is 16 years old. Malala and her family have lived under the Taliban boot for much of her short life. As a girl, she has been forbidden to attend school. The Taliban is known for crushing *any* attempt for girls to learn. They burn schools and kill teachers suspected of teaching girls.

In 2009, Malala—at the tender age of 11 or 12—began speaking out about the *need* for girls to learn. And to attend school. Through the BBC, she published a blog under a pseudonym, detailing life under the Taliban and speaking out against them. She then began writing under *her own* name—and giving interviews on television. All directed toward the need for girls to go to school.

On October 9, 2012, the school bus in which she was riding was stopped and boarded by Taliban assassins. They approached Malala and shot her in the head and neck. Malala clung to life and was sent to the U.K. for surgeries. On October 12, 50 Pakistani clerics—to their credit—issued a *fatwa* (religious ruling) condemning the attack.

Malala is now up and around. And she is speaking out. Against the cowards who are the Taliban. She is now under consideration for the Nobel Peace Prize. She deserves it. (In 2014, she won.)

February 8, 2013

Gratitude

He is a wise man who does not grieve for the things which he has not, but rejoices for those which he has.
~ Epictetus

It is interesting that many folks who have "everything" are unhappy. Yet those who have little or nothing can often be *very* happy. *Why?*

Part of the reason is that people who feel a sense of *gratitude* in their lives are more apt to be happy. *Fasten your seat belts.* Here's a TED Talk that made my eyes misty. This 9-minute program is on the subject of *gratitude* (www.ted.com/talks/louie_schwartzberg_nature_beauty_gratitude?referrer=playlist-give_thanks#t-2392).

We all have reason to be *grateful.* Yet how often do we ponder this sentiment? The talk ends with a powerful narrative by Brother David Steindl-Rast, a Benedictine monk, who expounds on why gratitude is such an important emotion. Among his comments: "Think of this day as the first day and the last day of your life.... Each day is a gift. Let your gratitude for this day flow through you and be a blessing to others."

Strong, compelling words. Inspiration to give. Reason to be *grateful.*

August 2, 2018

Empathy

Could a greater miracle take place than for us to look through each other's eyes for an instant?
~ Henry David Thoreau

The Cleveland Clinic is known as one of the great medical institutions in America and probably the world. Two years ago, the clinic produced a powerful YouTube video on empathy. I watched it for the first time in early March. And I've watched it several times since.

As I walk from the train station to my office, I'm sure I pass a thousand people. Probably more. They all walk in their own world. With their own thoughts. Dealing with their own issues. Health. Fears. Demons. It is important to realize that each one of us has a story. Each one of us lives with the cards that are dealt in the lottery of birth. And the life that is thus given.

Do me a favor and devote 4½ minutes to this video. It's hard to watch it and not feel a sense of empathy for the human condition. A sense of … *that could be me.*

Watch it here. You may want to watch it again.

https://www.youtube.com/watch?v=Xytn4fuxok4

April 14, 2018

All Saints Day

Sunday was All Saints Day. A celebration of all those men and women who have been canonized by the church. Do you have a headache? Then pray to St. Teresa of Avila (1515–1582). She is the patron saint of those who suffer from headaches. Are you a lawyer? Then St. Genesius of Rome (circa A.D. 300) is your patron saint. Though perhaps it's no surprise that St. Genesius is also the patron saint of comedians, actors and clowns.

Where do we find the saints of today? Do we need a window? Or can we use a mirror? As I have gone through life, plenty of people have been "saints" for me. Teachers, a judge, a college dean, friends, strangers. And then there are those who have been saints to all of us. Parents. Relatives. Founding Fathers. Men and women of the armed services. Clergy and laity. Charitable organizations. Volunteers. Teachers and tutors. None has been canonized, but many deserve the title "saint."

Who are the saints in your life?

November 9, 2017

Empty-Handed

Graham Greene's *The Power and the Glory* (1940) is set in Mexico in the late 1930s. The country has turned against the church. Priests, nuns and the faithful are executed. Public prayer is forbidden. Church bells are silent. One lone priest—the "whiskey priest"—escapes and goes on the run. He is being pursued by a methodical, and merciless, police lieutenant tasked with his capture.

The whiskey priest—an alcoholic who has sinned in varied ways—tries to remain faithful as he travels around, incognito, ministering to his flock *sub rosa*. But he is doggedly pursued by the lieutenant and narrowly escapes capture.

The book tracks the ills of a society that attacks and tries to destroy the church. And faith. In the end, the whiskey priest is captured. And condemned. He regrets not his imminent death but rather his failings. Green concludes with:

He felt only an immense disappointment because he had to go to God empty-handed, with nothing done at all.... He felt like someone who has missed happiness by seconds at an appointed place. He knew now that at the end there was only one thing that counted—to be a saint.

There are several lessons in this work. One is the war on religion (which we deal with in our own country). Another is the universal question of, *Why am I here*? And most the nagging question of, *Am I going to God empty-handed*?

I know many of you reading this are active in volunteering, contributing, helping, doing good deeds and working to improve the human condition. *But are we doing enough*? Think about it. *Could we do more to make the world a better place*? If every person—spurred by that simple query—did one *extra* act of kindness, charity or contribution each day, imagine how much better the world might be.

March 31, 2019

The Star Thrower

One of my favorite short stories is "The Star Thrower" by Loren Eiseley (1907–1977). The author gets up early one morning and goes walking on a beach by the ocean. The gray fingers of dawn touch the horizon. It is dark, but he can see that the sand is *covered* with starfish—live starfish being swept in by the tide. He keeps walking.

Off in the distance, on the beach, he sees the shadow of a figure that stoops—and throws. Stoops—and throws. The author continues walking.

And as he approaches the figure, he sees it is a young man. Who is picking up starfish and slinging them back into the sea. As he reaches the young man, he stops and watches.

The author looks at the young man and says, "Look at the beach. It's covered with starfish. What you're doing doesn't make any difference." The young man looks back as he picks up a starfish. "You see this one? It makes a difference to him," he says, and throws the starfish into the waves.

This message is so powerful it brings tears to my eyes. What are your talents? What lights your fire? What do you do to *make a difference*? We are each blessed with special gifts. Abilities. We may not be able to throw a starfish into the sea. But we may be able to throw a lifeline to some person. With a kind word. A generous deed. It may not mean much to us. But it may make *all the difference in the world* to someone else.

April 21, 2013

The Open Door

I belong to an Episcopal church in my neighborhood. I am invigorated by the services, educated by our adult education programs and strengthened—in all respects—by just *being there*.

Our church is like others—in shape, liturgy and message. But there is one thing that sets this church apart. *The doors of the church are never locked.* They are open, 24/7.

Members of the church can stop in. Folks who are *not* members can stop in as well. At 10 at night. Or 3 in the morning. *Everyone* is welcome. To pray. To think. To ponder. Donna and I will sometimes stop in. In those off hours when we've gone in, the sanctuary is usually empty. Except for us. Which makes our visit more personal.

I like to think that the doors of all *faith traditions* are open to the public. And yet I am aware that is not the case. I remember one pastor, years ago, haughtily suggesting that unless I was of his faith, his denomination *and his synod*—the doors to my salvation might well be *closed*. That's tough to stomach.

I wonder what the Archangel Gabriel would have to say about *that*. I bet *his* doors are open … 24/7.

March 28, 2019

Annual Christmas Message

For unto us a child is born, unto us a son is given … and his name shall be called Wonderful, Counselor, the mighty God, the everlasting Father, the Prince of Peace. (Isaiah 9:6)

And Joseph also went up from Galilee, out of the city of Nazareth, into Judaea, unto the city of David, which is called Bethlehem (because he was of the house and lineage of David). To be taxed with Mary his espoused wife, being great with child. And so it was, that, while they were there, the days were accomplished that she should be delivered. And she brought forth her firstborn son, and wrapped him in swaddling clothes, and laid him in a manger; because there was no room for them in the inn. (Luke 2:4–7)

Here we are again! Christmas [insert year here]. Mercy—the days are often long, but the years go fast.

Our best wishes to all of you for a happy and blessed Christmas, New Year and holiday season!

Make a Difference in the World

I want to make a difference in the world. So do you. But the clock is winding down. So just what can we do? I ponder this question. I often pray about it. Share it with others. I recently happened across some quotations on this very topic. Let me share a few with you—to consider.

> "We rise by lifting others."
> ~ *Robert Ingersoll*

> "No act of kindness, no matter how small, is ever wasted."
> ~ *Aesop*

"One person can make a difference, and everyone should try."
~ *Jacqueline Kennedy*

"We can change the world and make it a better place. It is in our hands to make a difference."
~ *Nelson Mandela*

"The purpose of life is not to be happy. It is to be useful, to be honorable, to be compassionate, to have it make some difference that you have lived and lived well."
~ *attributed to Ralph Waldo Emerson*

"I have one life and one chance to make it count for something.... My faith demands that I do whatever I can, wherever I am, whenever I can, for as long as I can, with whatever I have, to try to make a difference."
~ *Jimmy Carter*

"There is no limit to the amount of good you can do, if you don't care who gets the credit."
~ *Ronald Reagan*

Let's make a difference in the world. As Lao Tzu put it, "The journey of a thousand miles begins with the first step."

Take a step.

November 20, 2019

A Prayer

I've been walking to the train station every weekday for 40 years. As I walk, I don't listen to music. Or books on tape. I ponder the day ahead. Plan. Think. And normally, I say a prayer. Over the years, the words have evolved a bit, but it is always the same in tone and tenor.

Lord, thank you for this day. Forgive my sins and hear my prayer. I pray, Lord, that you will bless this world and your children who live in it. I ask you to help, heal, comfort, feed and defend the poor, the hungry, the homeless, the sick, the dying; those who are victims of abuse, hatred and violence; those who are lonely and depressed; those who are disabled and disfigured; those who can't hear, those who can't see, those who have MS or are paralyzed, those who suffer.

Speak to each one of us, Lord, and remind us of your presence, your divinity and your Holy Word.

Speak to me, Lord, and let me know how to use my time for the greatest good. Guide me, lead me, push me—but whatever you do, use me to Your service.

Bless my family. Bless them all with health, safety, happiness, wisdom and faith in You. Help our grandchildren to grow up strong and good. Let them love and be loved. And let them be remembered for their contributions to this world, to your Kingdom, to their families and to humanity. Amen.

And then I add a few words for friends and relatives who are ill or struggling. I don't need a script for this. It's hard-wired. We all deal with challenges, stress and now a pandemic that knows no bounds. At this holy time of year, perhaps some of these words can be used—and give comfort.

April 11, 2020